Mohamed M. Keshavjee was called to the Bar at Gray's Inn, London, and Osgoode Hall Canada. He did his LLM at London University in Alternative Dispute Resolution (ADR), Islamic Law, International Protection of Human Rights and Arab Comparative Commercial Law. He attained his doctorate in Law in ADR at School of Oriental and African Studies, London University, and has lectured to LLM students on ADR in diasporic Muslim communities at the London School of Economics. In 2010, he attended the Harvard Program on Negotiation under Frank Sander and in 2012 he trained family mediators in the European Union to conduct mediation in cases where The Hague Convention on International Child Abduction is inapplicable. Keshavjee is internationally recognised for his expertise on ADR among Muslims and has been invited as a keynote speaker to address several conferences on mediation. He has contributed chapters to influential books dealing with diasporic Muslim communities and legal pluralism in Europe. From 2000 to 2010 he coordinated, and lectured in, all the Ismaili Muslim community's training programmes on family and commercial mediation worldwide. He has also lectured on family mediation to students at the Muslim College in London.

Dr Keshavjee's exploration of the use of alternative dispute resolution services (ADR) by a Muslim community in a London area is a deeply insightful study of a Muslim community's approach to the settlement of disputes in sensitive family matters. The study focuses on the services available to this community in their local area and their strong preference for resolving family disputes privately, outside the culturally alien arena of English family law. Religious law – the Sharia – has an important role in Muslim approaches to conflict resolution. Dr Keshavjee's book is of great interest to scholars and practitioners alike. It not only provides a conceptual bridge between Muslim culture and religion and Anglo-American forms of mediation and negotiation, it also provides an essential bridge between theoretical literature on ADR and ADR in practice, applied in a particular cultural context. There are many invaluable insights gained from the author's experience of training mediators in Ismaili communities worldwide. This book is an essential resource for all mediators working with Muslim and cross-cultural families, to develop the great potential of mediation to enhance the well-being of Muslim communities, not only in the United Kingdom but all over the world.

Lisa Parkinson
Member of the Hague Conference Group of Experts advising on the 'Guide to Good Practice on Mediation' under the 1980 Child Abduction Convention

In this pioneering study of the Muslim community in the London borough of Hounslow, Mohamed Keshavjee, a British-trained barrister, explores the way Sharia law can exert a positive role in Britain's Muslim communities through its emphasis on mediation and conciliation in resolving personal and family disputes. With clarity and sensitivity he examines the interface between the British legal system and the informal Sharia-based models adopted by Muslims as they navigate the difficult waters between the majority culture and the divine imperatives of Islam with its manifold local traditions. This book, which does not hesitate to venture into problematic areas such as forced marriages and domestic violence, is a valuable antidote to the hysteria surrounding much of the media comment on the 'introduction' of Sharia law in Britain.

Malise Ruthven
Author of *Islam: A Very Short Introduction*

This pioneering work by Dr Keshavjee highlights a number of issues that diasporic Muslims have to grapple with to resolve their family disputes. The book demonstrates how traditional methods of dispute resolution can be judiciously combined with modern dispute resolution processes. Appropriate training programmes that respect the cultural sensibilities of the immigrant community and the public laws of the host countries where Muslim minorities are settled today are particularly effective in this respect. The book makes a major contribution to greater cross-cultural understanding.

Makhdoom Ali Khan
Constitutional lawyer, author and former Attorney General of the Islamic Republic of Pakistan

Islam, Sharia and Alternative Dispute Resolution

Mechanisms for Legal Redress in the Muslim Community

Mohamed M. Keshavjee

I.B. TAURIS

LONDON · NEW YORK

Published in 2013 by I.B.Tauris & Co Ltd
6 Salem Road, London W2 4BU
175 Fifth Avenue, New York NY 10010
www.ibtauris.com

Distributed in the United States and Canada Exclusively by Palgrave Macmillan
175 Fifth Avenue, New York NY 10010

Library of Islamic Law, Vol. 6

ISBN: 978 1 84885 732 2

A full CIP record for this book is available from the British Library
A full CIP record is available from the Library of Congress

Library of Congress Catalog Card Number: available

Typeset in HoeflerText by Newgen Publishers, Chennai

Printed and bound by CPI Group (UK) Ltd, Croydon, CR0 4YY

In memory of the late

Dr Alex Quaison Sackey,

President of the nineteenth UN General Assembly

for recommending the academic world to me

Contents

Foreword

This pioneering ethnographic study of family dispute resolution processes in a Muslim community within the Hounslow area of London provides a rich and suggestive counterpoint to a predominantly occidental ADR literature. As the author notes, Muslims in Britain today comprise some 3 million people. On the whole, they do not, as Mohamed Keshavjee confirms, make extensive use of local procedures available under the common law. This is entirely understandable when one considers the inevitably ethnocentric character of these locally developed arrangements. We see instead predominant, if eclectic, use of the Sharia.

Today, with a growing recognition that a vigorous, if qualified, legal pluralism must be the route forward for the present and the foreseeable future, studies of this focus and quality are indispensable. Keshavjee is a born ethnographer, with a sharp and careful eye for the detail.

At a time when Muslim indigenous ADR processes are seriously misunderstood vis-à-vis Western legal processes, this study makes a valuable contribution to the engendering of greater international understanding in the field of informal justice today.

Simon Roberts
Professor of Law at the London School of Economics
and Political Science

Acknowledgements

In the endeavour of transforming my doctoral dissertation into a book that could be used by ADR academics, lawyers, law students and practitioners, as well as be interesting to general readers, I have had assistance from a number of people and I would like to express my gratitude for their contribution. Among these, I count Amin Kassam's continuous editorial support and advice invaluable. Without his help, my task would have been daunting. The Institute of Ismaili Studies, London provided useful support to ensure publication of this work. I am deeply grateful to Dr Farhad Daftary and his team for this. I am particularly grateful to Kutub Kassam for meticulously reading the manuscript and suggesting extra sources where these would be helpful. I am also grateful to Raficq Abdulla for spending hours on reading the text and making valuable suggestions. His experience as a member of the Muslim Law Shariah Council panel for some 25 years, helped provide some very useful insights. Alex Wright of I.B.Tauris has been supportive throughout. His initial encouragement spurred me on to undertake this endeavour. Of course, while all the people mentioned here provided valuable comments and input, the responsibility for the contents of this book remains solely mine.

I received cooperation and help from a number of people while doing research for and writing the doctoral dissertation on which this book is based. Those people were mentioned in the dissertation, but I would once again like to express special gratitude to all of them.

List of Figures

Introduction

The applicant before the Sharia 'court' was a young British woman of Pakistani origin living in a London borough. She was married to a Pakistani civil servant and wanted an Islamic divorce, which is the prerogative of the husband within a normal marriage contract under Islamic law. She could obtain a civil divorce in the United Kingdom courts, but that would not be accepted by many of her fellow religious adherents, and she would not be able to marry an observant Muslim in the future.[1] In return for the divorce, she was prepared to hand back to her husband everything he had agreed to give her on marriage, an arrangement known as a *khula* divorce; but her husband had refused to cooperate unless she gave him £15,000. During the course of the negotiations, the wife's father had died, leaving her a bequest of £150,000, and the husband had then increased his demand to £50,000. Subsequently, she had appealed to the Sharia 'court' to intervene in the matter.

After deliberating on her case, the Sharia 'court' wrote to the husband in Pakistan, informing him it would ensure reimbursement of the marriage expenses he had actually incurred and asking him to specify those expenses. When the husband replied with a sum that was clearly exaggerated, the Sharia 'court' invoked two important principles of classical Islamic law – *darura* (necessity) and *maslaha* (public interest) – and exhorted him to take due cognisance of his wife's situation. However, the husband would not agree to a compromise. The 'court' had no power to compel him to comply, but its founder, Dr Mohamed Zaki Badawi, an Egyptian scholar-imam, knew the then Pakistani President General Zia ul-Haq personally, and warned the husband that if he continued to be unreasonable he would ask the President to intercede. The husband then agreed to settle the matter for £5,000.

This case, which was heard by the Sharia 'court' in the late 1970s, is an illustration of how different the day-to-day actual implementation of Sharia law can be from the image conveyed by sensationalist reports in the media focusing on practices such as whipping and stoning among some of the more conservative Muslim societies. Zaki Badawi used an arguably extra-legal manoeuvre – the threat to use a personal connection to Pakistan's former ruler – to increase pressure on the defendant since the Sharia 'court' had no right of enforcement against the husband. By so doing, he protected the rights of the woman in the interests of equity and justice.

This was the second case brought before the Sharia 'court', which later became known as the Muslim Law (Shariah) Council (UK), or the MLSC. Since its formal inception in the mid-1980s, the MLSC has increased its membership to 15, of whom three are secular lawyers trained in Britain. It has also broadened its scope immensely, encompassing the different *madhaib* (schools of law) of Sunni Islam as well as Shi'i (Imamia) schools of jurisprudence.[2] Zaki Badawi explained the advantages of this fusion to me: 'We advanced a great deal on the Imamia *madhab*, because the Imamia are very good in some aspects.[3] Also, we often drew upon the Imamia as well as the Maliki *madhab* to find a solution to a particular problem.'

The Sharia instructs any group of Muslims living in a non-Muslim society to select one person from among them to be their leader as well as some other knowledgeable people to help them resolve their disputes in accordance with the Sharia (Badawi, 1995). It was in the context of this second provision that, in 1978, Dr Mohamed Zaki Badawi, then imam of the Regent's Park Mosque and Director of the Islamic Cultural Centre in Regent's Park, started to resolve conflict-of-law issues in collaboration with a small group of imams.[4] The most prevalent issues were family matters. One common problem was refusal by a husband to give a *talaq* (divorce by repudiation) to his former wife after she had obtained a divorce in the secular courts. While this made her eligible for remarriage in accordance with the laws of the United Kingdom, it did not do so under the Sharia. The man, for his part, could remarry according to UK laws as well as the Sharia, since men are allowed to be polygamous under the Sharia. This problem, referred to as that of the 'chained spouse', was creating serious difficulties for Muslim women in Britain and elsewhere in Europe. Operating from offices in West London, the MLSC entertained applications from Muslim women facing the 'chained spouse' problem. This was often done through the imams of the various mosques with which Zaki Badawi's organisation was affiliated. At the time of publication, some 350 matrimonial dispute cases were being referred to the MLSC each year.

In Islam, divorce is perceived as a reprehensible act and is only a last resort. This is based on the *hadith*[5] that states, 'of all things legally permissible, *talaq* is the most blameworthy' (Coulson, 1969: 84). However, marriage in Islam is viewed as a civil contract and its dissolution is accepted when a relationship has broken down irretrievably. Therefore, the MLSC's willingness to help women who have already obtained a divorce from secular courts because they can no longer continue their marital relationship is within the bounds of Islamic law.

To hear the cases of 'chained spouses', Zaki Badawi headed a panel of scholars, including the three lawyers trained in England, one of whom was a woman. In each case, the husband would be sent a letter by the MLSC stating that the Qur'an exhorts people to live in harmony, but when that is not possible, Muslims 'are not allowed to hold forcibly a woman, as a wife, against her wishes'. The letter requested the husband to do one of three things: to make every possible effort towards reaching a reconciliation; failing that, to grant his wife a divorce; and in either case, to contact the MLSC to present his side of the issue. The letter stated that if the situation remained unchanged over a reasonable time, the MLSC would dissolve the marriage. It normally issued three notices. The final notice cautioned the husband that 'if the Council does not receive a reply from you within 21 days (31 days, if overseas) of the date of this letter, it will be construed as a definite act of intention to harm (*darar*) the interests of the woman concerned, which would be valid grounds in Islam to dissolve the marriage'. Usually,

3

husbands ignore the notices, with the result that the MLSC proceeds to hear the applications in their absence.

According to its literature, the MLSC also provides conciliation and mediation services. Processually, the MLSC operates as an arbitration tribunal. It advises reconciliation, but in practice that does not always seem to take place since a civil divorce petition has already been heard or is being heard simultaneously in an adversarial arena. In effect, the MLSC is asked to grant a declaratory judgement – pronouncing an Islamic divorce based on, and following, a divorce granted under the laws of the United Kingdom. Examination of its records shows that the grounds for the civil court divorce as well as the Islamic one are in many cases almost the same.

In order to address the fullest spectrum of Muslims in Britain, the MLSC draws upon the wider heritage of Muslim law, employing the most humane interpretation of the law. It does this by allowing disputants to choose from the different schools of Islamic jurisprudence allowed by Islamic law (*takhayur*), including where necessary, the principles of Shi'i law, to resolve problems. Its ecumenical approach, coupled with professionalism, has given it a pre-eminent place in alternative dispute resolution (ADR) for Muslims in England. According to Badawi (1995: 77), 'We have quietly established ourselves as consultants for the Courts, and have been approached by a number of solicitors.'

The MLSC was also approached in the case of *Akmal* v. *Akmal*, involving a 14-year-old girl who had been taken to Pakistan and forced by her father to marry against her will. She returned to Britain and, ten years later, decided to end the marriage, asking not for divorce but for annulment. The civil court granted her petition, but the case disturbed many Muslim parents because it undermined their authority to compel their daughters to get married. In asking the civil court for annulment of her marriage, the young woman rejected the MLSC's advice that she should petition for divorce because society could not be changed overnight by appealing to 'another law superior to our law, but rather you achieve change by education' (Badawi, 1995: 77). However, it was significant that the MLSC was approached for advice from an Islamic perspective.

The MLSC has handled a number of cases concerning inheritance and the distribution of wealth within the family where one child or heir is preferred to another. In 1979, before its formal establishment, it negotiated with the authorities over inheritance, and was advised by legal specialists that a Muslim could divest of his estate in accordance with Islamic law through a will. It negotiated with a lawyer who agreed to draft wills for £7 each, and the MLSC agreed to pay the cost for the first 100 applicants to encourage Muslims to come forward. Only 17 did so and a delegation of Muslim women asked the MLSC to end the service 'because it militates against our interests. We are better off under English intestacy law' (Badawi, 1995: 80). Thus, in that case, it would seem Muslims were prepared to eschew the provisions of the Sharia if it did not serve their interests.

Muslims are not the only minority community in a Western country who use faith-based arbitration to resolve interpersonal conflicts. Jews also use religious courts, known as *bathei din*.[6] Research into faith-based arbitration in the United States by Wolfe (2006) and Zelcer (2007) identifies features and issues that arise in such courts that are common to both Muslims and Jews. Six main themes emerge that are of relevance to this study.

First, Islamic and Jewish tribunals are of special interest because marriage and divorce are likely to come within their ambit, yet the religious doctrines used to resolve these issues are viewed by some in the two communities as antiquated and prejudiced against women. For instance, in Judaism only a man can grant a divorce, called a *ghet*, and he must grant it willingly. If the husband refuses to give his consent to a divorce, the *beth din* cannot terminate the marriage and the wife is unable to remarry. If the woman does remarry, the relationship is considered adulterous and any offspring born of the marriage are considered illegitimate under Jewish law, preventing them from marrying within the Jewish faith.

An interesting development in this connection was the enactment of the Divorce (Religious Marriages) Act 2002, an addition to the Matrimonial Causes Act 1973 (the Act that deals with divorce in England).[7] The Divorce (Religious Marriages) Act 2002 provides that, where a Jewish man applies for a civil divorce, a civil court may adjourn his application until it has proof that he has given his wife a religious divorce (by *ghet*). The Act facilitates matters where the husband wants a civil divorce but wants to punish the wife by not giving her a religious divorce; however, it does not assist the case of a Jewish woman who wants a civil divorce while her husband does not. In such a case, a Jewish woman may obtain a civil divorce but cannot force her Jewish husband to give her a *ghet*, so she will still be unable to remarry within the Jewish faith. The Act states that it may be extended, through secondary legislation, to other religions (such as Islam, although a Muslim wife may have avenues such as the MLSC for obtaining a religious divorce in a diasporic Muslim community) but no such secondary legislation has been passed as yet.

The second commonality between Muslim and Jewish use of faith-based arbitration to resolve interpersonal conflicts is that the benefits of using such arbitration in a family dispute are considered to outweigh the disadvantages because, from a legal perspective, to quote Wolfe,

> religious arbitration systems are actually necessary to deal with religious disputes because resolving religious conflicts through secular courts leads to inconsistent results and limited relief for religious people. The inconsistencies can be seen clearly in the way courts treat the enforcement of religious documents like the *ketubah*, *maher* agreements, and Jewish prenuptial agreements, and the response of courts to Jewish men who refuse to grant their wives religious divorces. (Wolfe, 2006: 451.)

Third, faith-based arbitration using religious law raises human rights concerns. Legitimate fears that extremist religious laws and cultural attitudes would take over any type of independent faith-based arbitration system have driven some to believe that such an arbitration regime would be harmful to vulnerable parties. Fourth, according to Wolfe, the proper response to the criticism of religious arbitration is not to ban it entirely, but to implement greater oversight procedures, because through heightened oversight religious communities will be able to preserve their culture and heritage while the state will be able to fulfil its duty of protecting citizens.

Fifth, evaluation of the processes is very important. Zelcer points out that 'Statements of ex-litigants [because there will always be one person who was satisfied and one who was aggrieved] must therefore be taken with a grain of salt'. However, 'when these complaints are numerous and widespread, we have no choice but to listen to them and try to derive solutions to prevent them from recurring' (Zelcer, 2007: 102).

Finally, as Zelcer observes, though it would be ideal as a community to 'put our efforts and allocate resources to create a single outstanding *bet din* that will be used by the entire community', unfortunately, that will never happen, as 'there are too many diverse groups who will never give up their rights to run their own *bet din*' (Zelcer, 2007: 110).

The present study found these themes in the faith-based ADR processes among the Muslims in Hounslow as well. It also found that the notion of trust in a diasporic Muslim community encompasses a particularly broad range of issues because of concerns over patriarchy and diverse interpretation of religious laws. This includes confidentiality, trust in the mediator, trust in the process, trust in oneself, trust in the other, but above all, trust in the community as a whole to subscribe to a form of Sharia that is true to its original purpose and compatible with contemporary needs. In Hounslow, the concept also includes trust in an institution such as the MLSC to make decisions that transcend geographical areas of the Muslim world, schools of Islamic law and particular interpretations, and yet remain authentic and relevant. The importance of trust is demonstrated by the recent ADR controversy in Canada, where the Ontario provincial government initially allowed faith-based communities to apply their own religious laws in family-based arbitration but subsequently had to repeal the law because Muslims in the province could not agree on a common interpretation and application of the Sharia (Boyd, 2004). The issue attained national proportions, involving Muslims across Canada.

Britain has generally shown a degree of tolerance and has for some time now been officially propounding a policy of multiculturalism or cultural pluralism. In 1966, the Home Secretary announced that integration of ethnic minorities no longer entailed 'assimilation', but rather equal opportunity coupled with cultural diversity in an atmosphere of mutual tolerance (Jenkins, 1967). The Swann Report (1985: 6) articulated this vision of a 'genuinely pluralist society which is both socially cohesive and culturally diverse':

> seeking to achieve a balance between, on the one hand, the maintenance and active support of the essential elements of the cultures and lifestyles of all the ethnic groups within it and, on the other, the acceptance by all groups of a set of *shared values* distinctive of the society as a whole (emphasis added).

The same point was made by the Chief Rabbi, Dr Jonathan Sacks, in his Reith Lectures in 1990 when he outlined his vision of a pluralistic society:

> think of a plural society; not as one in which there is a Babel of conflicting languages, but rather as one in which we have to be bilingual. There is a first and *public language of citizenship* which we have to learn if we are to live together. And there is a variety of second languages which connect us to our local framework of relationships: to family and group and the traditions that underlie them. If we are to achieve integration without assimilation, it is important to give each of these languages its due […] For everyone, it means settling for less than we would seek if everyone were like us, and searching for more than our merely sectional interests: in short, for the common good (Sacks, 1991: 66, 68, cited in Poulter, 1995: 81; emphasis added).

Citing a number of common law cases as examples to demonstrate that the English legal system responds positively to the needs of a multicultural society, Poulter asks whether such a pluralistic philosophy has any limits. He posits that it is not likely that English law will adopt a policy of 'cultural relativism', whereby any practice or any tradition of any minority community will be automatically accepted and upheld by English law. He feels that limits will be imposed on the basis of 'shared values' or 'public language of citizenship'. He suggests that the place to find these 'values' and this 'language' would be in very widely ratified and accepted human rights treaties, particularly the International Covenant on Civil and Political Rights, which has 167 states parties, 67 by signature and ratification and the remainder by accession or succession, and the Convention on the Elimination of All Forms of Discrimination Against Women.[8] However, several Muslim countries that have ratified the Convention have attached reservations to the article dealing with marriage and family relations on the ground that the Sharia accords wives not 'equality' but 'equivalent rights'.

With regard to a demand made by the Union of Muslim Organisations for a completely separate system of Muslim family law in England, Poulter (1995: 84) states that 'there is no question, it seems, of the British Government acceding to this demand'. He suggests that some issues are far too intractable to be resolved by minor accommodations in English law. He singles out polygamy, divorce by repudiation (*talaq*) and marriage between Muslim women and non-Muslim men as such issues.

Poulter suggests some practical solutions that are of significance to this book. He sees no reason why the state should not encourage settlement of family disputes by Muslims themselves, through mediation, conciliation and informal arbitration by local or national organisations such as Sharia courts or councils, provided certain key points are borne in mind. Among those points, he includes the proper addressing of gender-based power imbalances and proper concern for the welfare of individual children and their future upbringing, which should not be determined simply on the basis of their age or sex. Furthermore, Poulter sees 'no reason why such religious or community organisations should not receive some government funding' (1995: 86). I am in accord with Poulter on this point, particularly where there are credible institutions dealing with dispute resolution in a professionally sound way.

Against this background, the establishment of the MLSC falls under the Sharia category of 'public interest' (*maslaha*), its aim being to protect the five essential values of Islamic law, namely, religion, life, intellect, lineage and property. According to Shah-Kazemi (2001: 9), these functions are performed by the MLSC in a specific manner. The principle of 'protecting religion' is upheld through promotion of the observance of Islamic social and familial tenets, for example when facilitating the capacity to divorce and remarry. The principle of protecting life is upheld by enabling and promoting safe relationships, free from harm and abuse; protection of the intellect through promotion of learning; protection of lineage by protection of the family; and safeguarding of the welfare of children and of property through protection of the home.

The MLSC's work can be seen as a modern-day expression of the concept of *ijtihad* [9] – a concept pivotal to Muslim modernity – through ongoing interpretation of the Qur'an, something that the Sharia permits. By celebrating diversity and respecting pluralism, the MLSC has the potential of restoring to Islamic law its essential ethical principles of equality, justice and freedom. This approach, which is in the best spirit of the famous *hadith* of the Prophet Muhammad (Pbuh) that 'difference of opinion among my community is a sign of the bounty of God', could once again bring to the fore the ethics of the faith. Though this would not be done by Islamic law being implemented directly, as in a Muslim state, it would, in Poulter's words (1995: 87) 'be the best way forward in the creation of a cohesive multicultural society in England today'.

Focus and scope of this book

I learned about the case of the woman seeking divorce from her Pakistani civil servant husband, which was summarised at the beginning of this chapter, while conducting research into alternative dispute resolution among Muslims in Britain for a PhD in Law at School of Oriental and African Studies, University of London. I was employed by an international development organisation in France and the free time available for the research was limited. Therefore, I decided to focus on one Muslim community, in the Hounslow area of London, and spent several months spread over a number of years interviewing Muslim residents, Zaki Badawi, imams, mosque trustees, community elders, staff of various dispute resolution organisations and academics specialising in dispute resolution. With the research extending from 2001 to 2009, I also had the opportunity to witness some of the changes in the community at first hand.

There were several reasons for locating this research in Hounslow. To begin with, a study of this kind requires a fairly organised group of immigrant Muslims, preferably homogenous in culture and linguistic background as well as constituting a good critical mass. The Hounslow Muslim community of some 19,000 people, predominantly from the South Asian subcontinent, meets this criterion. Second, unlike a community following diverse jurisprudential schools with a variety of ADR practices, which would have diffused the focus of the study, the Hounslow Muslim community largely belongs to the Hanafi school of Sunni Islam.[10] The area also has a smaller group of recently arrived immigrants from Somalia, most of whom belong to the Shafi'i school of Sunni Islam.[11] However, because their different racial, ethnic, linguistic and cultural background creates its own specific issues, the Somali segment of the population is not the focus of the study on which this book is based.

Third, while most areas of Muslim settlement in the United Kingdom would reflect the main difficulties faced by any immigrant Muslim community going through the process of acculturation in Britain, Hounslow has the advantage of proximity to various national institutions providing ADR services. Fourth, and most importantly, a study of this nature requires sufficient access to people and issues, which is not easy to obtain because of the sensitivity of a subject involving religious law, cultural sentiments, community institutions and interpersonal relationships. While studying for an LLM degree at London University, I had conducted a small ethnographic study in Hounslow and therefore had already established a trust relationship with some of the people in the area. The present study was able to build on that relationship.

Finally, the Hounslow area refers its jurisprudential matters to the MLSC, with which it has a privileged relationship. This study became possible largely through the relationship of trust developed between the MLSC and myself, more particularly with its head, Zaki Badawi. Dr Badawi assigned his senior scholar, Maulana Shahid Raza Naeemi, to assist me. Many issues concerning the Sharia, as they relate to the area and to the Hanafi school of jurisprudence, could only be elaborated upon by Maulana Raza.

Before beginning the research, I faced two basic questions: How does one define a 'Muslim' for the purposes of a study of this kind, and can the dispute resolution processes that the study identified be appropriately termed 'Muslim', regardless of interpretations, cultural affiliations or other variables? In an era of increasing religious resurgence, with renewed emphasis on orthopraxy and a clamour for more visible symbols of identity – often concerning personal appearance and dress – the questions assumed an added complexity. With regard to the 'definition' of a Muslim, I decided to take a pragmatic approach and to utilise a generally accepted formula which is also used by the MLSC. It operates on the basis that whoever affirms the fundamental Islamic testimony of truth, the *Shahada*, that there is no God but Allah, and that Muhammad (Pbuh) is His Messenger, is recognised as a Muslim. Such a formula has validity in all the jurisprudential schools and interpretations of Islam and is fully in accord with Islam's juridical history, which says that once a person affirms the *Shahada*, he/she is a Muslim. It is then only up to Allah to judge whether he/she is a good Muslim or not. Taking any other basis as a premise would have been grossly erroneous and could result in unnecessary theological controversy. Thus, the many diasporic Muslims who do not strictly adhere to regular praxes or a specific dress code, a segment referred to by Haddad and Lummis (1987: 171) as 'unmosqued', were not excluded from the research. With regard to the second question, while for practical purposes this study refers to the dispute resolution processes that it analyses as 'Muslim', it does so with the caveat that this is only how that particular community actually identifies those processes.

In this context, Lawrence Rosen's seminal anthropological work on the Islamic law courts of Morocco (Rosen, 1989), which explores the cultural basis of judicial discretion in a *qadi* court, was informative. While his study of the factual operations in a modern Islamic law court in the Arab world is illuminating, it is problematic, insofar as it cannot be held as representing 'Islamic' dispute resolution processes across the Islamic world. Its main focus is one small court in one area in Morocco.

It is important to note that, while the research for this study was conducted in the Hounslow area, the Muslim community there by no means lives in a discrete, hermetically sealed geographical entity or ghetto. For example, some of the respondents in this study live in nearby Southall but utilise the mosque in Hounslow for services and other communal interactions. One ADR agency that covers the area, Relate, is based in the London borough of Harrow. The Black Sisters are based in Southall but also provide services to residents of Hounslow.[12] The MLSC, which has its offices in Ealing Common, is the main point of reference for the Hounslow Mosque imam.

All in all, I conducted and recorded some 50 in-depth interviews of between 60 and 90 minutes each. To ensure confidentiality in view of the sensitivity of the subject matter, the names of almost everyone were withheld in the original thesis. Zaki Badawi was mentioned by name because he was an axial influence on the research and a respected public Muslim figure in the UK and elsewhere. Badawi also said specifically that he had no objection to being named because many of his statements were already in the public domain. Two lawyers, Raficq Abdulla and Soli Osman, also gave permission to use their names.

I interviewed a broad range of people and tried to ensure that the sample was as inclusive as possible. It included the main functionaries of the MLSC, the three imams of the mosque, a few trustees, some elders, some women, a police officer, the solicitor to the Hounslow mosque trustees and some younger members of the local Muslim community. In addition, I interviewed four academic specialists in Islamic law and legal pluralism. I was unable to interview disputants despite assiduous efforts to do so.[13]

The ethnic and class backgrounds as well as the cultural and customary practices of the Hounslow Muslim community reflect those of much of the Muslim diaspora in Britain. Alternative dispute resolution based on the Sharia is used to resolve interpersonal disputes in all Muslim communities, although the degree to which the Sharia and its jurisprudence are considered immutable may differ among some groups.

How generalisable are the findings from this study to other Muslim communities in the United Kingdom? Immigrant Muslims in the UK have many commonalities. Among other things, they share a religion focused on the Sharia; where they originate from the same region (almost 80 per cent of British Muslims come from India, Pakistan and Bangladesh) they share cultural and customary practices, and some even come from the same ethnic and class backgrounds. Therefore, certain findings of this study apply to many of them. For example, the Sharia features in the interpersonal disputes of all Muslim communities and, in addition to observing the laws of the land, Muslim communities also resort to various customary practices that are often conflated with the Sharia.

The receptivity to mediatory practices and their efficacy is dependent on a number of factors. First, mediation is more likely to be acceptable if the community in question is acculturated to the host environment. That predisposes the community to take a more creative approach to its religious laws and view them as coexisting with the laws of the land, with an understanding that nothing can be done that would violate the public laws of the country of abode. Second, receptivity and efficacy depend very much on the extent to which a Muslim community has decided to make the United Kingdom its definitive home. That helps them to shed many cultural prejudices and to view the future as a horizon instead of being burdened by the past. Third, the level of education and socio-economic status of the community, particularly the education of females, would also play an important role. It would help the community to appreciate the value of mediation as a process through which greater gender equity could be fostered. As Walker (2009: 2) suggests, 'Family mediation is a product of social change and heavily influenced by societal values and the specific approaches to family breakdown that have been adopted in each country'.

The findings of the study on which this book is based may not be generalisable in a number of areas, namely where a significant portion of the community considers the Sharia and its jurisprudence as being wholly a-temporal and immutable; where a community views the laws and values of the society in which it presently lives as being inimical to its own personal law and its value system; where a community views its existence in the UK as temporary and the UK norms and laws as being alien to its social ordering and ethical worldview; and where a community is unprepared to engage with the complex and multifaceted processes of acculturation and their impact on issues such as gender relationships, women's rights, issues of youth and so on.

My research showed that most Hounslow Muslims regard Britain as their home and that they view their religious laws as coexisting with the laws of the land, accepting that nothing can be done that would be in violation of UK public laws. They have also undergone significant cultural changes. For example, I came across a number of cases where families had sent young women for further education and where women were beginning to play an important role in community affairs.

Sharia councils are one of several informal ADR mechanisms used by Muslims in Western countries; they are resorted to in cases that are complicated by religious or cultural factors that could affect the social standing of the parties concerned. The ADR approach to dispute resolution is not limited to Muslims and Jews; it has become an increasingly important social movement in Western countries over the past 50 years, helping to ease the pressure on the civil justice system, which is being flooded by cases as societies become more and more diverse and complex. The advantage of ADR is that it takes into account the socio-cultural history and practices of the community in which a dispute occurs.

While some interesting and useful research on ADR has been done by a few Muslim writers in the West over the past decade,[14] relatively little is known of conflict resolution among the 200 to 300 million Muslims in overseas communities who constitute sizeable minorities in the United States, Canada, the United Kingdom and continental Europe, as well as in India, China, Russia, Eastern Europe, South America, and other areas of the world. At the time my research was undertaken, it was one of the few studies of ADR carried out in the United Kingdom through wide-ranging interviews in a Muslim community.

Better understanding of the Muslim diaspora in the West is particularly important currently, because there is a growing public impression, fed by some politicians and sections of the media, especially in Europe, that Muslims are unable to fit into Western society. In the contemporary geopolitical context, Muslim minorities in Western countries are perceived to constitute an unintegrated segment of the population, and any genuine attempt on their part to introduce principles of their faith in the resolution of their disputes is viewed with suspicion by governments, the media and significant parts of the non-Muslim populace, who regard 'the Sharia' (as they perceive it) as being antithetical to the liberal principles of Enlightenment on which the laws of Western countries are generally based.

This message is conveyed in various ways, ranging from criticism of the way some Muslim women dress to condemnation of Muslims and Islam as a whole. For example, in 2006, Jack Straw, then leader of the House of Commons in the UK, said he would ask Muslim women wearing the face veil to lift it when they wanted to talk to him at his constituency office in Blackburn. He told the press four years later that he had only been 'seeking to generate a debate within a framework of freedom' and that he still talks to female constituents who refuse to lift their veil. This is in contrast to Philip Hollobone, MP for Kettering, who said in July 2010 that he would refuse to hold meetings with veiled Muslim women at his constituency office unless they lifted their veil.[15] 'God gave us faces to be expressive. It is not just the words we utter but whether we are smiling, sad, angry or frustrated. You don't get any of that if your face is covered,' he was quoted as saying. At the other end of the spectrum is Dutch MP Geert Wilders, who says 'Islam is merely not [sic] a religion, it is mainly a totalitarian ideology' and wants the Qur'an (which he puts on a par with Adolf Hitler's *Mein Kampf*) to be banned.[16]

My research on which this book is based draws upon three principal areas of discourse: alternative dispute resolution, Islamic law and society as found in the diaspora, and relations between the dispute processes of a local Muslim community and the national legal system, and the wider structures of society. It shows that such statements are based on insufficient knowledge of Islam and Muslims, and on a stereotypical perception of Muslims globally as a monolithic bloc. It provides evidence that the Muslims in Hounslow are already adapting to British society without abandoning their religion and that a substantial portion of Islamic law can be used in the West as an adjunct to the established courts to protect human rights and provide justice. My hope is that my research will increase understanding of the cultural sensibilities of Muslims in the context of ADR and help to improve the conceptualisation and design of ADR training programmes for Muslims in the West. It will obviously also have some bearing on how Muslims in those areas respond to ADR.

Although ADR in general, and mediation in particular, holds great potential for Muslim communities globally, it is more relevant in diasporic settings than in Muslim-majority countries. Given the circumstances that Muslims in Britain have faced over the last four decades, and the creative options they have developed to fit into British society without abandoning their identity, an argument can be made that there is a greater possibility that real creativity in the field of ADR and its ability to bridge the Sharia with different Western legal systems can take place more easily in diasporic settings. Such settings afford the opportunity for Muslims to develop innovative ways of resolving their disputes while ensuring that their ADR processes, using religious law, respect the public laws of the countries concerned. Such possibilities also impart to Muslim communities renewed vigour to speak to their contemporary needs with a voice that is authentic but not ossified in time.

Such a response is not inimical to a faith that has always espoused universalism as a founding creed and has creatively engaged with the different circumstances, situations and societies it has encountered in its evolution. According to Jomier (1989: 37), 'Islam is a clear stream, with well-defined characteristics, which are the same everywhere. But the soil over which the stream flows can be varied. Moreover, in each case, the water will take on the colour of the shores, the sand or the earth which forms its bed.' Similarly, mediation has well-defined characteristics which are the same everywhere, and it, too, like a clear stream, will take on the colour of the shores, the sand or the earth over which it flows. Laws of countries constantly change and reflect the needs of different societies at different stages in their evolution. Customs evolve, but where they assume immutable proportions, instead of becoming the 'living faith' of the dead they can become 'the dead faith' of the living (Pelikan, 1971). In an ever-interdependent and evolving world experiencing rapid globalisation, there is a need for more dialogue between all the stakeholders in this great social movement, a need for us to draw wisdom from the past but not be unnecessarily imprisoned by the past. We need to combine the wisdom of the past judiciously with the needs of the present to create a vocabulary that speaks to us for today and for the future.

This book has the potential to serve several purposes. It provides Western governments with an actual case study of a Muslim community and its legal ordering. It gives Family Court judges and ADR organisations an insight into the types of issues they may have to handle with regard to the cultural sensitivities of a diasporic Muslim community. It indicates the type of training government institutions could impart to the imams of the mosques to enable them to play a meaningful role in conflict resolution in the context of the multifaceted issues faced by diasporic Muslim communities. Through such training and practices, the imams could contribute to a culture of social harmony and negotiated settlement, thus reducing the potential of a culture of disenfranchisement, anger and conflict. Such training can be carried out with a minimal financial burden on governments – a critical factor in the present global recession – by encouraging mosques to utilise their own congregation-generated funds for this purpose. Finally, the book puts forward a successful example of legal pluralism in Britain, which could provide inspiration for similar initiatives in other countries.

The Muslim Community in Britain

The Muslim presence in Britain goes back at least 300 years, to the time of the East India Company, which recruited seamen from Yemen, Gujarat, Sindh, Assam and Bengal, who later settled in various parts of the United Kingdom. By the nineteenth century, there were already a number of Muslim businesses in England, of which one of the best known was the fashionable 'Mahomed's Baths', founded in Brighton by Sake Deen Mohammed (1750–1851). Following the opening of the Suez Canal in 1869, seamen from Yemen settled in small communities in Cardiff, Liverpool, London, South Shields and Tyneside. They set up *zawiyah*s (places of prayer generally associated with Sufi Islam)[1] which, in addition to being places of congregation, became centres for celebration of rites of passage such as birth, marriage, circumcision and funerals. In the 1920s and 1930s, many of the seamen in the United Kingdom merchant navy were Muslims and a large number of them stayed on in Britain after the Second World War. Some ten years later, those pioneers acted as points of contact and sources of assistance for the substantial chain-migration (migration of spouses and dependents) from East and West Pakistan that took place in the 1950s (Runnymede Trust, 1997).

Groups of Muslim intellectuals also emerged in Britain in the late nineteenth century. From 1893 to 1908, a weekly journal, *The Crescent,* was distributed from Liverpool by William Henry Quilliam, a lawyer who became a Muslim in 1897 after spending time in Algeria and Morocco. He became famous throughout the Islamic world as the author of the influential *The Faith of Islam*. Various Muslim countries welcomed and honoured him. The Ottoman Sultan made him *Shaykh al-Islam* for Britain and the Shah of Persia appointed him Persian Consul in Liverpool (Lewis, 1994). Quilliam also set up the Islamic Institute and the Liverpool Mosque, as well as institutions for the care of children and orphans.

Britain's first mosque was established in Woking, Surrey in 1889 with funds provided by Shah Jehan, ruler of Bhopal in India. The mosque became the base for the *Muslim India and the Islamic Review*, which was renamed *The Islamic Review* in 1921. Those associated with the journal included Khwaja Kamal-ud-Din, a barrister originally from Lahore, who was viewed by the British press as the spiritual leader of all Muslims in Britain; Lord Headley, a civil engineer who had lived in India and converted to Islam; the Rt Hon. Syed Ameer Ali, an Indian jurist and well-known Islamic scholar; and Abdullah Yusuf Ali and Marmaduke Pickthall, both well known for their influential translations of the Qur'an.

In 1910, a group of prominent British Muslims, including Lord Headley and Syed Ameer Ali, met at a central London hotel and, with the help of His Highness the Aga Khan III, established the London Mosque Fund. In 1941, the East London Mosque Trust purchased three buildings in Stepney and converted them into London's first mosque. Meanwhile, major purpose-built mosques had been built in Birmingham, Glasgow and Manchester. The site for the Regent's Park mosque in London was donated by the British Government in 1944 in recognition of a similar donation made by the Egyptian government to the Anglican community in Cairo, but the building was only completed in 1977 (Runnymede Trust, 1997).

The last quarter of the nineteenth century and most of the twentieth century witnessed a steady flow of Muslim students from various colonial territories, and after the colonies became independent, from member states of the British Commonwealth. One of the most famous Muslim students to study law at the Inns of Court in London was the founder of modern Pakistan, Mohammad Ali Jinnah, whose portrait in oils still hangs at the entrance to the Great Hall and Library of Lincoln's Inn (Wolpert, 1984).

While the connection of Muslims with the UK goes back some three centuries, large-scale migration to Britain began only in the 1950s. According to Peach (1990) the probable Muslim population of Britain in 1951 was about 23,000. By 1971 it was about 369,000. Migration was encouraged because there were major labour shortages in Britain, particularly in the steel and textile industries of Yorkshire and Lancashire, and mainly for night shifts. The migrant workers earned 'wages for labouring jobs in Britain in the early 1960s [...] over 30 times those offered for similar jobs in Pakistan' (Shaw, 1988: 9). Actually, or in effect, invited by employers, they were Commonwealth citizens and had full rights of entry, residence and civic rights. They came mainly from the Mirpur district of Azad Kashmir in what was then known as West Pakistan, from the North West Frontier region of Pakistan, or from the Sylhet area of northeastern Bangladesh, known then as East Pakistan. In all these largely rural areas, there was a long-standing tradition of young men migrating for long periods of time to work and save money for their families back home (Lewis, 1994: 16).

Migrant workers also came from India, and about one-sixth of those were Muslims in the 1950s and 1960s. A high proportion of them came from three districts of Gujarat: Baroda, Surat and Bharuch, areas with a long tradition of migration and trade, especially with East Africa (Lewis, 1994). The migration to Britain was thus from a rural setting to an urban one as well as to a different country and culture, and it involved an increase in wealth and income as well as a change in occupation (Runnymede Trust, 1997: 14).

About 15 per cent of the 150,000 Asians who came from the East African countries in the late 1960s and early 1970s were Muslims with family roots in Pakistan or Gujarat. Substantial communities from Turkey and Middle Eastern and North African countries also began to be established in the 1970s. Later, Somali, Iranian, Arab, Turkish and Bosnian communities settled in many British cities. More recently, following the collapse of socialism in the former Soviet Union and the subsequent civil wars in Yugoslavia, a number of Central Asian and Eastern and Central European Muslims have settled in Britain. According to Nielsen (1991), there were at least 5,000 converts to Islam in Britain in 1991, about half of whom were of African-Caribbean origin. The 2001 census showed that Muslims, at around 1.6 million, made up 3.1 per cent of the population of England, and their number increased to two million by 2010. According to the 2011 Government census Muslims today at 2.7 million people represent a rise of 4.8 per cent since 2001.[2] The largest group originated from Pakistan, followed by those from Bangladesh, India, Cyprus, Malaysia, Arab countries and parts of Africa. Britain has seen a growing number of refugees during the last 20 years and many of them are Kurdish, Iraqi, Somali, Afghan, Bosnian and Kosovar Muslims. The 2001 census found that approximately 75 per cent of the total British Muslim community were of South Asian origin, and over 90 per cent of Pakistanis and Bengalis classified themselves as Muslims.

On average, the non-white Muslim population is much younger than the white non-Muslim population (Coker, 2003). South Asian communities – Muslim as well as non-Muslim – in Britain have a higher proportion of people under the age of 20 and a lower proportion over the age of 60 than in the majority population. Because of this, they are bound to increase in size over the next 20 years, both absolutely and relatively. It is estimated that the Pakistani population will eventually stabilise at about 900,000, and the Bangladeshi population at about 360,000, towards 2020 (Ballard and Kalra, 1991). Given the present geopolitical realities and the political situation in many Muslim countries, it is likely that many more Muslim minorities will be seeking asylum in Britain and Western Europe in the next decade.

In the early days, most Pakistani migrants to Britain saw themselves as temporary visitors who would one day return to their country of origin (Anwar, 1979). By the 1960s, however, they began to see themselves as settlers rather than temporary residents, and established families. A major impetus for this change was the Commonwealth Immigration Act 1962, which closed the door to automatic entry for Commonwealth citizens, forcing families to choose between being together in Britain or being divided between Britain and Pakistan for long periods. According to Lewis (1994) migrant numbers also increased dramatically in the 1960s because of fear among wives, often fed by rumours, that their husbands had married a second, British wife (Shaw, 1988). Between 1961 and 1966, the Pakistani population grew by over 400 per cent, from about 25,000 to 120,000. Between 1973 and 1981, a further 82,000 people came as settlers, almost all of them dependents of men already in Britain (Runnymede Trust, 1997).

The voucher system introduced by the 1962 Act contributed to the rapid generation of a Muslim middle class by creating 'B' vouchers, as they were known, for people with professional backgrounds. From 1965 to 1967, 'B' vouchers were issued to 1,264 doctors from Pakistan, 577 teachers and 632 engineers and scientists (Runnymede Trust, 1997). South Asian Muslims also established a wide range of small businesses, including some 8,500 Bangladeshi restaurants. In 1996, the Bangladeshi catering industry employed about 60,000 people, more than steel, coal and ship-building combined, and had an annual turnover of £1.5 billion (Bowen, 1966).

According to Lewis (1994), most South Asian communities in Britain evolved in four phases: pioneers, followed by what is known as 'chain-migration' of generally unskilled male workers, and then migration of wives and children, and finally, emergence of a British-born generation. The voucher system was suspended in 1965. However, since there was still a demand for labour into the late 1960s, 'an increasing number of Mirpuri men [from the Mirpur district of Pakistan Punjab] began, following one of their periodic trips home, to bring their fourteen- and fifteen-year-old sons back with them to Britain. Young enough to be permitted to enter as dependents – and thus avoiding the bar on males – it would not be long before they left school and started work' (Ballard, 1990).

These loopholes were eventually closed and the migration of single men ended with the Immigration Act of 1971. After that, dependents could only enter the United Kingdom if they came at the same time as the breadwinners. The third and fourth phases of the immigration experience then accelerated, with the arrival of wives and children and the emergence of British-born communities.

Not all Muslim communities, however, have followed the four-phase pattern of community formation sequentially or simultaneously. Another set of South Asian communities merged all four phases into one. Those were people expelled by, or fleeing from, the increasingly oppressive nationalist and racist regimes in Africa. Pressure had been building on Asian minorities in Kenya from 1965, and in Uganda from 1969 (culminating in Idi Amin's expulsion of Asians in 1972). Thus, by 1981 there were 155,000 South Asians of East African origin in Britain, of whom possibly 15 per cent were Muslims (Clarke et al., 1990). Similarly, in the 1980s and 1990s, political circumstances in Somalia, Bosnia, Afghanistan and Iraq led to thousands of people seeking asylum in Britain, collapsing the four-phase evolution process trend even further. As a result, Muslims in Britain today are a microcosm of the Islamic *umma* worldwide.[3]

British Muslims established a wide range of community organisations in the 1960s. They began to become more self-consciously 'Islamic' in their sense of identity and more observant in the practice of their faith. The factors underlying this included their desire to build a sense of communal identity in a situation of material disadvantage in an alien culture; to keep generations together and transmit traditional values; and to access inner spiritual resources to withstand various pressures, for example, racism, Islamophobia and the threat to their customs and cultures from Western materialism and permissiveness (Runnymede Trust, 1997).

Interface between the Sharia and United Kingdom laws

Muslims today comprise a diverse, but significant, religious minority in Britain; many of them have a close affinity to their religious law, the Sharia, which governs most aspects of their lives and constitutes the most critical element in any discussion on the application of the principles of their faith to their contemporary needs. While there have been some modifications to the application of the Sharia in the Islamic world, Muslims still regard its family law aspects as an 'integral part of the scheme of religious duties' (Coulson, 1964: 147). Consequently, for many Muslims the classical doctrine of medieval Islam remains inviolate as expressing the only standards of conduct valid in the eyes of God; any deviations from this norm, condoned as legal practice in certain areas, 'were never recognised as legitimate expressions of Islamic law' (Coulson, 1964: 147).

Coulson wrote the preceding in 1964, but this issue still lies at the heart of the challenge facing Muslims in Western societies in 2012: how to reconcile their religious law with their obligations as citizens of a secular, non-Islamic, nation-state (Ansari, 2002: 22). This matter also came up for discussion at a 2004 conference on Islam in Britain, where it was stated that Muslims in Britain want greater recognition of their faith, with the introduction of Islamic law for civil cases.[4]

It is in the realm of the family that this challenge is most strongly felt. The family is a central institution in Muslim society. In Britain, families today have to cope with problems of rapid urbanisation and the pressures of living in cramped and stressful conditions in towns and cities. These conditions of contemporary life have an impact on Muslim family relationships. Although there has been an alarming increase in divorce rates among Muslims, their marriages tend to be on the whole more stable than Western ones because they are based on an entirely different set of assumptions, which reflect the Muslim notion of the cosmos: as there is order and balance in the universe, there should be a similar natural pattern in society, including the household. In a conceptual sense, one mirrors the other, with each individual member playing an equally significant role in his or her own capacity, which is related to the other members of the family (A. Ahmed, 2002).

The proper behaviour and responsibilities of all members of the family are constantly emphasised in the Qur'an and the *hadith* (Prophet Muhammad's sayings and actions). Dignity and modesty are encouraged in the family. The father, mother, children and elders all have a positive and defined role to play. The model of ideal behaviour comes from early Islam. The Prophet is held as the example of the ideal son, husband and father. According to Ahmad (1974: 13), 'The family is a divinely inspired institution that came into existence with the creation of man. The human

race is a product of this institution and not the other way round.'
Not surprisingly, the most intricate rules and regulations guide
Muslim family life. Almost a third of the legal injunctions in the
Qur'an deal with family matters, covering different generations.
A Muslim family is traditionally an extended family, normally
with three or four generations within its circle (A. Ahmed,
2002: 151).

The areas in which a Muslim family normally faces difficulties
in Britain include marriage, *mahr* (the contractual sum due to a
woman in the event of divorce), *iddat* (the period of abstinence
after divorce), custody of children, mixed marriages, plural marriages, change of faith, and inheritance.

Marriage is an essential part of the Islamic way of life.[5] It is the
only way in which a man and a woman may lawfully have sexual
contact and establish a stable relationship based on mutual love
and affection, together with psychological, emotional and spiritual support. Marriage is as essential to keeping the relationship
between the two individuals and families prosperous and happy
as it is to preserving the human race, Islamic values and traditions (Ahsan, 1995). United Kingdom law recognises a Muslim
marriage only when it is certified by one of the few mosques or
Muslim organisations licensed to issue civil marriage certificates.
The marriage also has to be registered at a Registry Office. Ahsan
observes that in Islam both sons and daughters have the absolute
right to select their partner and fashion their future life within
the framework of the faith. Even in arranged marriages they can
reject the parental choice if they feel that the parents are abusing
their trust and resorting to an 'un-Islamic' practice. However, in
practice, marriage partners tend to be selected by parents rather
than by the man or woman involved.

Forced marriages are decreasing and no longer a serious problem in the Hounslow area, according to a young Muslim graphic
designer and other people interviewed. A Muslim solicitor confirmed that they are also not very common in the UK as a whole.
However, he added:

There still remains a fine line between 'arranged marriages'
and 'forced marriages'. The latter still occur in some parts of

Britain, but secularly trained Muslim lawyers, when advising on such issues, remind parents of the laws against abduction and kidnapping.

In the recent past, instead of seeking a marriage partner locally, many Muslims imported a son-in-law or a daughter-in-law from their country of origin, often members of their own extended family. Tensions generally arose when the groom was uneducated, came from a remote village, was unable to speak English and knew nothing of British culture and traditions. In many cases, such sons-in-law lived for a long time as guests of the bride's family and obtained unemployment benefits to supplement the family's income. Sometimes tensions reached such a peak that life became intolerable, and in a few cases the marriage ended in divorce. Muslims in Britain have learned through experience that consultation and finding a marriage partner from among the new generation brought up in Britain are the way to avoid mismatches from 'overseas marriages' and traumas caused within the family by 'love matches'. Recent changes to the United Kingdom immigration laws have also contributed to this (Ahsan, 1995).

In dissolution of marriage, too, the interface between the Sharia and UK law is marked by some disparities. Although marriage is described in the Qur'an as a strong and binding contract, it is not a sacrament or indissoluble. Islamic law permits divorce, but only as a last resort and refers to it as 'the most abominable of permissible acts' (*abghaz al mubahat*). Contrary to popular belief, it also allows a wife the right to divorce in certain circumstances. A woman can repudiate her marriage under a form of divorce known as *khula*;[6] or initiate a divorce if she has been given the right to do so in the marriage contract (*tafwid*); finally, she can also divorce if the husband turns out to be impotent, fails to maintain the wife properly or deserts her for a long time. Muslims are allowed to implement a gradual process towards dissolution of marriage through divorce when all possibility of reconciliation has been exhausted. However, once the irrevocable decision has been taken, Islamic law makes the separation mutually amicable and exhorts the husband to be especially generous financially towards the wife and not take back from her whatever he has given her, even if it be a 'heap of gold' (Qur'an, 4: 20).

Because Muslim divorce is not recognised by UK law, if a Muslim couple decide to divorce they have to go to a civil court. However, according to Zaki Badawi, under Islamic law the divorce has to be 'Islamised' before the woman can marry again. From as early as 1983, the Union of Muslim Organisations has been asking unsuccessfully for the application of Islamic law in such matters within the Muslim community (Ahsan, 1995: 24).

Mahr is another area where UK law does not recognise a right inherent in Muslim marriage. The Qur'an commands men to 'give women their dower', which is a contractual sum stipulated in the marriage contract and payable to the wife by the husband. According to Coulson (1964: 14),

> the basic concept of marriage under some forms of the customary law was that of a sale of the woman by the father, or other near male relative, who received, qua vendor, the purchase price paid by the husband. The effect of this is simple. Qur'anic rule, then, is to transfer the wife from the position of a sale-object to that of a contracting party who, in return for her granting the right of sexual union with herself, is entitled to receive the due consideration of the dower. She is now endowed with a legal competence she did not possess before.

Potential conflict between principles of Islamic law and the laws of the United Kingdom also exists with regard to *iddat*, the period of abstinence during which the wife has to remain unmarried after dissolution of marriage by divorce, death or any other cause. The *iddat* is four months for a widow who is not visibly pregnant and three months for a divorced woman who is not visibly pregnant. The main objects of *iddat* are to ascertain whether the wife is pregnant and, if so, to determine the paternity of the child; in the case of divorce, to give the husband an opportunity to return to his wife if divorce is revocable; and for a widow to mourn her dead husband. During the *iddat*, the divorced wife is entitled to full maintenance from the husband or members of his family. The widow in mourning is not supposed to engage in normal activities such as employment or to move about freely. Normally, in Muslim countries, members of the extended family look after the household of the widow; however, in Britain, problems arise if the widow has no near relatives and has to look after the children herself. Because *iddat* is not recognised by UK law, a working widow has no right to take leave of four months and ten days from her work; nor does she have a right to full social security support during the period (Ahsan, 1995).

Islamic law also differs considerably from UK laws over custody. Young children (boys up to the age of nine, and girls up to puberty or the age of marriage, depending upon the specific school of law) remain in the custody of their divorced mother. As long as she is nursing the young children and looking after the others, it is the father's responsibility to bear the full cost of their care. In addition, he alone is responsible for their accommodation, clothing and food, even though they are in the mother's custody or home (Ahsan, 1995). Considerable conflict occurs over this, particularly in mixed marriages.[7] The problem becomes more complicated when a Muslim father abducts an infant and takes him/her to his Muslim country of origin. With the majority of Muslim countries not being party to the 1980 Hague Convention on the Civil Aspects of International Child Abduction, this can be traumatic for the mother even if she has converted to Islam. In a few cases, the situation is reversed, with the mother being the abductor.[8]

A Muslim man is allowed to marry a non-Muslim woman provided she is one of the People of the Book (*ahl al-kitab*); that is, Christian or Jewish. However, a Muslim woman cannot marry a man of any other religion, including Christianity and Judaism, unless he converts to Islam. On the face of it this regulation seems discriminatory, but if one looks at the underlying philosophy of Islamic law, this is not so. In Islam, the husband is the head of the family and the children born of such marriage belong to the religion of the father. Where the husband is non-Muslim and the wife Muslim, the children cannot be brought up as Muslims. The marriage of a Muslim woman to a non-Muslim man is viewed as null and void even if it is validly solemnised according to the laws of the non-Muslim state. This principle has implications for *mahr* (dower) and the rights of a non-Muslim wife to have control over her property, as well as for custody, access and inheritance. A non-Muslim wife cannot inherit any part of the estate of her Muslim husband, because it is the convention for an heir to profess the same religion as the person from whom the descent is traced. She can, however, be given up to one-third of the estate through a will (Ahsan, 1995). The Sharia does not allow Muslims to marry polytheists or atheists.

Polygamy is another area where UK laws clash with Islamic law. A Muslim man is allowed to marry up to four wives, under some strict conditions, whereas UK law allows only monogamy. Islam does not permit extramarital relations or living together outside wedlock. The common-law wife, unmarried mother or bachelor father is regarded as an abhorrent aberration (Ahsan, 1995).

Change of faith is also an area of conflict between Islamic law and UK laws. Many indigenous British people have embraced Islam over the past few years, but immigrant Muslim communities in Britain have been unable to provide the necessary emotional, psychological and material support to such newcomers to the faith. If the husband is the convert and his wife remains Christian or Jewish, the marriage may continue; if she is of another faith, the marriage will be nullified under Islamic law. If it is the wife who adopts Islam, the husband is invited to do so as well; if he refuses, the marriage is invalid under Islamic law. In a number of cases the husband has refused to convert as well and the resulting break-up of the family has been difficult for all parties, particularly the children.

Muslims in Britain also face difficulties in the field of inheritance law. The Islamic law of inheritance is very comprehensive and is postulated on a different world view than that of secular modern English law. It aims to provide justice to all members of the extended family in accordance with their religious rights and responsibilities. Since the allocation of shares to different members of the family has been determined by the Qur'an, it is not feasible for Muslims to alter the system to conform with the law of the land. Because Western laws of inheritance are different from the Sharia, if a Muslim wishes to divest of his property according to the principles of Islamic law, he has to do so through a will. Some Muslims use their wills to authorise well-qualified and knowledgeable individuals to distribute their property according to Islamic principles (Ahsan, 1995).

Pressures of rapid acculturation

A large proportion of British Muslims are from the rural areas of the South Asian subcontinent. Many have been in Britain for only 40 to 50 years. They have come to accept the UK as their home, establishing a wide range of community organisations. However, over time they have begun to feel more self-consciously Muslim, projecting a corporate Islamic identity in opposition to an alien and often hostile environment. The 2001 census showed Britain's Muslims to have the youngest age demographic with one-third under 16 years and 50 per cent under 25 years. The first data release for the 2011 census does not provide a population count by religion but the data on local authorities recording the highest population growth suggests such a social trend.[9] This segment would constitute an integral part of a 'burgeoning British-born second generation' (Ballard, 1994b: 6).

Like their counterparts in the United States, Muslims in the United Kingdom are experiencing rapid acculturation (Haddad and Lummis, 1987). Educated in the British education system, young Muslims adopt norms of the host culture that seem to be at odds with those of their parents and what are considered to be appropriate to Islamic obligations. This often leads to inter-generational conflict, most visibly within the family arena, which is regarded by most Muslims as the bastion of their religious and cultural values. Thus, young Muslims face a number of pressures from different and often conflicting directions, including the mosque, family, youth organisations, extremist Muslim organisations and Islamophobic messages from the media (Runnymede Trust, 1997). Against this backdrop, they have to deal with day-to-day issues that exert severe pressures on their parents, community leaders and themselves. The second generation of Muslims in Britain are beginning to question the relevance and meaning of elaborate social and religious rituals, segregation of the sexes and imposition of dietary restrictions. Many have come to discover that some of their parents' beliefs are not religious but have arisen from local customs (Mirza, 1989; Lewis, 2007).

The experiences and identities of Muslim women are also relevant to this study. Muslim women in the diaspora have to grapple with a stereotypical image of themselves, largely created by Western scholarship and buttressed by Western media portrayals. This creates 'a false impression that the subordination of women is somehow a specifically Muslim characteristic' (Ansari, 2002: 14). Ansari notes that 'This picture of submissiveness and oppression is far removed from the lived experience of most Muslim women in Britain.' The different communities of which they form a part have constructed their own variations of gender relations, shaped by cultures and social structures derived from their regions of origin and underpinned by their own interpretation of patriarchal religious ideology. However, that still does not obviate the larger issue faced by Muslim women as to whether their roles are really scripturally assigned.

This issue is particularly apposite with regard to arranged marriages: are they sanctioned by religious law or a function of culture? Though arranged marriages among young Muslims in Britain are declining – 67 per cent for women aged 16 to 34, as compared with 87 per cent for women over 50 (Modood and Berthoud, 1997) – such marriages have been more common among South Asian Muslim communities than among those originating from other geographical areas (Bridgewood, 1986: 199, 208). Since the 1980s, various organisations have emerged in England to deal with some of these issues; for example, the Muslim Women's Helpline, a voluntary body set up in London to provide counselling and welfare advice to Muslim women[10] and the Southall Black Sisters. This study draws upon some of their insights and experiences.

The mosque is an important arena of socialisation, which gives rise to some difficulty because many imams and religion teachers have received their secular and religious education outside Britain. It is common for Muslim children up to the age of 14 to regularly attend mosque schools where religious education is mainly imparted by rote learning. Often, there is also a widespread perception in Muslim communities that the imams are not able to help teenagers to deal with the major social and ethical issues they face in Britain.

Muslim youth organisations, too, play a significant role in shaping the identity of young Muslims in Britain. Often, the young find a discrepancy between the types of issues brought up within the youth organisations, and what they are taught about their faith and its practice at home as well as by imams and religion teachers (Lewis, 1997, Lewis, 2007). This becomes a source of conflict, both in the home as well as in religious schools. Extremist Muslim organisations that publish their ideas in English in pamphlets and online also exert some influence on the youth. Frequently, either implicitly or explicitly, they are critical of various aspects of tradition that they feel are culture-bound or located in a geographical or temporal context far removed from the present. They also tend to be anti-Western in their rhetoric and their stark world view without nuances tends to appeal to some younger Muslims, who feel that at least they are able to capture a clear picture of the reality of their lives and develop a practical agenda (of resistance and struggle) to deal with it.

The media, with their constant Islamophobic messages, which today have a global and instantaneous reach unparalleled in human history, play a major role in undermining the self-image of young Muslims in Britain and create a feeling of antipathy towards Muslims in the wider society. The impact of these developments is not only felt at the individual level; it also reduces young Muslims' confidence in community institutions, the family and the faith itself. According to a young Muslim teacher, 'The distorted image portrayed by the media is so profound, it is believed by Muslim elders that 60–80 per cent of young Muslims will never practise Islam other than [...] rituals' (Runnymede Trust, 1997: 17).

Muslim youth growing up in Western countries inevitably tend more or less to take up the mores of the dominant culture in which they are living and in which they are being acculturated. Due to shortage of good educational materials portraying a broader humanistic and civilisational dimension of Islam, there is often a tendency to resort to a more textually oriented, simplistic and dogmatic approach to the faith. According to a young Muslim female graduate I interviewed, this sometimes takes the form of dressing in a manner compatible with 'Islamic' principles. At other times it takes the form of rejecting whatever may be 'Islamic' because of its perceived strong normative and dogmatic stance. The confusion often leads to intergenerational tension, with the parents espousing a more communitarian ethic while the youth veer towards greater individualism. Finally, there is the street culture of young people who, when either unemployed or with little or no prospect of employment, often resort to gang formation and anti-social activities. With a large proportion of all British Muslims being under the age of 25, to be concerned for British Muslims is to be concerned with Muslim *youth*.

Runnymede Trust (1997: 18) presents a number of suggestions from various people and institutions on how to deal with Islamophobia and its devastating consequences. These include creation and development of a national body to represent British Muslims to government and other public bodies; production of more high-quality books about Islam for schools and libraries, which involves persuading major publishers to commission Muslim writers for this purpose; taking steps to ensure that imams and other religious leaders have appropriate training and expertise to help young British Muslims to cope with the problems and pressures of modern secular society; encouraging Muslims to train as teachers, including, but not only as, teachers of religious education; and training in media relations. There is an important need to provide awareness-raising seminars and training for journalists. It is also vital for Muslims to be involved in making a range of TV and radio programmes and writing articles for the press. Media-monitoring projects need to be set up that enable Muslims to make educated and informed critiques and complaints about inaccurate, misleading or distorted media coverage. Voluntary welfare projects should be established to help non-Muslims as well as Muslims. Also, Muslim organisations should make common cause with non-Muslim organisations and secular bodies. Islamic financial institutions should be established to fund apprenticeship and training, and more Muslims should be encouraged to start well-planned business initiatives.

Problems of recognising the Sharia

By and large, Muslims communities in Britain have been able to cope with their problems despite the great pressures arising from their interface with a Western, liberal society, with its challenging secular values and perceived permissiveness. In their endeavour to create a 'space for Islam' for themselves, they have even asserted that it is their human right to have communal autonomy to apply Islamic law to their family or personal matters.

In 1975, Sheikh Syed Darsh, the Al-Azhar-educated head cleric of the Regent's Park mosque in London, stated:

When a Muslim is prevented from obeying this law he feels that he is failing to fulfil a religious duty. He will not feel at peace with the conscience or the environment in which he lives and this will lead to disenchantment. [...] They [that is Muslims] believe that the British society, with its rich experience of different cultures and ways of life, especially the Islamic way of life which they used to see in India, Malaysia, Nigeria and so many other nations of Islamic orientation, together with their respect for personal and communal freedom, will enable the Muslim migrants to realise their entity within the freedom of British society. When we request the host society to recognise our point of view, we are appealing to a tradition of justice and equity well established in this country. The scope of the family law is not wide and does not contradict, in essence, the law here in this country. Both aim at the fulfilment of justice and happiness of the members of the family. Still, there are certain Islamic points which, with understanding and the spirit of accommodation, would not go so far as to create difficulties in the judiciary system. After all, we are asking for their application among themselves, the Muslim community, as our Christian brothers in Islamic countries are following in the family traditions and the Christian point of view. The Qur'an itself has given them this right (Pasha, 1977).

According to I. Ahmed (2002), such autonomy would give rise to serious legal, philosophical, theoretical and political problems related to current Western notions of justice. Islamic laws and practices regarding marriage provide examples of such issues. As observed earlier in this chapter, the recognised schools of Islamic jurisprudence view marriage as a central institution of Muslim society. In legal terms, marriage is not a sacred bond but a civil contract between two free individuals. However, the consent of the guardian is considered necessary by some jurists while others do not consider it obligatory for an adult female. A girl may not be coerced into marrying someone of whom she does not approve, but since traditional law does not prescribe an age limit, even very young individuals can be married. In such cases, it devolves upon the guardian to decide the terms of the contract.

In addition, a Muslim male is allowed up to four wives at the same time if he has the resources to look after them equally. A man can dissolve a marriage by pronouncing his intention to do so three times in a prescribed manner. There are different ways of doing it, but in principle a man can secure a divorce at will, even when he is advised to seek reconciliation (Amin, 1989). Women can apply for divorce under exceptional circumstances, though that does not mean that a woman can secure a divorce at will. Normally, she has to be ready to pay an agreed sum of money to the husband, who must agree to her proposal (Doi, 1984). These provisions could be seen as being antithetical to civil laws on monogamy and gender equality.

As noted earlier, inheritance is another area where there could be problems. In Islam, the distribution of a deceased father's assets among his children follows the principle that the share of the female children is one-half that of the male children. Further, while Muslim wives are entitled to a share, non-Muslim wives are not. However, a husband can gift some property to his non-Muslim wife through a will or testament. The property of a Muslim may not be inherited by non-Muslim children or parents. The property of an apostate cannot be inherited, nor can the property of a Muslim be passed on to an apostate. As regards children born out of wedlock, according to the Hanafi school, the illicit child cannot inherit from the father but may inherit from the mother's side. Children of a deceased son are excluded from inheriting the property of the grandfather; instead, the share is distributed among the siblings of the deceased son. Finally, although Muslims are encouraged to take care of orphans, there is no right to adopt a child. An adopted child cannot inherit the property of the adoptive parents; however, a part of the property can be left to such a child through a testament.

The Sharia laws pertaining to family matters obviously differ radically from the laws of the United Kingdom. I. Ahmed (2002) observes that only a monogamous marriage is legally recognised in Europe and that any restriction on marriage between a Muslim and a non-Muslim cannot be condoned by a European legal system because Western countries have ratified the International Convention on the Elimination of All Forms of Discrimination Against Women (1979). Article 16 of the Convention unequivocally places women on par with men in matters of marriage and allows them to choose a spouse freely. Similarly, divorce, the rights of a child (both within or outside of wedlock), inheritance and adoption are matters in which traditional discriminatory practices have been eliminated.

I. Ahmed (2002) points out that practical application of the Sharia would not be a simple matter. Who would be competent to interpret the Sharia? And which school or *madhab* of the Sharia would take precedence? Who would be competent to interpret and enforce Muslim family law? Would non-Muslim judges be competent enough to consider cases involving Islamic law or should the State set up separate courts with Muslim judges to try cases involving disputes over family matters? Even more intractable would be problems stemming from mixed marriages. There would be a possibility of some Muslims preferring to seek redress from the mainstream legal system or the conflicting parties might appeal to the two different legal systems. Who should decide which court is appropriate for a Muslim? On the theoretical and philosophical levels, the demand for communal autonomy poses serious challenges to current understanding of multiculturalism and pluralism.

Muslim law rulings on family matters are underpinned by ontological and epistemological values embedded in the Sharia that identify Revelation and community consensus as superior to individual reason (I. Ahmed, 2002). In sharp contrast, Western European legal systems have been reformed in the light of the

Enlightenment values of rationality and secular humanism. The human rights of individuals are a centrepiece of such reformed law. How and whether these diametrically opposite approaches can be reconciled into a coherent system of law is a matter on which additional serious work needs to be done. Ahmed further cautions that any concession to Muslim separatism, under the garb of communal autonomy, would give rise to a profoundly negative response against Muslims from the wider society, deriving from xenophobia in general and Islamophobia in particular.

With regard to adherence to religious law, it is worth noting that even among Muslim states there is no agreement on how best to apply the Sharia, including its rulings on family matters. Saudi Arabia and Iran apply the Sharia in a more or less complete sense. Mauritania, Libya and Egypt base their legal praxis on the Sharia in principle, but not consistently in practice. The United Arab Emirates, Oman and Pakistan recognise the Sharia as the supreme law of the land but deviate from it in practice. Twenty countries retain Sharia courts for personal law, while 14 make reference to it in personal law codifications. Nine Muslim-majority countries have abolished all reference to the Sharia. These include Eritrea, Senegal, Turkey and the former Soviet republics with a Muslim majority, namely Kazakhstan, Kyrgyzstan, Turkmenistan, Tajikistan and Azerbaijan (I. Ahmed, 2002: 32).

Before continuing this discussion of the Sharia, it is instructive to trace the beginnings and growth of the Muslim community in Hounslow, particularly with regard to the central position of religious faith in their lives and how they have adapted to modern British society.

Overview of the Hounslow
Muslim Community

The migration of Muslims into Hounslow and the community's development are inextricably linked with economic changes in the area. Therefore, it is important to begin with a brief outline of Hounslow's economic history, showing how labour shortages combined with changes in the immigration law to create favourable conditions for immigrants in the second half of the twentieth century.

The borough of Hounslow, comprising a total area of 22.59 square miles and stretching some ten miles from east to west, and over five miles from north to south, is the eighth-largest of the 33 London boroughs. It is situated in the Lower Thames Valley in West London, on the north bank of the River Thames (Hounslow, 1990). In 2001, it had a population of 212,341, of whom 19,378 were Muslim.[1]

As early as the fifteenth century, brick-making was an important activity in the area and it developed into a major industry by the end of the nineteenth century. The opening of the Hounslow loop railway line in the mid-nineteenth century gave impetus to the rapid development of the borough. Major industries, such as breweries, distilleries, gasworks, sawmills and chemical works were established in nearby Chiswick, Brentford and Isleworth. As in the rest of the country, production of consumer goods rose sharply in the immediate aftermath of the Second World War, but there was a major setback within 18 months because six years of war had exhausted the national resources, including personnel and machinery in the mining industry, and there was a severe national energy shortage (Marshall, 1995: 90). In the winter of 1945–46, the Ministry of Fuel ordered all but the most essential industries to shut down and drastic restrictions were imposed on domestic consumption of electricity. The fuel crisis led to massive unemployment, with 10,000 workers losing their jobs within a few weeks.

Even after the energy shortage eased, industry faced yet another critical problem: shortage of labour. A newspaper reported a director of the Champion Spark Plug Company as saying: 'Shortage of labour is an acute problem [...] if I could get them, I could start fifty new employees tomorrow.'[2] In June 1946, the Minister of Fuel and Power, Emmanuel Shinwell, warned that too few ex-servicemen were taking 'productive jobs' because they had high expectations of entering self-employment or of finding white-collar jobs with good career prospects. Others shared his concern that the labour force was 'shy of the dirty industries' while other employment with more attractive conditions was available.[3]

Following Britain's move away from coal and steam power and decline of the older riverside industries, new factories emerged along the Great West Road running towards Heathrow airport, which bordered Hounslow. Most of the industries established before 1945 have disappeared. Since 1951, Heathrow has been London's major airport and its continued expansion has stimulated the development of new types of commercial and industrial activities within Hounslow – particularly in high-technology, computer and electronic industries – as well as aggravated the problems faced by more traditional industries, which have been unable to compete with the relatively high wage rates offered at the airport. In the spring of 1965, attempts by several local employers to recruit labour from as far afield as South Wales, North England and Scotland 'met with little success', according to the Local Employment Committee's quarterly report.

In the 1960s, as the Greater London Council implemented a policy to reduce congestion and air pollution by discouraging further development of manufacturing industry, industries began to move out of Middlesex county, in which Hounslow is located. As a result of the relocation of several big manufacturing companies and closures caused by an increasingly competitive market, unemployment in the borough of Hounslow more than doubled between January 1980 and January 1981. Almost 2500 people went on the dole. It was in this changing economic landscape that many Muslim immigrants made a life for themselves in the Hounslow area, beginning in the 1960s, when industry and the rapidly expanding Heathrow airport, were experiencing a shortage of labour.

Growth of the community

In 2001, at the time of my research for this study, some 19,378 Muslims lived in the Greater Hounslow area. The majority, who are the focus of this study, follow the Sunni Hanafi school of Islamic jurisprudence. Ethnically, most of them are from Pakistan and mainly comprise two groups: Kashmiris[4] and Mirpuris.[5] A few are from other areas, such as Gujarat in India, Central Africa and East Africa.[6] There are also small numbers of Shi'i Muslims, including Ismailis, in the Hounslow area.

Asian settlement in the Hounslow area goes back to the 1950s, and in some cases even earlier, when students from various parts of the British Empire lived there. Although the 1921 census shows the total number of Asians in the whole of Middlesex county to be 84, it would not have been unusual to see Asians in the adjacent Isleworth area during the 1920s (Chippendale, 1993). The major Asian influx into the area started in the 1960s as part of the larger Muslim migration to Britain. In the case of Hounslow, the migration was mainly due to the labour shortage in the area, and more particularly the labour needs of Heathrow airport and its allied services. It is not coincidental that of the early Muslim pioneers in the area, three – Raja Yakub, Assen Shah and Haji Gondal – were employed by the British Airport Authority.

As previously noted, the first immigrants to the UK intended to return to their countries of origin after some time. However, the 1962 Commonwealth Immigrants Act forced Muslim immigrants in the United Kingdom to make a choice as to where they wished to make their definitive home, and that changed their perspective. Thus, immigration law played a major role in Muslims' settlement patterns in the UK as well as in the nature and resolution of their interpersonal conflicts.

Of particular note is the 'primary purpose rule'. According to Sachdeva (1993: 7), the 'primary purpose rule' is an element of British immigration control peculiar to the situation of a country which has quite desperately been seeking to control secondary immigration, that is, settlement of spouses and other family members after the primary immigration or labour migration was officially stopped. The legal core element of the 'primary purpose rule' is that the application of a male or female spouse or fiancé(e) for settlement in Britain should be refused if the primary purpose of the marriage is to obtain entry to the UK. A crucial contributory factor to the 'no win' situation in primary purpose cases is that the onus of proof rests upon the applicant, who has to satisfy the Entry Clearance Officer (if abroad) or the Secretary of State (if applying to stay from within the UK) that gaining entry to the UK is not the primary purpose of the marriage.

By 1970/71, the greater Hounslow area already had a small, but burgeoning, Asian population in which Muslims were the majority, encompassing some 2,500 to 3,500 people. The following year saw another major influx of Asians as a result of their expulsion from Uganda. Many of these new immigrants were Muslims. While the earlier influx was largely of semi-skilled workers, with some from the middle professional level who found work easily with the British Airports Authority, the later influx was largely of professional people and small businessmen (Bhatia, 1973), who settled in various parts of London and other areas. It was their entrepreneurial vigour that helped to revitalise the retail trade in Britain over the next three decades.

The nascent Muslim community in Hounslow faced many of the problems Muslims faced elsewhere in Britain. The initial preoccupation of the Muslims in Britain was to construct a Muslim identity for themselves in the UK. Generally, this took the form of 'setting up the infrastructure of continuity and belonging'

(Sardar, 2005: 22). The first task of the community was to ensure that they were able to meet together at least once a week (on Fridays) to offer congregational prayers. Raja Yakub, one of the early settlers in Hounslow, made a room in his residence available for this purpose, providing lunch after the prayers. Yakub, then in his late 30s, was from Abbotabad in Pakistan. He had arrived in England in the late 1950s with his wife and eight children. An aircraft maintenance engineer by profession, he secured a job with the British Overseas Airways Corporation, which later became British Airways. The room in Yakub's house was a temporary arrangement and the community's elders in Hounslow made the construction of a mosque their major preoccupation.

The early community experienced relatively little interpersonal conflict, and that was largely as a result of the preoccupation with resettlement in a new country. However, pressures were exacerbated in some cases by practices such as forced marriage of daughters, often resulting in marital problems and subsequent divorce, which was perceived socially as besmirching the honour of all the parties concerned, including the parents. Problems such as these and others were normally referred to either the *biraderis*[7] or the community elders, who would try to resolve the matter internally. The main interest of the elders always was to preserve clan cohesiveness and harmony, and therefore internal disputes were kept confidential within the circle of close community or clan members.

Other preoccupations of the community at that time included a search for more 'Islamic' ways of doing things. Those ranged from finding or establishing shops selling *halal* (Islamically lawful) food and placing children in schools with norms compatible with 'Islamic' principles as understood by the community, to ensuring that their marriage ceremonies were communally recognised and the community's customs and practices, particularly those having legal implications, conformed to the laws of the United Kingdom (Ahsan, 1995). Many found that their professional qualifications were not recognised in the UK and those who could afford the fees took courses to obtain British qualifications. The immediate preoccupation for most of the immigrants was to find a job as soon as possible. In many cases, remittances had to be sent to India and Pakistan to support extended families there, which often led to conflict between spouses in those initial years. Additionally, racism in the form of 'Paki-bashing' was on the increase and bricks were sometimes thrown through windows and obscene, anti-immigrant graffiti was scrawled on walls. The older generation, having given up their countries of origin and being left with no alternative but to make the best of their situation, tolerated those indignities. However, the younger generation, either born or brought up in England, were not prepared to accept the violations of their rights (Anwar, 1991: 32). The riots in Southall in 1982, which subsequently spread to Brixton, were the turning point. They unleashed the pent-up anger in the community and even some of the older generation started exhorting people to retaliate for all the insults from 'Paki-bashing' thugs.

In addition to socio-economic and racial difficulties, there were also emotional problems. Those who had migrated with their families had some kind of support mechanism, but those who were single faced serious problems of isolation, loneliness and depression. For the initial immigrants, suitable jobs were difficult to obtain and many people experienced a dramatic decline in their confidence and self-esteem.

For the youth in the area, particularly boys in their later teens, life was somewhat different from that of their elders. Though in some cases it was hard, their social life was largely shaped by themselves. In addition to the Friday congregational prayers, followed by lunch, there was the attraction of nearby Southall, which had established a reputation as a major Asian centre in the West London area, showing Hindi films, selling Indian groceries and other products and catering to a cosmopolitan palate. The cinemas became a main centre of attraction. For the solicitor Soli Osman, then a law student at Isleworth Polytechnic and head of its cricket team, political activity was a major extra-curricular occupation. The Vietnam War and South African Apartheid were increasingly the focus of protests, and he organised lectures at his college featuring prominent speakers such as the South African activist George Peake who had been a political prisoner on Robben Island, South Africa.

Members of the community helped to deal with some of the early settlement problems. In addition to those mentioned earlier, there were Dr Khan, a dentist and president of the Pakistan Welfare Association,[8] and his wife, known popularly as Bhabi Khatija, a doctor who played an active social role in the Association and is still a social worker today. Dr Khan, since deceased, also inspired members of the community to get involved in the community activities and to serve others.

Inevitably, family conflicts were high on the list of problems. Most of the disputes at that time involved conflicts between spouses. Tensions usually arose as a result of greater earning capacity, particularly when one spouse's desire to send money to his or her relatives back home was opposed by the other. For example, a young woman brought up in England would be forcibly married to a man from Pakistan or India, who might not be of her educational level. That would often lead to serious compatibility problems, exacerbated by the expectation that the girl would provide for her husband's extended family, most of whom were still in his country of origin. Many problems were also caused by the overwhelmingly patriarchal attitude of men who refused to accept changing gender roles. Family disputes were initially referred to clan elders, who would try and settle the matter internally among their group.[9] This practice is still followed by some individuals, but it is no longer common. Often, the pressure to make a compromise as part of reconciliation was greater on the woman. The divorce rate in the community was very low, about 2 per cent, because it was an issue of *izzat* (family honour).

In the early days of settlement, facing a plethora of socio-economic issues, most Muslims in the Hounslow area were not preoccupied with the role of the Sharia in their dispute resolution processes. If the Sharia did arise, in most cases it would be in the context of forced marriages and the issue would be whether such marriages were sanctioned by religious law or constituted a cultural practice.[10]

In the late 1980s, the greater Hounslow area witnessed another major influx of immigrants, this time of Muslims from Somalia fleeing the murderous regime of Siad Barre, the military dictator who had overthrown the civilian government in 1969. According to an official of RAAD, a limited company that provides advice on education and employment to refugees and asylum seekers in West London, there have been Somalis in England since the eighteenth century. Being nomads, they kept going back and forth between England and Somalia. 'Uncles who were married to English women kept in contact with their relatives back home'. The RAAD official said that there were some 400,000 Somalis in Britain in 2005. In West London alone, there were an estimated 80,000, with the largest concentrations being in Brent (20,000), Ealing (15,000), Hillingdon (7,000) and Hounslow (6,000).

The Somali community, especially the men, according to her, were facing serious social problems. The men were perceived to be underachievers and had lower self-esteem than the women. An estimated 30 to 50 per cent of families were collapsing, largely because of lack of understanding between spouses and problems of integration. The situation was exacerbated by many of the women having to raise their children with relatively little support from their husbands, and by the racism encountered by Somalis. The greatest difficulty they faced was the lack of a support system of the kind they had in Somalia, where community elders and relatives played a major role in dispute resolution. The culture of counselling was non-existent and going to a lawyer was taboo. Many of the problems of the younger generation emanate from the fact that they were born during the crisis of war and are now 'sandwiched between two cultures', according to the RAAD official.

Struggle to build a mosque

A mosque is often where a Muslim community normally organises its identity. It is there that the children learn the rudiments of faith; their rites of passage, those attendant on birth, marriage and death, are performed at a mosque. While the nascent Hounslow Muslim community was trying to contain its conflicts and challenges, it also laid down the principles of a community organisation and spent much of its time trying to establish more permanent structures. Among those, the construction of a purpose-built mosque became a priority. However, it proved to be more of a challenge than they had expected.

In the early 1980s, the community set up the Hounslow Jamia Masjid Trust, which campaigned to build a mosque on a piece of land adjacent to the Heathland School in Hounslow. However, in 1985, the Hounslow planners rejected the proposal. Following an appeal by the Trust and a public inquiry in September 1985, the Inquiry Inspector gave the go-ahead to the Trust on the condition that they widened the road along which the mosque was to be built, undertook to do landscaping, tree-planting and fencing, and provided parking for cars. Many objections were filed by Heathland School and the neighbours about potential traffic congestion and noise. To those, the Inquiry Inspector responded: 'Despite details of accidents given and problems experienced, I do not accept that the situation is already intolerable at all times.' She felt that there was little prospect of early morning prayers attracting more than about a dozen people from outside the site.[11]

Over the next few years, the Trust tried to find financial resources to build the mosque; unfortunately, initial funding anticipated from the Middle East did not materialise. Further hearings took place, with more impassioned objections from both the Heathland School and the Heathland Residents Association. Those were finally overcome with the assistance of various civic authorities and city councillors. In August 1992, the government decided to back the Hounslow community and gave the Trust the go-ahead to start construction. Although not fully completed, the mosque, named the Jamia Mosque, was used for Ramadan prayers in 1993 and the local congregation raised £200,000 for the project. Regular prayers were offered there for the first time in January 1998, when the project was finally completed.

The Jamia Mosque has contributed significantly to consolidation of the Muslim community's identity in Hounslow. Besides constituting the focal point of its social and cultural interactions, the complex also houses a faith-based primary school attended by some 120 students. The school, which is coeducational, teaches the national curriculum and provides Islamic education (consisting mainly of learning to read and recite the Qur'an and learning the Arabic language). The imam of the mosque trains the teachers in the Islamic dimensions while seven teachers, two of whom were brought up in the UK, teach the other, secular, subjects.

The Jamia Mosque has also given the first-generation immigrant Muslims in the area a greater sense of belonging and rootedness, while for the younger generation it has become an important focal point of religious formation and identity. On a weekday, between 50 and 75 male worshippers attend the afternoon prayer session (*zuhr*) which is often followed by a *khutba* (sermon) by the imam in English. On one occasion, in May 2004, the sermon touched on conflict resolution. The imam told the congregation that Abu Bakr, who later became the first caliph, was once talking to someone in the presence of the Prophet Muhammad when an argument ensued and Abu Bakr lost his temper. At that point, the Prophet walked away. When asked why he had done that, the Prophet replied that when Abu Bakr kept his composure, even the angels were with him, but when he lost his temper they abandoned him; therefore, he, too, had followed suit.[12]

Outlook of the younger generation

The younger generation are facing newer problems. While most young Muslims are able to relate to the imam, they view their lives somewhat differently from the way their parents did. According to respondents in their late 20s and early 30s, young Muslims respect the world their parents lived in and belonged to, and the values they espouse, but they do not necessarily share their universe entirely.

The story of a brother and sister in the area is instructive.[13] Both attend prayers at the Hounslow mosque. Feisal, born in Asia, arrived in England in 1974 with his parents and sister at the age of five. His father had been a tailor and his mother had kept the home. In England, his father became an antique dealer and his mother trained as a counsellor, a vocation which she still practises today, mostly as a volunteer. Feisal grew up in the area, studied osteopathy, worked for a few years in Munich with an educational consultant group and then went to Damascus to study Islamic art and calligraphy. He is now back in Britain. Ayesha, his sister, also born in Asia, was three months old when her parents migrated to the UK. She went to an all-girls school in Ealing and, on her own accord, decided at the age of 13 to wear the *hejab* (a headscarf worn by some young Muslim women). Subsequently, she obtained a BSc (Hons) in Geography from the Open University.

During his early days in England, Feisal's extended family, including uncles and aunts, constituted his 'community'. He also had a few friends from other communities (including English boys) with whom he got on very well. Over time, English became the only language in which he was fluent. His life was comfortable but he felt a growing communication gap with his parents. He received his early religious education in a *madrassa*, which in those days largely consisted of recitation of the Qur'an and Arabic lessons. The teachers were imams who had come to England from the South Asian subcontinent. 'We grew up questioning a lot of the time,' he reflects. 'It was not Islam that was speaking, but culture [that the imam was interpreting]. Islam gives you much more freedom than culture'. For him, Islam goes beyond the five pillars,[14] and ethical engagement with society constitutes an important part of his understanding of the faith.

According to him, many young Muslims today participate in internet chat rooms where they question establishment views and conventional norms. Sometimes, as many as 6,000 participants read a query online and those who have views on the subject respond.

With regard to dispute resolution and whether he, as a British Muslim, would want to avail himself of the help that can be given by the community, Feisal feels that the 'wisdom' of elders is very important. Asked whether he would go to the imam for help to resolve a dispute, his response was: 'When I was young, these types of issues were settled within the family. At that time I saw it negatively. But as I grew up, I began to view my cousin-brothers and cousin-sisters more in a trust relationship. For me to trust someone takes a long time. On the other hand, I do have a cousin-sister and she was having some matrimonial problems and the family members came up with some traditional approaches. At that time, the mosque here was not organised. Ealing was undergoing some conflict, so she went to Regent's Park Mosque and she was advised by the imam about her Sharia rights and was able to resolve her problem equitably.'

Asked why his cousin-sister had not gone to a UK-trained secular lawyer, his response was: 'She was brought up in a culture where to speak about these things is taboo. The general feeling is to solve problems within a family, because if you do not do so it can reflect on you later on. It could affect your chances of a remarriage.' Feisal believes that people are more willing to bring their problems out into the open now.

Similarly, he does not see forced marriage as being that prevalent any more. He recalls that when he was young, his mother tried to find a suitable partner for him. The procedure was that they would visit his aunt, and when she served them tea and biscuits, on the tray there would be photographs of 15 eligible young women. Feisal was to look through them while his aunt and mother were conversing. Indignant at the suggestion, he accompanied her on the visit but assiduously avoided looking at the photographs. Since then, he has never experienced any pressure from his family.

Feisal believes that many modern British Muslim women have a strong sense of communal identity. 'If you wear a *hejab*, it does not mean that you are forced to do so. You do it out of volition. In fact, women (sometimes professional women) come to my mother and say, "We want to get married. Can you suggest any suitable partners?" I have not heard for many years of girls in this area being forced into marriage.' However, 'young girls still face certain constraints as a result of the culture; they cannot go out whenever they want to, and when freedom is denied there is greater resistance. Compromises have to be made. It is not part of the religion. But I have seen many young women who feel a sense of frustration.'

His sister, Ayesha, has a different perception of the community, particularly of domestic conflicts, based on her life experience. When she was experiencing matrimonial problems, her mother referred her to a religious scholar at the MLSC. He was extremely helpful and was able to help her get a divorce. Simultaneously, she took counselling from a Buddhist counsellor. 'He tried to influence me, but I kept a filter [with regard to my faith].' She also consulted a secular lawyer in Southall about initiating divorce proceedings in court. With regard to custody of her two children, from the beginning she did not want to prevent her husband from having access to them. 'Islamically, the father is responsible for the children at all times. I did not want to indulge in spite or anything like that, because that only serves to hurt the children. I have seen many women suffering as a result of that attitude.'

She went to secular institutions to register her claim for child maintenance because men often renege on their obligations and she wanted to safeguard her children's rights. She also wanted the MLSC to grant her an 'Islamic' divorce. 'Deep in my heart, I am a Muslim. I wanted my *nikah*[15] to be annulled.' The MLSC charged her £100 for securing the divorce.

Like her brother, Ayesha says there are fewer forced marriages today. 'When I was young it was happening, but now things seem to be changing. Perhaps this is due to greater media coverage today.' Asked why she felt forced marriages were still a problem, she cited the case of a family where, because one daughter had been married off to a relative of the mother, the father insisted that the other daughter should be married off to one of his relatives. 'But things are changing. Parents are beginning to realise their mistakes as they see more divorces taking place.'

Asked whether women would feel inclined to go to the imam of the mosque for help, Ayesha's response was: 'Generally, when women are suffering abuse, they want to hear that they have been wronged. Often, imams do not say that'. She says the imams are always accessible, but they need to go for training in matrimonial dispute resolution and interspousal relations, and to form a network, so they can help the community better.

Both Feisal and Ayesha consider themselves to be 'British Muslims'. In some ways, they seem to epitomise well-educated young Muslims across Britain.[16] In November 2004, the *Guardian* newspaper commissioned an ICM poll to gauge the mood of Britain's younger Muslim generation and invited 103 young Muslims to discuss the main issues shaping their lives and their futures.[17] The participants in the discussion were described as being among the success stories of two decades of integration. They were mostly from humble backgrounds, had gone to university or obtained other qualifications and were working as accountants, pharmacists, social workers, journalists, civil servants, lawyers, nurses and entrepreneurs. According to the newspaper, they have drawn from their faith a powerful social conscience; the majority of the participants devote a considerable amount of their time to volunteering in community organisations and political campaigns.

The main concern for them is how to accommodate diversity and equality within Western democracy – which, according to the Swiss-born scholar Tariq Ramadan, 'is a chapter which has to be written in Europe'. The discussions with the *Guardian* reflected a plurality of voices and created 'an unmistakable impression that this is a generation which relishes the heavy responsibility they bear [...] It is the quest for justice for a marginalised, misrepresented, impoverished and increasingly beleaguered community that spurs them on.' The *Guardian*/ICM poll found that 36 per cent of British Muslims are leaving school with no qualifications and a fifth of those between the ages of 16 and 24 are unemployed. Of the total Muslim population in Britain, 40 per cent are in low-skill jobs, and nearly 70 per cent of Bangladeshi and Pakistani children live in poverty. Thus, with a third of the Muslim community being under 15, a British Muslim generation is coming of age with the experience of deprivation.

Based on a sample of 500 British Muslims, the poll found that a clear majority wanted Islamic law introduced in England for civil cases relating to their community. Some 61 per cent wanted Islamic courts – operating on Sharia principles – 'so long as the penalties did not contravene British law'.[18] The newspaper observed:

This generation is being called to explain their faith to a secular society which has long since lost all interest in God, angels, prophets and holy books. What does it mean to 'put God first in everything' as one participant described British Muslims' distinctive contribution to British society. [...] Frequently, issues that the vast majority of Muslims have little interest in debating, such as homosexuality and abortion (such is the consensus, there is nothing to debate) or the role of women (why do they keep asking us about this? they complain) are settled by faith – which only deepens incomprehension among non-Muslims.

Young people comprise about 30 per cent of Hounslow's Muslim population, with a marginally higher proportion of girls than boys. The issues they face today are very different from those faced by their predecessors some 30 years ago. According to a Muslim solicitor, Soli Osman, if a Black lawyer became too vocal or visible in the 1960s he tended to get into trouble with the police or the judiciary. Today, with many more South Asians, Africans and Caribbeans in the judiciary and government, the situation has changed. Increasing numbers of Muslims, both men and women, are joining government service. Many youths are now entering professions such as law, accountancy and medicine. It should also be noted that, as in the rest of British society, girls tend to perform better in their studies than boys.

Soli Osman points to another difference between young Muslims of his generation and those today: 'In our days, when a youth made a phone call to a colleague from university, it was to find out about a demonstration somewhere or something similar. Today they are on their mobiles checking on property prices and mortgage rates.'

However, young people do have their frustrations in Hounslow, where some of them have been trying unsuccessfully to have the physical space of the mosque utilised more comprehensively in a way that reflects the needs of the local community beyond the five daily prayers. 'Islam is a way of life, and the activities in and around the mosque have to reflect this all-encompassing nature of the faith,' observed a young media professional. The trustees of the mosque, conservative by temperament, initially resisted such demands vehemently; on one occasion, the confrontation led to a scuffle, which led the young professional and some others to form an organisation to cater for the multifaceted needs of young Muslims ranging in age from 7 years to the early 20s. One of the co-founders of the organisation, a financial analyst with a leading international firm headquartered in the City, was elected a mosque trustee in 2006. In his mid-20s and originally from Birmingham, he became the youngest mosque trustee.

Wider utilisation of the mosque complex could have an important bearing on the future of ADR in the community. Soli Osman, while sympathetic to the sentiments of the elders, also recognises the need for the mosque to play a more encompassing role, one that would be more responsive to the changing needs of young Muslims. He would like to see the mosque encourage more debate on issues in a spirit of mutual tolerance and understanding. He suggests that the mosque complex should include a community centre for youth, providing facilities such as a canteen, an internet café and a room where young people can be taught how to prepare their CVs and receive advice and counselling. The impact on ADR of the provision of such physical space would be threefold. First, young people would begin to attend the mosque more regularly and find a niche for themselves in its activities. They would thus be better prepared to become the community's future leaders. Second, they would start talking to each other and discussing common issues – primarily inter-generational communication problems, which are a major source of dispute in the community. Third, young people would be shielded from ideological radicalisation because they would be within the community's overall embrace (Husain, 2007).

Soli Osman emphasised that the mosque trustees have established bulwarks against radicalisation. First, no residential facilities are available, so no itinerant preachers are allowed to take up residency within the mosque compound. Second, the trustees have chosen the imams very carefully. Third, and most importantly, the majority of the congregation in the mosque are Barelwi Muslims from Pakistan, who espouse a pious and more tolerant interpretation of the Hanafi school of Islam, respectful of other Muslim communities, including the Shia and the Sufis.

It is noteworthy, however, that Britain's first home-grown Muslim suicide bomber came from the Hounslow area. His radicalisation, it is suggested, did not take place in the mosque but was brought about by external forces. Commenting on this in the context of a larger phenomenon plaguing British Muslims, Husain (2007: 262) observes that this '21-year old travelled a path of rejection, confrontation and ultimately violence'. Referring to another recruit from Derby who joined the Hounslow bomber, Husain notes, 'Neither came from unemployed, disenchanted inner-city Muslim communities. Both had middle-class backgrounds.' According to him, 'the recruitment [...] came about against a backdrop of increasingly radicalised young Muslims in communities across Britain'.

According to Soli Osman, the suicide bombing shocked the young men's parents as well as the Hounslow Muslim community as a whole. 'It was a freak incident.' Following the bombing, the mosque trustees recognised that there was a great need for interfaith dialogue and invited a number of religious leaders to the mosque, including a representative each from the Sikh, Hindu, Christian and Jewish communities, and the imam gave a talk on the fact that Islam deplores suicide. At one of the meetings, Soli Osman related Prophet Muhammad's last address to his followers, extolling equality of all races, and particularly between men and women. It is interesting to note that the new organisation formed to deal with youth issues was able – for the first time – to get the trustees to sponsor an open-day exhibition at the mosque with non-Muslims invited.

It is clear that young Muslims in the area, and indeed elsewhere in the UK, are facing (to borrow from human rights vocabulary) 'third-generation problems'.[19] Muslim families in Hounslow today are experiencing newer types of challenges requiring a new mindset. In addition to those already mentioned, the Muslim solicitor Soli Osman adds that there are other important factors to be taken into account when one considers the role of Muslims in the modern, mainly secular society of the UK. These are the impact of education and socialisation on traditional notions of authority that go to the very heart of family life; issues such as how a young British-born Muslim girl views the notion of familial authority and what happens when her parents invoke either religion or culture to justify the differential treatment they mete out to their sons and daughters; how the greater emancipation afforded to women in England, many of whom now work and earn their own keep, is viewed by families that espouse a more traditional and patriarchal view of gender roles; and how people from a traditional pre-modern, rural, society, taken out of a rural setting in Pakistan or India and transplanted into an urban area in the Occident, view notions of gay and lesbian rights.

It is in this context that some background to the religious law of the Muslims – the Sharia – is important to this study. Besides its positive legal dimension, the Sharia is underpinned by its essential higher purpose – the *maqasid al-sharia* – which encompasses the protection of five main interests: religion, life, lineage, property and rationality (Weiss, 1998: 78). The Sharia often gets used instrumentally in Muslim societies. In some cases, it is a positive force; in others, when it is exploited and used for political or ideological purposes, it can become negative. Whatever role it plays, it is implicated as part of the law of the society in which the disputants negotiate and constitutes 'the law', in the shadow of which all negotiations take place (Mnookin and Kornhauser, 1979; Palmer and Roberts, 1998: 93).

4

The Sharia, Religious Law of Muslims

The term 'sharia' literally means 'road', 'path' or 'way' to a watering hole. Since many Arabs were desert-dwellers during the time of the Prophet Muhammad, water and direction were essential for life. The Sharia is divine law (that is, in general terms its origin is divine and its focus is faith).[1]

For Muslims, the concept of law is a far broader concept than it is in the English and other secular legal discourses. It includes details of conduct in the narrow legal sense, minute matters of behaviour as well as issues related to worship and ritual. The individual believer's perspective on the law becomes a central element of self-definition for a Muslim, and it has thus evolved as one of the controlling elements of the Muslim community's identification as a whole (Rippon 1990: 74). A Muslim has various relationships based on his faith. First, his or her relationship with the Creator, which is a vertical one normally mediated through prayer and is known as *ibadat* (acts of worship). Then there is his or her horizontal relationship with fellow human beings; this is a transactional one, known as *mu'amalat* (interpersonal acts). Furthermore, there is the relationship between a Muslim and the environment, a fiduciary one characterised by *amanat* which means trust. According to Masud (1996: 269), 'For Muslims, obedience to Islamic law is voluntary. This approach to religion – obedience to revealed laws by choice and the surrender of individual will – is the essential meaning of Islam: submission'.

The Qur'an refers to a *shira* (law) with the injunction: 'Obey God and His Prophet and obey those who hold authority among you' (4:59), but its legal verses are not extensive. In all, they amount to some 600 verses out of a total corpus of some 6000, and the vast majority are concerned with the religious duties and ritual practices of prayer, fasting and pilgrimage. According to Coulson (1964: 12–13), 'no more than approximately eighty verses deal with legal topics in the strict sense of the term'. He adds that, 'Although the regulations, which are of a more specifically legal tone, cover a great variety of subjects ranging from women's dress to the division of the spoils of war [...] they often have the appearance of *ad hoc* solutions for particular problems rather than attempts to deal with any general topic comprehensively.' Assessing whether the Qur'an is a legislative document or not, Coulson makes the point that 'it does not expressly provide solutions for all the legal problems inherent in the organisation of a society [...] Later events, indeed, were to show that the Qur'anic precepts form little more than the preamble to an Islamic code of behaviour for which succeeding generations supplied the operative parts.'

Islamic law, like other legal systems, developed within the context of history and was subject to historical forces. However, there is still a tendency today for some scholars and many Muslims to take an ahistorical approach to it – a factor that tends to ossify the very spirit that underpins the purpose of the Sharia, the understanding of which should be the driving force in its evolution. For Coulson (1964: 1), 'Muslim jurisprudence, in its traditional form, provides a much more extreme example [than Western jurisprudence] of a legal science divorced from historic considerations.'

During his lifetime, the Prophet Muhammad, through whom the Qur'an was revealed, not only set out the message of the faith but also interpreted it and its practices to the nascent Muslim community. For Muslims, the Prophet was both a medium of Revelation and an interpreter of the message of God. Examples of Muhammad's guidance abound, including those on the laws of inheritance. Following his death, people turned for guidance to his closest companions, and more particularly his immediate successors – Abu Bakr (d. 634), Umar (d. 644), Uthman (d. 656) and Ali (d. 661) – popularly referred to as the '*khulafa rashidun*', the 'rightly guided caliphs'.

Ali, the fourth caliph, was also the first Imam (spiritual leader) of the Shi'i Muslims. The Shia believe that before the Prophet's death, he appointed his cousin and son-in-law Ali as successor to lead the Muslim community. This is disputed by the Sunnis, who maintain that the Prophet made no such appointment and it was up to the community to select its leader. This difference of opinion on the succession to the Prophet eventually led to the division of Islam into its two main branches. Today, the Sunnis comprise the majority of the global Muslim community (*umma*).

Although the formation of systematic schools of jurisprudence in Shi'i Islam took place two centuries or more after Sunni Islam, its legal and doctrinal principles were founded as early as the eighth century by the fifth and sixth Imams, Muhammad al-Baquir (d.ca. 732) and Ja'far al-Sadiq (d. 765). It is on account of the seminal contribution of the latter in particular that Shi'i Law is often referred to as Ja'fari Law. In general, there is little difference between the legal and juristic forms of Sunni and the Shi'i schools of jurisprudence, except in two important respects. In Shi'ism, the Imams are considered the authoritative interpreters of the Qur'an and the Sharia, and their teachings and sayings carry as much significance as the *hadith* of the Prophet. In principle, therefore, the law is meant to be continuously reformed and reinvigorated by the Imams as long as they are living and accessible to their followers. This is no longer the case in Twelver Shi'ism, whose Imam is believed to be in temporary concealment, unlike in Ismaili Shi'ism, whose line of Imams has continued to the present day.

Another distinctive feature of Shi'i jurisprudence is that, in the physical absence of the Imam in Twelver Shi'ism, interpretation of the Law has become the function of *mujtahid*s, that is, those members of the religious hierarchy who have acquired a high degree of expertise in legal theory and practice and are permitted to exercise *ijtihad* or dispense independent opinion on matters of Law. Whereas in Sunni Islam, the 'gate of *ijtihad*' is reputed to have been closed since the eleventh century when the four canonical schools of Law became established, in Twelver

Shi'ism it remains open for *mujtahids* to interpret and apply the Law. This accounts for the importance accorded in Shi'i jurisprudence to *'aql* (reasoning) as one of the four pillars or sources of Law, alongside the Qur'an, the *hadith* and *ijma* (consensus). There is no similar tradition of *mujtahids* in Ismaili Shi'ism, for it is their living hereditary Imams in direct lineal descent from the Prophet who exercise ultimate authority in the interpretation and application of the Law according to new circumstances that arise in every generation.

Following the assassination of Ali in 661, the caliphate was claimed by Muawiyya, who was from the Quraish tribe and a member of the Umayyad clan. The locus of power at that point in history shifted from Medina and Kufa to Damascus. This period of rule by the Umayyad caliphs (661–750) saw a massive expansion of Islam, with Muslim influence consolidating its presence in areas formerly ruled by the Persian and Byzantine empires. The emerging discipline of Islamic law interfaced creatively with pre-existing cultures and legal systems; where possible, it absorbed pre-existing legal institutions and notions, such as the *muhtasib* (agronomus of the Byzantine tradition), giving it a new 'Islamic' orientation. Even the concept of *wakf*, so important an institution in Islamic law, was of Byzantine origin.[2] Over the whole of the Umayyad period, standards and norms of foreign law (Sassanian Persian as well as Roman law) gradually influenced Islamic legal practice, so that Muslim jurisprudence in the mid-eighth century could take them for granted when conscious knowledge of their origin had been lost (Coulson, 1964).

New issues arose as Islamic influence spread to other parts of the Middle East and Islamic suzerainty began to apply to new populations that were conquered. Therefore, Muslim jurists and jurisconsults had to elaborate approaches to the understanding of the Sharia and come up with rules of positive law that could be applicable to new human situations that the nascent polity was beginning to face. This process, which took place in various centres of Muslim settlement (Medina, Kufa, Damascus, Qum and Cairo) over a period of three centuries, was known as *usul al fiqh*, which broadly translates as 'legal methodology'.[3] It fell upon the *ulama* in Sunni Islam to make sense of the eternal message contained in the Qur'an. For Shi'i Muslims, the interpretative role devolved on their hereditary Imams descended from the family of the Prophet Muhammad, through his cousin and son-in-law Ali and his wife Fatima, the Prophet's daughter.

For legal interpretation, Sunni jurists, known as the *fuqaha*, relied on original sources, particularly the Qur'an. This was supplemented by the *sunna* or conduct of the Prophet. The term *sunna* literally means the 'beaten track,' which originally included the traditions of ancestors, a tribe or a city. Its usage was often combined with a normative sense of ideal behaviour (Schact, 1993). Over time, the *sunna* of the Prophet was transmitted through the *hadith* or reports of his sayings and narrated from generation to generation. This search for understanding and formulation of a suitable jurisprudence based on the Qur'an and the Prophet's *sunna* also coincided with complementary, often countervailing, discourses in various Muslim centres on issues such as the role of reason as opposed to revelation in the understanding of faith.

Differences abounded due to the ongoing evolution and needs of the newly evolving community, reflecting different interfaces and influences. Medina, being an oasis town, represented a more 'settled' approach to issues, while Kufa, at the confluence of major cultural crossroads in Iraq, reflected a more cosmopolitan worldview. Each exegete depended on the *hadith* of the Prophet that was most relevant to the case he espoused. Proponents of diversity often quoted the Prophet's saying that 'differences of opinion among my people is a bounty of Allah', while those who saw *ijma* (consensus) as constituting an important cornerstone of legal interpretation turned to another saying of the Prophet, that 'my community will never agree on an error'. With the passage of time, the evolution of the law reflected this dynamic process, where legal pluralism and diversity were accepted and celebrated. As a result, a number of legal schools developed; some were based upon a more literalist approach while others engaged with both the text and rational thought in order to arrive at norms and dispositive principles appropriate to the time and acceptable to a particular group.

Over a period of some three centuries, through the *usul al-fiqh*, Muslim jurists formulated a process whereby they could arrive at understanding of the law on an ongoing basis and create a *fiqh* appropriate to their particular needs. From the middle of the eighth century, a number of juristic scholars emerged whose independent interpretations of the words and actions of the Prophet Muhammad stimulated the development of separate legal schools in Islam. The study of Islamic law initially developed as local legal traditions in various prominent cities during the early centuries of Islam, which then evolved into systematic schools of law, generating a vast literature as well as the establishment of courts and official institutions (Masud, 1996). Thus, jurisprudence became a highly technical process, and disputes about method and juridical opinions crystallised into various legal schools designated by the names of prominent jurists who founded them.[4]

The legal school that followed the Iraqi tradition was called Hanafi, after Abu Hanifa (d. 767). According to Sachedina (1996: 264), 'the *Hanafi* school is known for its endorsement of reason and logic as legitimate sources in the application of rules to the practical questions of life. Abu Hanifa's unusual ability to broaden the juristic practice with the use of analogy and "juristic preference" allowed *Hanafi* jurists to carry out meticulous investigation of legal sources to formulate their juridical decisions.' The Hanafi school of Islam is followed today in some parts of the Middle East, Turkey, Eastern Europe, China, as well as South, Central and West Asia.

Other schools of law also evolved, either simultaneously or sequentially. Those that followed the rulings of Malik ibn Anas (d. 795) became known as Malikis. Malik, in his legal formulations, depended upon the well-established practice of the early associates of the Prophet in Medina. Although in his legal doctrines he was bound by the *sunna* of Medina, he also utilised analogical deduction in cases not treated in the Qur'anic Revelation in order to arrive at a rule. Maliki jurists regard 'juristic preference' and 'public interest' as valid sources of juridical decisions. The Maliki school is followed today in North and West Africa and some southern parts of the Middle East.

The Shafi'i school of Islamic jurisprudence was founded by Muhammad ibn Idris al-Shafi'i (d. 820) whose influence spread widely in the Muslim world. The school was the result of a synthesis conducted by a single scholar who was thoroughly familiar with the doctrines of the Maliki and Hanafi schools. According to Sachedina (1996) Shafi'i adopted the essential thesis of the Malikis regarding the centrality of the Medina legal opinions as a juridical source. From the Hanafis, Shafi'i accepted the role of independent sound judgement and used it as a tool for analogical inference in his legal theory. Shafi'i's contribution lies in his magnificent synthesis of legal theory in Islamic jurisprudence. The Shafi'i school is followed today in Egypt and some other parts of the Middle East, East Africa, East Asia and the coastal areas of South Asia.

The fourth school of jurisprudence in Sunni Islam, the Hanbali, is associated with Ahmed ibn Hanbal (d. 855) who compiled a work on the *sunna* of the Prophet that became the source for juridical decisions of his school (Sachedina, 1996). It contains more than 40,000 reports on various topics, not necessarily all legal. The Hanbalis are found today mostly in Saudi Arabia.

As noted earlier, the Shia underwent a different model of legal development. All Shia accept that their Imams are the authoritative interpreters of both the outer and inner meanings of the Qur'an and the Sharia. The Imams are thus regarded as the custodians of the Qur'an and the Prophet's *sunna*. Among the Shia, there are the Ithna Asharis (Twelvers), the Zaydis and the Ismailis. In addition to the Qur'an and the *sunna* as sources for deriving religious practice, the Shi'i legal theorists regard human reason as a decisive basis for determining the scope of divine purpose for humanity. They believe that natural reason guides a person to ethical knowledge and can objectively determine good and evil as rational categories. For them, reason is needed to provide a more categorical verdict on religious injunctions. Such a verdict could only be derived from an absolute religious authority resembling that of the Prophet and his legitimate successors, the Shi'i Imams or their representatives. Hence, in practice, the role of reason was confined to extracting the general principles from the Qur'an and the *sunna*, and inferring rulings through the use of reason. Among the Shi'i schools, the Ithna Ashari school is followed in Iran, Iraq, Lebanon, Bahrain and South Asia, and the Zaydi school is followed in Yemen. The Ismailis are settled in the Middle East, Central and South Asia, East Africa and, more recently, in North America and Western Europe.[5] Historically, Ismailis adhere to the Jafari *madhab* of Shi'i Islam while taking into account other related *madhaib*, an adherence that continues under the leadership of their living, hereditary Imam.[6]

With regard to meting out justice, the *qadi* courts, which played an important formative role, did not occupy an exclusive space in Muslim daily life during this process. In addition to the *qadi* courts, there were three other significant institutions for the administration of law: the *hisba*, *nazar fi'l-mazalim* and *ifta*.

Hisba courts had summary jurisdiction and they were presided over by the *muhtasib*, who was an inspector of the market and a general guardian of morals. He was also a controller of weights and measures, prices and quality of merchandise. He ensured that the religious and moral laws of Islam were observed. Like the *qadi* courts, the *hisba* courts were established as early as the time of Umar (634–44), the second caliph (Masud, 1996) and manuals for the function of a *muhtasib* were also written. This institution still exists in different forms in some Muslim societies today. In Pakistan, for instance, the office of the *muhtasib* has been established since 1980 to hear public petitions against government offices and officers.

Mazalim courts, separate from regular courts, were established by the Abbasid caliphs.[7] The *mazalim* courts were headed by the *nazar fi'l-mazalim* (investigator of complaints), an office originally designed to hear charges of miscarriage of justice, which thus acted as a check on judges. Later, the office emerged as a parallel system of justice, especially for lawsuits, as a result of the *mazalim* courts having powers that the *qadi*s did not have: the right to double-check and investigate evidence, restrain acts of violence and refer people to binding arbitration (Rippon, 1990). Initially they were presided over by the caliphs, but later judges were appointed to them. *Mazalim* courts were not governed by the Sharia or *fiqh*, but by the principles of *siyasa* (administrative laws). Procedural laws for these courts were set out in books separate from *fiqh* texts, usually with constitutional and administrative laws. Ibn Taymiyya, the noted Hanbali Sunni scholar of the fourteenth century, appears to have been the first jurist to have tried to systematise this branch of the law, which was secular in nature as recorded in his book *al-Siyasat-al-shariyya*.

During the Mamluk period in Egypt (1250–1382) jurists known as *mufti*s were attached to *ifta* courts. A *mufti* was a jurist who rendered opinions about Islamic law. He differed from a judge in that the opinion of a judge was enforceable, while that of a *mufti* was not. Both judge and *mufti* were considered equal as far as qualifications were concerned. In the fourth century of Islam, manuals were written describing the qualifications of a *mufti*, together with the cautions, requirements and etiquette for writing a *fatwa* (legal opinion).[8] Unlike court judgments, *fatwa*s were systematically recorded and collected, a practice that still continues today. There were two types of *fatwa* books; the first contained questions and answers and the second contained the accepted opinions of great jurists. Following the development of schools of law, the jurists classified this second type of literature as lower in authority than the texts written by the founders of the schools (Masud, 1996).

An important concept of Islamic law, which is pertinent to this study, is the notion of *ijtihad*. According to Rauf (2000) *ijtihad* is often translated as interpretation or interpretive effort. In its widest sense, it means the use of human reason in elaboration of the law and covers a variety of mental processes, ranging from interpretation of texts to assessment of the authenticity of the Prophetic traditions (Coulson, 1964). Its provenance is in both the Qur'an and the *hadith*s. The example of Muadh Ibn Jabal is often cited in the *hadith* to illustrate this principle.[9] Muadh was designated head of a group of missionaries (*du'at*) that the Prophet had commissioned to teach Islam to the people of Yemen at the request of the Kings of Yemen. The Prophet is reputed to have put the following questions to Muadh:

'According to what will you judge?' 'According to the Book of God,' replied Muadh. 'And if you find nothing therein?' 'According to the Sunna of the Prophet of God.' 'And if you find nothing therein?' 'Then I will exert myself to form my own judgement.'

The Prophet was pleased with this reply and said: 'Praise be to God who has guided the messenger of the Prophet to that which pleases the Prophet.'[10]

This concept of the application of reason to the solution of legal issues is a complex one, comprising many different levels of inquiry. Even a *faqih* (an expert in Islamic jurisprudence) who feels bound by the teachings of his masters often encounters situations for which no clear precedents can be found, thus making it incumbent upon him to exercise at least limited *ijtihad* to resolve the case before him. Even within a given school, there is often much discussion among the leading authorities as to the correct solution, and in that situation the *faqih* would have to decide on the most appropriate ruling. By the late eleventh century the idea had begun to spread that the 'gate of *ijtihad*' had closed and that future jurists were not entitled to develop new theories of jurisprudence, or even to depart from the established rulings of their *madhaib* (schools) where these were applicable to the case before them.[11]

Sulh: negotiated settlement

Regardless of the differences among the various schools of interpretation in Islam, one matter on which there is near unanimity is the concept of *sulh* – negotiated settlement – which is based on verses in the Qur'an, principles derived from the *sunna* of the Prophet, the sayings of the Imams and Muslim juridical thought (Keshavjee, 2002). Three verses of the Qur'an refer to it:

> If you fear a breach between the two, appoint (two) arbiters, one from his family, and the other from hers; if they wish for peace, Allah will cause their reconciliation: for Allah has full knowledge, and is acquainted with all things (4:35).

> Allah commands you to render back your trusts to those to whom they are due; and when you judge between man and man, that you judge with justice; verily, how excellent is the teaching which He gives you! For Allah is He who hears and sees all things (4:58).

But no, by your Lord, they can have no (real) faith, until they make you judge in all disputes between them, and find in their souls no resistance against your decisions, but accept them with the fullest conviction (4:65).

Arbitration, or *tahkim*, is an integral part of *sulh*. *Tahkim* is well known in Islamic law. What is not settled is whether or not the award given by an arbitrator is binding on the parties. One set of Muslim jurists hold the view that *tahkim* is a form of conciliation, which is close to *amiable compositeur* and not binding on the parties. The other view is based on the second and third verses given above: that an arbitral award is binding because the parties authorise the arbitrator to judge; therefore the arbitrator's judgement must be of a binding character. The Prophet is known to have recognised arbitration. In one reported case, he appointed the arbitrator and accepted his award. He also advised the tribe of Bani Qarnata to have a dispute arbitrated (El-Ahdab 1993: 14).

Among the Sunni schools of law, the Hanafi and Shafi'i hold that arbitration is very close to compromise and the arbitration award is binding only if the parties agree. Thus, for them, arbitration is like conciliation. The Maliki and Hanbali, for their part, hold the view that the decision of an arbitrator is binding unless it contains a flagrant injustice. However, once the arbitral award is filed in the court of a *qadi*, it becomes binding if the *qadi* (judge) finds no fault in it (El-Ahdab, 1993).

According to articles 1847–50 of the *Majallah al-Ahkam al Adliyyah* (known popularly as the *Majelle*)[12] the validity of an arbitration agreement is subject to a number of conditions: the dispute must have already arisen (that is, future disputes cannot be covered in anticipation) and the dispute has to be defined very clearly (in order to avoid uncertainty); there must be an arbitration agreement; the arbitrator must be appointed by name (if, for instance, the parties agreed that the arbitrator should be the third person encountered on the road or the fifth person to enter a particular place, the agreement would be void); and the arbitrator must be mentally and physically competent to act as such, possessing the capacity to act as a *qadi*. However, Shafi'is give the arbitrator a lesser status than that of a *qadi*; he is removable by the parties, whereas a *qadi* is independent of the parties' choice or will.

Islamic law has specific principles for deciding who is competent to be an arbitrator, and most Muslim countries have either arbitration acts or codes of civil and commercial procedure dealing with this issue. Islamic law does not require the arbitrator to adhere strictly to any procedural or evidential rules. It is considered enough if both parties are heard in each other's presence and the reasoning on which the award is based is provided to them.

With regard to enforcement, according to al-Mirghinani, the author of *Hedaya*, a very influential Hanafi treatise which is more than 800 years old:

> If the parties refer the award of the arbitrator to the qadi, and it be conformable to his opinion (that is, there is nothing illegal in it), he may cause it to be carried into execution, because it would be useless to annul it, and then pass a similar decree. But if it is contrary to his opinion, he must annul it.[13]

An arbitrator is allowed to correct any mistake in the award and to interpret it if necessary, but only up to the time it is registered in the court of competent jurisdiction. However, the court cannot sit in judgement over the merits of the award, except in cases of violation of natural justice or some Sharia principle, in which case it may order the award to be set aside.

The *qadi* of a Muslim state cannot set aside a foreign arbitral award except on the ground that it clashes with some principle of the Sharia. Many Arab countries have acceded to the Convention on the Recognition and Enforcement of Foreign Arbitral Awards 1958 (New York Convention). Article 37 of the Riyadh Arab Convention on Judicial Cooperation 1983, signed by 21 Muslim countries of West Asia and North Africa, provides for recognition and enforcement of arbitral awards in all the contracting countries.

According to Rashid (2004) one can infer from the Qur'an (4:35, which refers to the appointment of two arbiters, 'one from his family and the other from hers') that the duty of the arbitrator is to try to find a way to achieve reconciliation between the parties first, and if this fails then to opt for arbitration. Article 1850 of the *Mejelle* provides: 'Should the parties have authorised the arbitrators [...] to conciliate them, the agreement of the arbitrators is deemed a compromise [...] which the parties must accept'.

Thus, the role of authorised arbitrators is to act as agents of the parties in achieving a compromise between them after they have decided not to negotiate directly with each other. Article 1851 of the *Mejelle* adds to this provision:

> If a third party settles a dispute [put to arbitration] without having been entrusted with this mission by the parties, and if the latter accept his settlement, the award shall be enforced by application of Article 1453 [according to which ratification is equivalent to agency].

Arbitration seems to have greater traction in Muslim communities than mediation. Mediation field training that I have carried out in a number of countries between 2000 and 2010 indicates that the resolution of conflict is conceptualised very differently in certain non-Western cultures than in the West. In countries such as Syria and Pakistan, for example, 'mediators' tend to utilise a more 'directive' approach to dispute resolution and often play the role of adjudicators. Also, reconciliation features very prominently in the dispute resolution trajectory. Societies in transition could gain a great deal more by allowing the contesting parties more autonomy to resolve their own disputes, but that would need to be done gradually through an evolutionary process. It is in this context that a hybrid tool such as Med-Arb (Mediation-Arbitration) could prove valuable.

The concept of forgiveness

A related concept in Islam that has relevance to this study is that of forgiveness, which is also found in Judaism and Christianity. During an interview with me, Zaki Badawi pointed out that the

Qur'an gives an individual a choice between retaliation and seeking recompense. Like the other Abrahamic scriptures, the Qur'an calls for *lex talionis* when it says that 'the recompense for an injury is an injury thereto [in degree] (4:40). It adds, however, 'But if a person forgives and makes reconciliation, his reward is due from Allah; for (Allah) loves not those who do wrong.' Thus, in Islam, the spiritual benefit of forgiving far outweighs any recompense that just retaliation provides.

The Qur'an goes further in exhorting forgiveness and enjoining that help not be withdrawn from the wrongdoer when it says:

> Let not those among you who are endued with grace and amplitude of means resolve the oath against helping their kinsmen. Those in want, and those who have left their homes in Allah's cause, let them forgive and overlook. Do you not wish that Allah should forgive you? For Allah is oft-forgiving, most merciful (2:178).

In cases of homicide, the Qur'an, while invoking *talionis*, says:

> But if any remission is made by the brother of the slain, then grant any reasonable demand, and compensate him with handsome gratitude. This is a concession and a mercy from your Lord. After this, whoever exceeds the limits shall be in grave penalty (24:22).

One of the classic examples of forgiveness is a story from the *sunna* of the Prophet Muhammad that stands out in Muslim oral history. The Prophet used to take a particular route every day, and as he passed, a woman would deliberately empty her dustbin from a balcony above onto his head. He never said anything but continued on his way. On one occasion, she was not there when he passed. He inquired about her and was told she was ill. He felt sorry for her and sought permission to visit her. When he found that she could not even sit up to sip water, he helped her to do so. She asked him for forgiveness and it is said that he was moved by compassion and forgave her. His exemplary attitude touched her and she embraced the faith.

Stories such as this are an integral component of the oral history of Muslims in many parts of the world, and they often find expression in homilies or advice given to people in different social situations.

The Sharia: some issues in the UK

The place of Islamic religious law in relation to British Muslims has been a perennial topic of discussion among Muslim leaders in the UK. This concern is not unique to Britain or even to modern times. Yilmaz (2005: 39) observes that 'the juristic discourse on Muslim minorities with regard to whether or not Muslims may reside in a non-Muslim territory and under what circumstances, the relationships of these Muslims to *dar-al-Islam* [the domain of Islam] and the ethical and legal duties that these Muslims owe to Muslim law and to their host non-Muslim polity have been debated since the eighth century'. However, no clearcut guidance exists on how permanently settled Muslims should live in a quasi-secular non-Muslim state such as Britain, in which no safeguards have been provided other than freedom to practise one's faith (Ansari, 2002). According to Fadl (1994), the juristic discourse on the issue has not been dogmatic and Islamic jurisprudence has developed several mechanisms and concepts that facilitate compromise, such as duress (*ikrah*), necessity (*darura*) and public welfare (*maslaha*). The question then arises: when and why did the Sharia become critical to Muslims in Britain?

Many Muslims feel that important aspects of Islamic law are not addressed by the laws of the United Kingdom; for example, the giving and taking of interest is prohibited under Islamic law but permitted by UK law; and polygamy is permitted by Islamic law but prohibited by UK law. Some elements of the UK laws, for example, laws relating to usury, gambling and the sale and consumption of alcohol, appear to be in conflict with Islamic principles. Generally, however, Muslims have been flexible about these issues, and in specific areas of the law in the United Kingdom, Parliament has legislated to exempt Muslims from certain statutory provisions; for example, Muslims are permitted to slaughter livestock in abattoirs according to their own religious methods.

According to Poulter (1992), by the 1990s, while there was lobbying for state recognition of Islamic dissolution of marriage, the liberal principles of the English legal system – 'everything is permitted except what is forbidden' – were enabling Muslims to resolve many of their concerns in respect of family law according to Islamic principles within the framework of English law. Furthermore, the freedom allowed in English law to settle disputes out of court by means of an agreement negotiated with the help of lawyers and mediators has meant that disputes between Muslims in the field of family law have often been resolved on the basis of religious principles and values without resorting to the English judicial system. Such an agreement is legally enforceable once it has been reduced to a memorandum of understanding in keeping with general principles of mediation.

Schact (1993: 1) observes that, 'even at the present time, the Law, including its (in the narrow sense) legal subject matter, remains an important element in the struggle which is being fought in Islam between traditionalism and modernism under the impact of Western ideas" The current, highly conflicted, global geopolitical situation supports Schact's view. Muslims in the diaspora, as elsewhere, are constantly called upon today to demonstrate that the principles of their faith, as expressed in their religious laws, are compatible with the secular, liberal Enlightenment values generally espoused in the Western world.

Often, the conflict expresses itself in issues that touch on principles such as freedom of speech, freedom of religion, women's rights and the rights of the individual. In many instances, the issues that arise are genuine cases of concern and call for greater understanding, but it can be argued that some issues tend to be gratuitous; those issues lend themselves to easy polemics, leading to polarisation and evocation of identity politics. Responses given by both sides are often expressed in polemic assertions that claim conflictive certainty as opposed to compromise; for example, secular critics assert that the wearing of a *hejab* (head scarf) manifests a backward step in the status of women in Western society, whereas the *hejabi*s (those who espouse the wearing of a veil) argue that it is an assertion of their cultural and religious rights. Frequently, both parties are locked into entrenched and antagonistic positions, which leads to increased polarisation and radicalisation. In such cases, some Muslims defensively cite 'the Sharia', but often in a way that either ignores local context or appears ahistorical; not surprisingly, that approach fails to address their contemporary needs in a diasporic setting.

To understand this dynamic and the part that the Sharia can, and does, play in dispute resolution, it is also important to understand the role of a *fatwa* (legal opinion) in the resolution of an issue between two Muslims, or between a Muslim in a diasporic context and a third party. There appears to be no clear-cut understanding of what 'the Sharia' actually means for an average Muslim in the United Kingdom today, how it can be invoked meaningfully in a dispute resolution process and what role a *fatwa* can, and sometimes does, play. Some background on both these issues will help explain why certain fora are critical and how they relate to each other in their endeavour to resolve a dispute.

A national controversy in 2006 over a teacher wearing a *niqab* (facial veil) helps to illustrate the situation.[14] Aisha Azmi, a 24-year-old Muslim woman teaching British Pakistani children English at the Headfield Church of England Junior School in Dewsbury, refused to remove her *niqab* when teaching on the grounds that her faith obliged her to wear the facial veil, which covers the whole face except for the eyes. She had not worn the *niqab* during the job interview. The school suspended her on full pay and referred the matter to an industrial tribunal, which held that the Kirklees Council, which runs the school, was well within its rights to suspend her. She was, however, awarded £1,100 on the ground of victimisation.

The most interesting aspect of this case is that Azmi, a British-educated teacher, was following a *fatwa* issued personally to her by a Muslim cleric of the Tablighi community. The case thrust Azmi into the middle of a national controversy about integration, in which even the then Prime Minister Tony Blair, among others, expressed support for the school's action. The cleric, Mufti Yusuf Sacha, one of several hundred Islamic clerics in Britain with the status of a *mufti* (jurisconsult) opined that the wearing of a *niqab* was obligatory for women. At the tribunal hearing, Mufti Sacha, who teaches at the Tablighi mosque in Dewsbury and follows the teachings of the Tablighi Jamat, set out the religious position, which was accepted by both sides. He said that Azmi was required to wear a *niqab* in the presence of men who were not her blood relatives or whom she could potentially marry. His ruling on the veil was disputed by other Muslims. Mufti Abdul Kadir Barkatullah, who is affiliated to the Muslim Council of Britain, said: 'I am one hundred per cent sure that wearing the *niqab* is not obligatory on Muslim women. It is a matter of choice. It is more about habit than religion. The Tablighis observe the *niqab* very strictly.'

This example of the clash between what is perceived as Islamic law and what is considered acceptable in British society demonstrates the strong role that a *mufti* can play in a dispute and calls for an answer to the question: What is a *fatwa* and what role does it normally play in a dispute between two Muslims or between a Muslim and a non-Muslim?

The *fatwa*

The word *fatwa* has acquired a negative connotation globally, often being associated with a death threat because of the *fatwa* issued by the late Iranian cleric, Ayatollah Ruhollah Khomeini, against British author Salman Rushdie for his novel *The Satanic Verses*. The erroneous impression has been conveyed that the *fatwa* is a command that must be obeyed without question.

A *fatwa* is a considered religious opinion issued by a *mufti*, a jurisconsult who, through his knowledge and experience of Islamic jurisprudence and theology, becomes an authority in issuing such an opinion. Anyone who has reached that stage of learning can issue a *fatwa*. The authority of a *mufti* is generally legitimated through his learning and through popular support. There is no regulatory mechanism or licensing procedure for *muftis*, either in the Muslim countries or in the diaspora. Generally, it is the people themselves who invest a *mufti* with status and legitimacy.

A *fatwa* is not a universal statement, nor is it a divine construct. It can be changed, withdrawn, or even challenged by a counter-*fatwa* if, for example, the context in which the original *fatwa* was issued has changed or if another *mufti* or *qadi* does not agree with the position taken by the first jurisconsult. It is based upon certain original references from the Islamic texts, that is, the Qur'an, the *hadith* and the opinions of previous legal scholars. A *fatwa* cannot be a personal opinion, though, obviously, a *mufti's* decision will be coloured by his own predilections and the particular school of Islamic jurisprudence to which he belongs. In the United Kingdom, a *fatwa* carries no legal weight, but for a Muslim who respects the Sharia and Islamic values and theology, a *fatwa* would generally have some binding force if it was properly issued. This means that it has to be issued after taking into consideration all the sources as well as the context in which the *fatwa* is to be applied. The adoption of a *fatwa* is a voluntary act and the refusal to be bound by a *fatwa* does not, in any way, imply that the person is not a Muslim.

*Fatwa*s are often used in dispute resolution. Normally, they are issued when both parties to a dispute ask for them. At times, when a dispute cannot be settled, a *fatwa* can be issued at the request of only one of the parties. That, however, is very rare. A *fatwa* operates as a kind of *ratio decidendi*.[15] The role of the *mufti* and the effect of a *fatwa* in dispute resolution give rise to two important issues. First, how persuasive is a *fatwa*? It posits a legal opinion on an issue by way of a Sharia decision on it. It does not call for execution, yet anyone who executes what is called for in it could legitimately feel a sense of justification at having acted in accordance with the Sharia. Second, how authentic and authoritative is a *mufti* and how is the whole process regulated? In the general Islamic dispute resolution process, formal and informal, the ruling of a *mufti* is not normally challenged. A *fatwa* is not meant to be a personal opinion, yet it *can* be challenged – and often is – when it is used in an adversarial context. While the sources used for the *fatwa* are often the same, the interpretation placed on the same sources can, and does, vary between two or more *muftis*, depending on the context, the circumstances and the orientation of the *muftis*.

This question of who is authorised to pronounce a *fatwa* goes to the very principle of legitimacy and authority, and it has been a major issue in Sunni Islam for centuries. The matter becomes particularly urgent in a diasporic context. Governments of Muslim countries, especially in the Middle East, usually appoint one official *mufti*. While such a *mufti* enjoys official status, he does not have a monopoly. People also normally turn to other *mufti*s who have a reputation for learning. Also, people tend to have greater confidence in non-official *mufti*s because they perceive them to be free of governmental influence and closer to their concerns. In the United Kingdom, there are estimated to be some 100 *mufti*s from different schools of Islamic jurisprudence. They do not meet at any official forum, because none exists. They are not governed by any regulatory body or framework, as those, too, do not exist anywhere in the world.

Given that people often turn to a *mufti* for guidance on issues governing their daily lives and that many disputants feel bound by their opinions, more research and reflection is needed on this in the context of alternative dispute resolution among Muslims in the diaspora. This also raises issues about who speaks with authority for the entire Muslim population. It is not just on behalf of, but also to, the Muslim population. The various Christian faiths have a hierarchy of varying degrees of authority, the members of which are appointed through recognised systems of selection. This should not be confused with the appointment of secular judges, who have to undergo a rigorous process of training and peer group selection before being appointed. Even in the United States, where judges are political appointees, they still have to go through a validation process consisting of legal studies and practical experience as lawyers and legal experts. It seems that in most of the Muslim world the hierarchy is much more loosely developed, and therefore the problematic issue of legitimacy, validity and authority is inherent in the system. This has both advantages and disadvantages. It can be argued that in some parts of the Muslim world, where there is considerable ambiguity about what is legal or illegal in religious terms, individuals may take it upon themselves to make that decision, creating the possibility of chaos rather than certainty and order.

In most disputes, relevant *fatwa*s would already be available for application. If the dispute touches on a new issue for which a precedent cannot be found, a *mufti* has to do some extra work and issue a new *fatwa*. That would often involve a better understanding of the context, a reappraisal of the sources and an application of the principles of the Sharia to the particular circumstances. For example, the MLSC conducted a study of the issue of organ donation and transplantation, working with a team of UK scholars and doctors, and then decided to support it on the basis of the principles of *darura* (necessity) and *maslaha* (public interest). The *fatwa* is very important in the context of dispute resolution, as British Muslims today are facing new challenges and problems, and young people are tending to seek *fatwa*s on different issues from various sources and institutions, including the Internet. Some of these *fatwa*s are utilised in disputes and, since the competence of many of the *fatwa*-givers cannot be confirmed, their use is causing unease among some religious scholars. One of the scholars at the MLSC refers to such free-riding *fatwa*-givers as 'cosmetic *muftis*' and says that they are known to abuse their powers at times by manipulating the primary texts.[16]

The absence of a regulatory mechanism for issuing *fatwa*s is a serious problem, not only in the Muslim world but also in diasporic contexts. One of the internet's most contentious aspects is how it enables people to bypass channels of authority and authentic scholarly understanding of the law. Muslim internet users often seek quick and definite answers to queries regarding the practice of their faith in modern times, including responses to various ethical issues arising from medical advances. Chat rooms are often the loci of vigorous debates about whether answers are to be sought only from traditionally trained Muslim scholars (some of whom may be considered to be out of touch with current realities) or whether others are equally qualified to interpret the scriptural and legal sources according to their abilities.

Some perceptions of the Sharia

Understanding of the Sharia in a diasporic context by individual disputants, and how they apply it to the resolution of their interpersonal disputes, are often the factors that determine the fora to which disputants resort for resolution of their problems. The term 'Sharia' conjures up a number of possibilities for a Muslim in a diasporic context, and how it is understood varies according to the different sections of society. This is understandable; after all, even in a non-Muslim society an average person is not expected to know the law, notwithstanding the cardinal principle in English common law that 'ignorance of the law is no excuse'.

Legal practice in the first few centuries of Islam shows that the process was fluid and Muslim jurists were still debating the precise scope of religious law. By the early tenth century, the differences had been largely resolved, with the understanding that law is the command of God, and the acknowledged function of Muslim jurisprudence was simply the discovery of the terms of that command. This process culminated in the development of the classical theory of law, known as *usul al fiqh*, or legal methodology.

One of the difficulties Muslim societies face today is understanding of the distinction between the Sharia and *fiqh*. According to Yilmaz (2005), Sharia is the divine law whose principles are embedded in the Qur'an and *sunna* – a territory of considerable textual complexity, for there is no simple set of rules that constitute the Sharia, but rather a body of texts, including the Qur'an, *hadith* and legal texts of various genres that supply the authoritative base for Islamic legal thought and practice, but which inevitably need to be read, understood and finally interpreted in themselves because many of the texts are not immediately clear. *Fiqh*, on the other hand, is a product of human understanding, which seeks to interpret and apply the Sharia in space-time (Esposito, 1980). As mentioned elsewhere in this book, Muslims today tend to conflate the two, and the degree to which they are able to separate them will determine the level to which they are able to apply the principles of their religious law to their contemporary needs (Badawi, 1995). This analytical distinction, coupled with full acceptance of its implications, will help infuse Muslim ADR principles with the underlying purposes of the Sharia, which emphasises fairness, equity and justice (Abdalla, 2001).

The majority of people interviewed in the Hounslow area do not have a clear understanding of what the term 'Sharia' really encompasses. For potential disputants, 'the Sharia' comprises the principles of a God-given law that they have to abide by, but whose specific rules are more clearly understood only by the *ulama* (religious scholars). Some respondents showed a marked concern that its interpretation is largely patriarchal and will not ensure full justice for women. While some female respondents feel strongly that imams of their mosques are biased and therefore will not take their disputes to them, others disagree with this position and are prepared to ask an imam to intervene. Some of the female respondents mentioned that an imam's intervention has helped them.

The Sharia becomes important for British Muslims largely at particularly defining junctures in their lives, such as specific rites of passage like marriage, circumcision or funerals. Muslim men and women understand the importance of an Islamic marriage ceremony, without which a marriage cannot be Islamically valid; it is at such times that a Muslim will approach an imam to officiate over the ceremony. The same applies to divorce; a divorced Muslim woman generally is not able to contract an Islamic marriage with a Muslim man until her civil divorce, granted by a secular court, is 'Islamised' by a Muslim institution, and it is then that the woman resorts to the mosque, the MLSC, or any other Sharia Council for assistance.

It is common for some Muslims to conflate *urf* (custom) with the Sharia or *fiqh*, with the result that what is invoked as Sharia is not only not Sharia or *fiqh*, but a customary practice from their countries of origin and perpetuated in the United Kingdom as part of the religious law. This has caused some conflict, particularly in the realm of 'forced marriage', for which parents invoke 'the Sharia' as justification, even though Islamic law does not recognise the concept, let alone sanction it. Thus, customary ignorance muddies the principles of the Sharia and the rules of *fiqh*.

The average Muslim in the Hounslow area is not aware of what is happening in the field of personal law in Muslim countries, except by way of sensational media depiction and images deprecating 'the Sharia'. Some examples of this are the call for stoning of a woman accused of adultery in Nigeria (she was acquitted by a Sharia appellate court for want of evidence and due process), a call for excommunication of an author in Egypt, a call for the execution of an aid worker in Afghanistan accused of apostasy (*rida* in Islamic terms) and the whipping of a woman in Pakistan accused under the Hudood ordinances.[17] Very little is known of the constructive changes that have taken place in the realm of family law in the Muslim world during the twentieth century, and the transformation in 'jurisprudential thought from its traditional attitude of detached idealism to a functional approach to the question of law in society' (Coulson, 1969: 107). These developments give courts applying the Sharia discretion to deal with the problems of society 'so that they now assume, to a much greater extent than hitherto, the responsibility of organs of real social purpose' (Coulson, 1969: 108). Courts in Islamic countries, it would seem, are moving from a static, idealistic, impermeable interpretation and implementation of the law to one which is more pragmatic and responsive to the new pressures in the rapidly changing environment created by a globalising modernity.

This brings us to the MLSC's understanding of the Sharia. Because of its particular remit, coupled with the progressive worldview rooted in more scholarly and authentic knowledge of its founder, the late Zaki Badawi, the MLSC endeavours to keep abreast of Sharia-related developments in the Muslim world and examine their relevance and application. At the time of this research, the MLSC had on its panel of reviewers three UK-trained lawyers to ensure that the public law policy of the United Kingdom was not violated in any Sharia ruling. The way in which it makes its rulings on the basis of the Sharia is discussed in the next chapter.

5

The Muslim Law (Shariah) Council (UK)

The Muslim Law (Shariah) Council (UK) came into being after a Muslim woman who had obtained a divorce through a court in accordance with the laws of the United Kingdom found herself unable to marry another Muslim because her husband refused to grant her a *talaq* ('Islamic' divorce). The imams of the mosques were in no position to help women in such a predicament because they lacked knowledge of classical jurisprudence and how it could be applied in changing circumstances. However, the situation changed after the arrival in Britain of Dr Mohamed Zaki Badawi, an Egyptian scholar-imam.

In 1978, Zaki Badawi was Director of the Islamic Cultural Centre, which was affiliated to the Regent's Park Mosque in London, of which he was also the leading imam when he received a telex from the woman outlining her predicament. He consulted his two co-imams at the mosque, but both felt they could do nothing as they were in a non-Muslim country and were not a court of law. Zaki Badawi reminded his colleagues that, according to Hanafi jurisprudence, 'If Muslims live in a non-Muslim country, then the most knowledgeable amongst them should become like a judge to solve the difficulties between them according to the Sharia.'[1] Consequently, Zaki Badawi and his two colleagues formed themselves as a Sharia 'court' and informed the husband that he had three choices: he could divorce his wife; or, failing that, he could take her back; or, if that, too, was not possible, 'then we will grant her a certificate to break the marriage'. In the face of this authoritative instruction, the man capitulated and granted his wife the Islamic divorce.

Soon thereafter, the newly-constituted Sharia 'court' received another application, this time from a young Pakistani woman in the United Kingdom married to a civil servant in Pakistan who was refusing to grant her an Islamic divorce unless she paid him a substantial sum of money. As described at the beginning of Chapter 1, that case, too, was resolved successfully through the intervention of Zaki Badawi and his colleagues.

Approach of the founder of MLSC

According to Raficq Abdulla, one of the lawyers on the MLSC's panel, Zaki Badawi was able to constitute the MLSC because of his authoritative standing within the Muslim community, his deep jurisprudential knowledge and his background in Muslim diasporic societies. He understood the purpose (*maqasid*) of the Sharia and refused to be imprisoned by literal readings of its rules. His religious credentials to do so were impeccable and his arguments and the positions he took were based on a firm knowledge of the faith and its various doctrinal developments over the centuries. A graduate of Egypt's prestigious and long-established Al-Azhar University, he was able to draw from the foundations of classical Islamic jurisprudence and make its principles relevant to contemporary issues. He was able to do so without violating the fundamentals of the Sharia.

Mohamed Zaki Badawi was born in 1922 in a respected religious family who encouraged him to study religion. He joined Al-Azhar University, where he spent 23 years. Then he travelled to various parts of the Muslim world and taught and led communities in countries such as Malaysia, Nigeria, Singapore and Saudi Arabia. He dealt with seminal issues facing Muslim communities against a backdrop of rapid change in the twentieth century. In the early 1950s he studied psychology at the University of London, where he received his doctorate. In 1978, he returned to Britain when he was appointed imam of the newly built Regent's Park Mosque.

He also assumed the position of Director of the Islamic Cultural Centre, which was affiliated to the mosque.

During his first week in the country, he invited all the imams in Britain to a conference to discuss how they could collaborate on common issues affecting their mosques. To his horror, he discovered that 'None of them spoke English. None of them had any idea about other religions. None of them had any idea about Western culture at all. They lived in isolation all the time in the mosques. And finally, very few of them had studied Islam in the real sense of the word; and those who had, studied only one interpretation of the faith, one *madhab*.' Zaki Badawi realised that such a dire situation would result in an enormous vacuum of leadership in the future, because, 'although these people spoke to the first generation of Muslims [...] they were not able to speak *for* them. [They] spoke *to* them, but not *for* them'.

On leaving the Regent's Park Mosque, Zaki Badawi set up the Muslim College in West London, where he aimed to teach classical Islamic education to Muslims wanting to become imams. He also engendered in the student-imams a consciousness of the need to utilise a critical modern approach to education so that they could study other religions in addition to Islam. The College's objective was to instil understanding of the entire Islamic heritage as 'a treasure to look upon with respect. Not to try and do what most of our schools do – that is, being sectarian.' To achieve that, Zaki Badawi insisted that the College should have total academic independence and be apolitical and gender-neutral. Also, 'It should allow women and men equal opportunity to study.' When the Muslim College was established, he engaged a husband-and-wife team from Malaysia with appropriate academic qualifications to teach, thus entrenching the principle of equal opportunity for both genders right from the beginning. Since 1990, the College has trained over 150 students from 30 countries to become imams.

Since he founded the MLSC in the 1980s until his death in 2006, Zaki Badawi's contribution to the development of Islamic jurisprudence was seminal and he left an important imprint on the MLSC's own work. He instilled in the imams a new understanding of hermeneutics, emphasising that while the principles of the

Sharia are fundamental and fixed, the resultant jurisprudence or *fiqh* is not a static system, but a dynamic process. He stressed that, while the Qur'an and the *sunna* are immutable, 'the interpretation that comes from *fiqh* books is a human construct given by human beings. They can make errors. They are people of their own time.' Expounding on this concept, he often stressed, 'We can also make or have an opinion dealing with our own problems and our own time.' Most importantly, and of particular relevance to the present study, Zaki Badawi inculcated a new worldview in his student-imams. He stressed that his aim was to make Islam 'a native to this country, a native religion; that it should not appear to the British or to anyone else as strange.'

Zaki Badawi always applied both, Sharia principles as well as the *fiqh*. He would go back to the *maqasid-al-sharia* – the spirit behind the law – which is not dissimilar to the equitable principles that underpin English law. The principles themselves, as understood in Islamic legal discourse, point back to the original intent of the law rather than to the mechanistic application of the rules of a particular *madhab*. According to a lawyer on the MLSC panel, 'the MLSC would be able to defend any *fatwa* or opinion it gave – chapter and verse from the legitimate religious sources and legal texts – if required.' It avoids becoming enmeshed in an interpretation of the Sharia that is 'local or folkloric'. Instead, it tries to elicit, where possible, 'classical legal processes, thus avoiding the tremors of local cultures,' but remaining pertinent to the pressures and needs of time and place.

This approach was critical to a broader understanding of the faith and its relevance in a contemporary, diasporic setting, particularly in matters such as forced marriages and other interpersonal issues, where the MLSC was prepared to take a specific stand even though it might not be popular with particular segments of the Muslim community. As the founder and Chairman of the Imams and Mosque Council of the United Kingdom, to which many (though not all) British imams were affiliated, Zaki Badawi enjoyed a position of authority recognised by the other imams.

While he was widely respected, Zaki Badawi did not have paramount authority over all Muslims in Britain, so he faced an uphill task. As an obituary in a British newspaper succinctly observed, he did not have the title of 'Grand Mufti of Islam in Britain'. Had he had such a title, 'everyone would have understood that on matters of faith, his word ranked alongside that of the Archbishop of Westminster, the Chief Rabbi and the Archbishop of Canterbury. But with the collapse of the Ottoman Empire, the post died in the nineteenth century alongside Abdullah Quilliam, the last incumbent.'[2] Despite his extensive Islamic expertise, coupled with his leadership of some of the main United Kingdom religious institutions (many of which he founded) Zaki Badawi had to struggle with Muslim politicians, local imams and a host of other politically motivated and conservative-minded opponents.

ADR services offered by MLSC

The MLSC is widely known for the function that constituted its very raison d'être, that is, helping Muslim women who have a civil divorce from a United Kingdom court to obtain an 'Islamic' divorce. In addition, it provides counselling, mediation and arbitration services.

Counselling

The MLSC has provided counselling for many years, largely through one of its Muslim female counsellors, who came to the United Kingdom from Somalia in 1990. The counsellor worked at the MLSC since 1993. She has also trained as a psychodynamic counsellor at London University's Birkbeck College, specialising in refugee counselling.

According to this counsellor, most Muslims have a predilection to solve their interpersonal disputes privately at home, and in their former countries the extended family was very active in dispute resolution. However, that system broke down after migration. Members of the extended family are deeply affected by the bewildering multitude of pressures of modern, cosmopolitan city life in the United Kingdom and do not have the resources to help resolve family disputes anymore. Furthermore, neither *sheikh*s nor extended family members can provide disputants with the necessary papers to legitimise changed marital status. Hence, disputants have no alternative but to refer their problems to the MLSC. The scale of disputes has also changed. In their countries of origin, when Muslims went to a *sheikh* to arrange a divorce, no questions would be asked about maintenance and *mahr* (the contractual sum payable by the husband upon divorce); but the MLSC takes an active interest in these questions in each case brought before it. Clients are normally referred to the MLSC by the local imam. Sometimes they are also referred by lawyers practising within the legal systems of the United Kingdom.

Reconciliation between the parties figures prominently in the MLSC's dispute-resolution remit. According to the counsellor, 'We do not want all the Muslim families to end up in divorce. We have to do our best. People are doing their best to reconcile families.' Reconciliation is a recurrent theme among the ADR fora studied. Reconciliation is an important obligation for a Muslim institution and divorce is seen as the last resort, when no other alternative works. In the Islamic ethos, divorce is the most reprehensible of licit acts; it is tolerated rather than encouraged. For reconciliation to work, the counsellor has to take into consideration that the disputing parties are normally following two parallel tracks simultaneously. One is adversarial, through divorce proceedings in the civil courts; the other track is the mediatory one followed by the MLSC. However, the MLSC counsellor has found that reconciliation can, and does, often take place.

Generally, there is no contact between civil lawyers and the MLSC unless an issue is specifically referred to the MLSC. An example of such an issue would be a request for an opinion on the validity of *mahr*. When a husband refuses to pay *mahr* to the wife, the MLSC advises the wife to be practical. If she wants an Islamic divorce expeditiously, she is reminded that a protracted contest over their *mahr* is bound to delay the divorce. On Sharia matters, disputing parties generally want a legal outcome that is most favourable to their position. Some women argue that the Sharia is inimical to women; on the other hand, some men may accuse the MLSC of not representing the Sharia but supporting the laws of a non-Muslim country, which are perceived to be encouraging the break-up of marriages and marital homes.

The processes that the counsellor uses are an amalgam of existing ADR processes, but there is no clear-cut distinction in her mind between mediation and arbitration, or even between mediation and conciliation when in fact conciliation is being carried out. Mediation, in its purest form, is the facilitation by an impartial third party of a negotiated agreement by two or more disputants or their representatives in which the mediator does not decide the outcome of the dispute but facilitates communication and problem-solving by the parties themselves. Mediation has been supported on processual grounds – that it empowers parties and improves communication, especially in continuing relations – as well as substantive grounds, that it increases the probability that more information will be shared with third-party facilitation and thus increases the likelihood of analytic Pareto-optimal solutions (Menkel-Meadow, 2003: 282).[3]

Arbitration involves an impartial, independent third party hearing both sides of a matter and issuing a binding decision to resolve the dispute. Most types of arbitration have the following elements in common: parties jointly agree voluntarily to use the process; it is private and confidential; the outcome is determined by a third party (which could consist of more than one person) which is independent of the disputing parties; the process is final and legally binding; there are limited grounds for appeal; and hearings are often less formal than court hearings (that is, a quasi-judicial approach is taken to due process of law).

Conciliation refers to a process in which an impartial third party helps the parties to resolve their dispute by hearing both sides and offering an opinion on settlement. It overlaps with mediation, and the two terms, even though they have various differences, are frequently used interchangeably. A conciliator, like a mediator, is an independent, impartial third party who helps the parties resolve a dispute. Often, however, a conciliator will take a more active role in making suggestions or advising as to the best way to resolve the dispute. Mediators also do this, particularly with regard to shuttle mediation. One important difference is that conciliation is often used to describe a process in which the parties do not meet, but the neutral party works with them separately, usually over the telephone. All conciliation has the following elements in common: parties to the dispute must agree to participate, the process is non-binding and the parties are free to proceed to another dispute resolution method if they are not satisfied.

Conciliation is an important ADR tool for Muslims because of the general negative perception of divorce in the Muslim world, coupled with the fact that communitarian societies such as those in developing nations from which most British Muslims originate tend to be far more relational than Western ones and therefore value this concept. Members of such societies are not in the habit of making their own conflict-resolution decisions as done in the wider community and society. In such cultures, conflict, by its very nature, does not belong to individual disputants, with the corollary that its resolution, too, requires a more directive and communal type of handling, one that veers more towards the directive end than the facilitative end of the mediation spectrum. In some hadiths of the Prophet and sayings of Shia Imams, dispute resolution is likened to prayer, and Muslim dispute resolvers often tend to regard conciliation as a religious obligation and make every endeavour to exhaust its possibility before trying any other processual tool.

The MLSC counsellor often sees clients together with the senior scholar to deal with various issues, including anger management. When discussions become too stressful, they recess and allow the parties to compose themselves. When hearing a matter, the counsellor reiterates that she is not there to judge. 'I am here to facilitate,' she repeatedly emphasises, using a term that is compatible with mediation but also employed in the context of counselling.

One of the difficult issues the MLSC faces is that of domestic violence. Often, according to the counsellor, 'we will see a woman with a black eye sitting here in front of us, not accepting that she has been beaten up'. Despite this denial, which is connected to the client's sense of personal and familial dignity, she still wants a divorce. The MLSC then feels obliged to inform the police about the situation. The issue of wives denying that their visible injuries were caused by their husbands kept recurring during this research. It was alluded to by a Police Officer from Hounslow as well as by the imam of the local mosque. There is a cultural dimension to this reticence. Clients often blame themselves for the husband's violence; in addition, it is a matter of the family's *izzat* (honour) and therefore such violent and demeaning behaviour can never be revealed to a third party.

The MLSC's counselling expertise is used by members of the Muslim community for a number of reasons, of which the cultural context is the most important. The Western approach is individualistic, while the MLSC's approach brings the extra dimension of a respected institution which is faith-based; the disputants' trust in the MLSC's cultural understanding of their issues within the context of Muslim cultures and their confidence that it will try to solve their problem within this framework are important. For the counsellor, dispute resolution also involves enabling disputants to integrate into the host society: 'People have to be positive and to see the service we are offering as providing them with another language – fitting the two cultures together and allowing people to integrate both in their lives.'

Mediation and arbitration

Following the demise of Zaki Badawi in 2006, his colleague and deputy at the MLSC, the senior Islamic scholar Shahid Raza, has continued to provide mediatory services to clients living in the United Kingdom on an ongoing and largely non-fee basis.

Mawlana Shahid Raza (hereafter referred to as the Alim, meaning a scholar) was born in northern India and educated at Agra and Meerut Universities. He received his full Islamic education in India, attending the famous Jamia Naeemia seminary near Muradabad, in the state of Uttar Pradesh. He taught in India for some time before arriving in the United Kingdom in 1978 to serve as an imam in Leicester. In 1988 he moved to London to join the MLSC while remaining head imam of the Central Mosque in Leicester. He is also honorary director of the Muslim community's centre in that city.

Part of the Alim's general training at the Jamia Naeemia Seminary related to 'mediation' and 'reconciliation' – its general principles. After his arrival in England as an imam, he was called on to resolve disputes. Although he was hesitant to do so initially because he lacked professional skills in mediation, he did not have much of a choice. His skills improved gradually, through experience, listening and engaging with many people from diverse backgrounds. He often consulted his fellow imams in other UK cities and other mosques as well as respected elders in the community. After joining the MLSC, the Alim worked closely with, and under the guidance and supervision of, Zaki Badawi.

The Alim sees no clear-cut distinction between mediation and reconciliation as ADR processes in his work. 'My role as a mediator,' he told me, 'would be to try my best to reconcile the group or couple in a dispute.' For him, 'Reconciling means that I will try my best as a mediator to facilitate any reconciliation which may lead again to a happy life for the couple.' Two things are evident here. First, the Alim sees his role as being primarily to bring the disputing parties together again, to the status quo ante. Thus, in dealing with matrimonial matters, the Alim first looks for 'common ground' to 'mediate'. If that exists, 'we bring them together'. Second, in his mind there is no explicit distinction between mediation and arbitration at a conceptual level. Third, and most important, one has to keep in mind that the Sharia cannot be equated with 'the law' in a Western context. The Sharia includes ethical and faith norms beyond those that constitute law in the strict sense. 'It is incorrect to equate *Sharia* and law *simpliciter* as is often done' (Weiss, 1998: 8). Thus, to draw a clear distinction between law, and ADR as an alternative to it, may not always be useful. In Western societies, too, mediation today generally connotes bringing about an understanding between disputing parties. It does not always have a clearly defined connotation of a *discrete*, dispute resolution process with a clear set of principles where the control is supposed to be *exclusively* in the hands of the disputants themselves.

Despite this conflation, the Alim is very aware of certain basic principles associated with ADR, such as early detection in domestic abuse cases. If he feels that the safety of one of the parties is in jeopardy, he will not explore the possibility of 'reconciliation'. In this category, he also includes violence or apprehended threat of violence to a child or children. 'The psychological and emotional upbringing of the children will be paramount for us,' he told me.

The Alim only 'mediates' if both parties voluntarily accept his role as 'mediator'. Sometimes he sees the parties jointly and at other times separately, depending on the circumstances of the case. Secular lawyers rarely accompany the disputing parties to the MLSC; however, the Alim has found their involvement, when it does occur, to be generally constructive. They realise that 'there are certain considerations that go beyond legal considerations, some that are emotional, moral and spiritual as well'. Asked what that means, he cites cases of access to children, where the lawyers often tend to take a narrow stand that access should be highly restrictive and limited even if only a minor type of violence has been proved. The MLSC takes the position that even if a person is occasionally violent he is still the father of the child. 'He may not, by nature, be a violent person. He may show his fatherly emotions to his child, and that as well should be taken into consideration.' If, in such a case, there is concern for the child's safety, supervised access can be arranged. Thus, the MLSC, aware that the Sharia usually grants custody to the mother, always tries to ensure access to the father; it tries to achieve a balance as called for by the Sharia.

The Alim does not claim to be fully conversant with the principles of the Children Act 2000, but he observes that the MLSC has access to three UK-trained Muslim lawyers who could provide it with the necessary guidelines. The MLSC takes an eclectic approach to Islamic law and does not feel itself bound to one particular *madhab*, though its main orientation is the Sunni Hanafi school of jurisprudence. According to the Alim, this freedom is allowed by Islamic law under the principle of *takhayur*.[4] 'The purpose of the law is resolution of disputes, not the exaltation of a school of law.'

The MLSC does not conduct all-issues mediation, nor does it deal much with property issues. According to the Alim, its main remit is to 'reconcile' the parties in a family dispute so that they can live together again. It must be kept in mind that mediation and reconciliation are two different processes with different outcomes. It appears that the MLSC's main remit is to ensure that the parties make up with each other, though in reality that might be difficult as the application for divorce could be pending in the secular courts or may have been heard already, with the MLSC only 'Islamising' the decree. The MLSC leaves all the ancillary matters needing resolution to the parties themselves. Often, it asks clients to take their proposal for settlement to their respective lawyers to ensure that what they are proposing is compatible with the laws of the land; once that has been done, the MLSC approves the proposal in order to grant it legitimacy under the Sharia. Cases heard by the Alim take an average of three months to resolve. That would entail four to five sessions of one-and-a-half to two hours each. Sometimes cases are heard by the Alim and a female counsellor together, generally at the MLSC offices in West London. At times they are called to other centres; sometimes they are invited by outside agencies as religious advisors, but that is rare.

The MLSC does not deal with child abduction cases because they have a criminal law dimension to them and most disputants realise that the MLSC cannot easily play a role in 'reconciliation' or 'mediation' in such situations. According to the Alim, Islamic law recognises kidnapping, known as *ughwa*, as a crime. Abduction of a child therefore could be considered a crime in Sharia law. It could be a double crime, because it is taking away something which is jointly owned or is in joint custody. And taking away a child from the father or mother could be considered a crime against the child as well.[5]

The MLSC also does not handle maintenance cases, but it does support the woman and advises her to go to court and claim ongoing maintenance for the child and for herself. While the MLSC takes the view that this is in accordance with the Sharia, some scholars consider it 'un-Islamic' because, under most schools, a woman generally cannot claim maintenance beyond the *iddat* period – the three cycles of menstruation following dissolution of the marriage. Pressed on whether the MLSC's understanding is based more on *maqasid al-sharia* (purpose behind the law) than on a strict, textual understanding of the *fiqh*, the Alim's view is that maintenance is a wife's right and her entitlement. In an Islamic marriage contract the wife and husband are allowed to include an additional clause in the agreement. The wife has a right to enter into a marriage with certain conditions outlined at the time of the wedding. In the case of a civil marriage registered in Britain, however, the marriage is recognised with all the terms and conditions normally attached to it. If the civil marriage breaks down, the wife will have at least a 50 per cent share of the property. The MLSC will then advise the wife to take advantage of those considerations and seek her rights. According to the MLSC, this is not in any way un-Islamic.

The MLSC has taken a progressive approach to the application of the Sharia in a contemporary context. This is quite unusual and there are various reasons for it. First, its founder and chief inspiration, Zaki Badawi, was a fiercely independent individual who had impeccably orthodox training in the Sharia and consequently developed a deep understanding of this cardinal topic within the panoply of Islamic knowledge and sciences. He understood that the fundamental purpose of the Sharia was equity and justice.

Second, the MLSC is not affiliated to any sectarian, national or international institution. According to the Alim, the MLSC respects all scholars and viewpoints, and it is able to consult any Islamic theologian or scholar whenever the need arises. 'We feel that our independence is vital in order to offer the Muslim community in this country a resolution which is ideologically and emotionally of this country. [...] Our purpose is to provide Muslims living in this part of the world with a native Islamic solution to their problems. Maybe the Muslims who live in Egypt or Saudi Arabia or in Pakistan have their problems, but they have to resolve them in the light of *their* own environment.' Although Zaki Badawi was often called upon to provide mediation and arbitration services to high-profile clients, largely from the Arab world, the MLSC's focus under his leadership and since his demise has been primarily on the Muslim communities in Britain. The MLSC's approach to the Sharia is based very much on 'indigenous grounds', which implies taking the local context into consideration. It tells the disputants, 'Over here, we discuss your problems locally. We are ideologically here and we are geographically here.'

Third, the MLSC keeps abreast of what is happening in Egypt (an important country in the development of the Sunni schools of Sharia), the Middle East generally and the South Asian subcontinent. The Alim has a good idea of how the Sharia is evolving in those areas and the general feeling of Muslims in those areas about the changes. This is critical in a globalised world where there is constant free flow of ideas. Fourth, the trust that people place in the MLSC is very important. This is crucial in today's highly conflicted world where 'Islam' is often used for competing ideological purposes in both Western and Muslim contexts. In this regard, the MLSC's composition is also very important. It is a voluntary organisation. 'We are not sectarian,' says the Alim, 'We are not constituted on ethnic lines. We have a universal, all-encompassing nature, where we have members from so many countries. We are not Ahl-al-Hadith, or Salafi, or Wahabbi or Sunni. We are neutral. [...] Furthermore, we try to resolve peoples' cases on the grounds of Sharia, which is the common ground.'

Finally, trust is clearly vital in the MLSC's dispute resolution activities. Its set-up and attitude, according to the Alim, strengthens the confidence and trust of disputants. When people enter the premises, they notice that everything is 'fairly modern in nature and that the institution is well organised, well cultured, etc. It has a reception. It has a meeting room and all the necessary facilities.' The feeling of trust is further reinforced when female clients realise that they have the option of speaking to female advisers exclusively.

The process of how trust is engendered in a general mediatory context is graphically captured in Figure 5.1. For mediation within a diasporic, Muslim community, however, that conception needs to be expanded. Trust in the interpretation of the Sharia, as well as in the institution that is responsible for that interpretation, is as important to Muslim disputants as is trust in the mediator, in the process, in themselves and in the other. Therefore, Gadlin and Davis' triangle of trust would need to be significantly enlarged. Additional strands are required, such as the nature of the Sharia rulings issued; overall competence of the institution, based on the upgrading of knowledge and skill-sets of its officials; and overall confidentiality of the process. The triangle shows the progression of trust in straight, solid lines in a clearly defined progression from the beginning to a culmination point; in reality, however, things

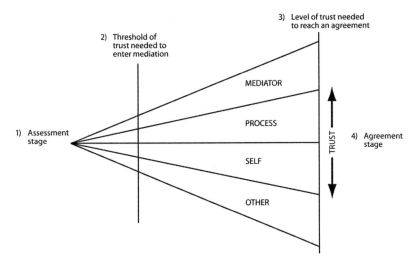

Figure 5.1 Growth of trust in mediation.
Source: H. Gadlin and A. Davis. (1998). 'Mediators Gain Trust the Old-Fashioned Way: We Earn It!', *Negotiation Journal* (January): 55–62.

do not work out so neatly. The lines are more likely to be gyrating, because, at any particular point in the trajectory of a dispute, trust in one of the indices can, and often does, suddenly plummet or soar, depending on the circumstances; for example, a spouse can take a child out of the jurisdiction without the consent of the other spouse in the middle of a dispute.

The MLSC occasionally handles forced-marriage cases referred to it from the Hounslow area, but the Alim does not see such cases as being on the increase. He perceives the problem as purely cultural: 'As we all know, in Islam forced marriages have never been recognised. During the last 1,400 years, we have had hundreds of denominations within Islamic societies, and I have never come across an opinion in any of these Islamic denominations that has sanctioned forced marriages.' He recalled an occasion when a UK court asked for the MLSC's opinion in the case of an Iraqi girl whose parents wanted to have her forcibly married to someone in Iraq. The MLSC responded that there was nothing Islamic in the practice and that the girl had the right to refuse the marriage.

The MLSC also undertakes mediation in inheritance matters. When a father asks for guidance on how to leave his estate equally between his daughters and his sons in view of the Sharia stipulation that his son's share of the inheritance should be twice that of his daughter, the MLSC advises him to transfer his assets equally to his children in his lifetime, which is allowed by the Sharia.

Declaratory functions of MLSC

As discussed earlier, the MLSC acts as a community-based court to 'Islamise' a divorce granted to a Muslim woman in a United Kingdom court. When a husband refuses to grant his wife the *talaq*, the wife files a petition to the MLSC by filling in a simple form. The MLSC then asks the husband to explain why he is denying his wife a divorce and thus causing her hardship. He is given three consecutive written notices over a defined period of time, with the caveat that if he does not respond, the MLSC will grant his wife the divorce on the basis that the Sharia forbids inflicting harm on an individual.

The bulk of the case processing takes place at the administrative level of the MLSC – largely through the Alim. Generally, all the papers, including evidentiary documents, are put together by the Alim and the file is then given to a panel of reviewers – twelve *ulama* (scholars, plural of Alim) and three UK-trained Muslim, secular lawyers – who deliberate on it. The lawyers on the panel ensure that any judgement or decision given by the MLSC conforms with English public law. At least four panellists are needed to make up a quorum. The mother tongues of the panellists include Arabic, Urdu and Punjabi, but the common language of deliberation is English. The *ulama* used to be largely of South Asian origin in the early days, but that is no longer the case.

The procedure followed by the MLSC panel is largely based on documentation. According to one of the lawyers on the MLSC panel, 'We [have] always dealt with cases as if we were a court of appeal; that is, we [have] generally considered documentation rather than heard witnesses.' Discussions with people generally take place before the panel's deliberations. The panel reviews the depositions made by the petitioner. If there is a defence, in most cases it is by the husband and the panel receives a written report embodying the defence. The files are fairly comprehensive and panellists can ask for more information if they need it. The panel arrives at a consensus through its deliberations, after which the head of the MLSC formulates the decision and has it communicated to the parties concerned. Over the years, the panel has heard hundreds of cases from the United Kingdom and parts of Western Europe. Some cases have also come from other parts of the world, including the Middle East.

One of the issues the MLSC may have to deal with is that of legal recognition of its rulings. Asked what would happen if the UK courts or a Muslim country refused to respect an MLSC ruling, the lawyer on the panel said it would create a conflict-of-laws situation. Various other questions could also arise with regard to the MLSC's authoritative status, let alone its judgements. For example, what would be the situation if a divorced woman wanted to return to a Muslim country and contract another marriage there, and her husband appealed the MLSC's decision in that country? Could the woman be charged with *zina* (adultery) if she went ahead with the marriage? Recognition of the MLSC's decrees has only been tested in a United Kingdom court once, in an arbitration matter.[6] It has never been challenged in a secular or even a Sharia court in a Muslim country. According to the lawyer on the panel quoted earlier, since the Islamic credentials of the MLSC are impeccable, it is unlikely that an MLSC decision would be lightly overturned on narrow technical grounds.

In the larger Muslim community that the MLSC serves, there is considerable trust in the institution. The lawyer attributes this largely to 'Muslims having a deferential attitude towards Sharia and law in a way [that is] slightly different from the Western world. In the Western world, the law is secular. Therefore, we have – an element, if you like – of coercion, supported, if not enforced, by the state, even in personal law.' In a diasporic Muslim context, things are rather different, whereby 'if the *ulama* pass [an] Islamic judgement, they [Muslims] are bound by their faith to accept the judgement.'

The lawyer sees great value in ADR and giving younger imams training in mediation to serve the Muslim communities in Britain. However, that will only be effective 'provided they [the younger imams] are capable of thinking beyond the narrow, strictly literalistic and legalistic understanding that they have of *fiqh*'.

Placing MLSC's work in perspective

The work of the MLSC has to be viewed mainly within the context of Islamic law and society in a diasporic community. Its work also has resonances with the whole notion of alternative dispute resolution, and it is here that its contribution to the reinterpretation of Islamic law in a contemporary context becomes both necessary and possible.

According to Pearl and Menski (1998) many disputes among ethnic minorities in Britain are settled in the context of informal or community conciliation, and senior members of families or community leaders participate in informal conciliation processes operating outside the traditional legal system through networks centred around religious and community centres. Over time, this has resulted in the organic development of certain customs and specific personal laws of ethnic minorities that may avoid official channels and the official legal processes (Jones and Gnanpala, 2000). One may legitimately ask whether this development is a form of legal pluralism or the development of a new, hybrid, unofficial law emerging from the dynamic interaction between English and Islamic systems of law.

Werner Menski, an academic who has specialised in Islamic family law in diasporic contexts observes that there is no single monolithic conception of this phenomenon. Each Muslim group develops its own approach within the principles of its own jurisprudential school, its history, its traditions, its interpretation and its own particular circumstances. The MLSC, under Zaki Badawi's stewardship and since his demise, has acted as a catalyst for a new approach to Islamic law in a diasporic setting by drawing on the principles of a number of schools, both Sunni and Shi'i. It can be argued that Zaki Badawi was able to do this with much greater facility precisely because he was in a diasporic setting.

Some Muslim countries, by their very constitution or political complexities, might find it difficult to allow such eclecticism.

Whether this development can be termed 'law' or 'ADR' is not clear. It appears to be more akin to the concept of 'unofficial law' postulated by the legal pluralist Masaji Chiba (1986: 1–9). According to Pearl and Menski (1998: 74), 'redefined unofficial Muslim laws in Britain have become hybrid obligation systems peculiar to British Muslims as a matter of social practice rather than legal fact.' In Britain today, through the process of legal pluralism, there is a 'new form of *Sharia*, English Muslim law, or *angrezi shariat*, which remains officially unrecognised by the state but is now increasingly in evidence as a dominant legal force within the various Muslim communities in Britain' (Pearl and Menski, 1998: 58).

Interesting questions arise as to the extent to which the notion of *angrezi shariat* is informed by local positive laws; and whether it is the development of 'Islamic law' in the stratosphere, which will look homogenous regardless of where the evolution is taking place. Professor Menski is not clear on this and the issue needs further research. For the moment, on the basis of the present study, it would be fair to assume that *angrezi shariat* is the outcome of the interface between United Kingdom official laws and the principles of Islamic law and various customary practices followed by various Muslim communities within a very specific juridical context.

As to whether there is a precedent with regard to these types of developments in Islamic law, Yilmaz (2003) views the work of the MLSC as a form of neo-*ijtihad*. He identifies five major characteristics of *ijtihad* in the United Kingdom context: it is exercised in a non-Muslim environment; it is unofficial and not recognised by the state but tolerated to a certain extent; new Muslim laws have been dynamically created in practical-life situations; the traditional Muslim laws are not disregarded or disrespected but reinterpreted; and *ijtihad* committees, but not individuals, exercise *ijtihad*. Most of the points Yilmaz makes are unarguable. However, while it is true that traditional Muslim laws are not disregarded or disrespected but reinterpreted, this does not apply in all cases, as for example, criminal laws. Yilmaz's assertion that *new* Muslim laws have been dynamically created in practical-life situations is also problematic and needs further elucidation. He does not give examples of new Muslim laws that have been created in such a manner.

In addition, the term 'neo-*ijtihad*' needs to be defined. *Ijtihad* means 'to exert', to use one's mind in order to make meaning of something. By its very nature, it gives rise to a reinterpretation – something that is 'new'. To refer to such a process as 'neo-*ijtihad*' is not really illuminating. According to Hallaq (1984) *ijtihad* has always been exercised in Muslim societies throughout history, and the very process of exercising it is often projected with a degree of diffidence and humility in deference to the great masters of *ijtihad* of the past. In the context of the MLSC, both the late Zaki Badawi as well as the Alim Shahid Raza expressed a sense of discomfort with the term 'neo-*ijtihad*' and showed a preference for the word 'reinterpretation'. To this extent, Yilmaz concedes that traditional Muslim laws *are* being 'reinterpreted' by the MLSC. Yilmaz's point that *ijtihad* being performed by committees instead of by individuals is something new, is fully conceded. Historically, according to Hallaq (1984) *ijtihad* was carried out by a *mujtahid* (one who exercises *ijtihad*); but in the twentieth century, Muslim governments endeavouring to undertake legal reform also resorted to *ijtihad* to make necessary changes to Islamic laws (Coulson, 1964). The reinterpretation by a committee in the United Kingdom could itself be viewed as an exercise in *ijtihad*.

The MLSC is making a small but not inconsiderable attempt to reinterpret classical Islamic law in a diasporic context through *ijtihad* and legal pluralism. The interesting point is that this process is actually taking place within the context of ADR and not as a result of a clash of legal systems. It can be argued that this approach makes the process more politically viable and acceptable because the Sharia is not being pitted against the laws of the land. Additionally, the principles of ADR resonate with the social purposes which underpin the Sharia, which, according to the *usul al-fiqh* (legal methodology) protect vital interests in the face of necessity (*darura*) relating to religion (*din*), person (*nafs*), offspring (*nasl*), property (*maal*) and reason (*aql*). The extent to which the

MLSC can restore to Islamic law the social purposes underlying its existence, through the development of appropriate Muslim ADR practices, is a much more complex question.

The MLSC is a positive manifestation of the Muslim ability to adapt to a changing context. This is nothing new. Islam, as a faith, began in a diasporic setting; out of necessity, some of the early Muslims emigrated to Abyssinia, where they lived in a Christian milieu; then the Prophet and his followers migrated to Yathrib, a city of Jews and pagans, which in due course became the first Muslim city of Medina. The Umayyad and Abbasid periods saw similar changes, and the Muslims were able to adapt to new circumstances. Forces of this nature are once again confronting Muslim diasporic societies today, requiring them to make appropriate adjustments. Neither a pure and dogmatic reversion to the past nor an indiscriminate abandoning of it in favour of outright secularism seems to be the answer. In the view of Coulson (1964) the solution may lie somewhere between these two extremes, 'in a concept of law as a code of behaviour which is founded upon certain basic and immutable religious principles but which, within these limits, does not neglect the factor of change and allows the adoption of such extraneous standards as may prove more acceptable to current Muslim opinion than indigenous tradition'.

The existence and practice of the MLSC is exemplary, but one that may be difficult to sustain over a long period. It fits the original Muslim paradigm whereby a courageous, charismatic, learned and effective leader of a Muslim community was able to do something that was creative and innovative in a diasporic setting, thus showing the ability of Muslims to adapt to a changing context. However, two important considerations need to be kept in mind. First, I found that the MLSC has become a victim of its own success as demand for its services has increased and the staff of the MLSC appear to be overworked. Second, and more importantly, the ability to mediate diasporic realities continues to remain a challenge for Muslim societies living in the Western world; continuing the bold changes initiated by the MLSC requires astute, informed and learned individuals like Zaki Badawi and an increase in diasporic communal self-confidence.

The issue of enforcement looms large for all the ADR fora in this study, including the MLSC. While it can be argued that in mediation the agreements arrived at by the parties themselves are often self-enforcing, this may be largely true where a more facilitative type of mediation is conducted and not necessarily where mediation tends to be more directive. According to Pospisil (1971) it is well established that between the body politic and the individual there are interposed various smaller, organised social fields to which the individual 'belongs'. These social fields have their own customs and rules and means of coercing or inducing compliance.

An emphasis on the capacity of the modern state to threaten the use of physical force should not distract us from the other agencies and mores of inducing compliance. For Moore (1978) the semi-autonomous social field is defined and its boundaries identified not by its organisation (it may be a corporate group, it may not) but by a processual characteristic, the fact that it can generate rules and coerce or induce compliance with them. The operation of the social field is to a significant extent self-regulating, self-enforcing and self-propelling within a certain legal, political, economic and social environment. Viewed from the inside, then, the social field is semi-autonomous not only because it can be affected by the direction of outside forces impinging upon it, but because persons inside the social field can mobilise those external forces, or threaten to do so, in their bargaining with one another. This is confirmed by the present study which found that, to quote Moore (1978), 'the legal rules are only a small piece of the complex'. Disputants and their families will want to play the game according to the rules – legal and non-legal – because the penalty for not doing so could be loss of *izzat* (honour), loss of status and social ostracism. Compliance is induced by the desire to stay within the community and prosper. According to Moore, it is not unreasonable to infer that some of those legal rules are obeyed at least as much because of the very same kinds of pressures and inducements that produce compliance with the non-legal mores of the social field, as because of any direct potentiality of enforcement by the state.

A number of problematic issues could arise with regard to the MLSC's declarations. For example, can an individual in the

United Kingdom obtain a prerogative writ of *mandamus* from a United Kingdom court to force the MLSC to perform an obligation or a writ of *certiorari* quashing a decision arrived at by the MLSC? Divorce changes a person's legal status and that change can have very important property ramifications; therefore, where a person feels an injustice has been committed, he or she could apply for a prerogative writ. It is arguable that if the parties were only married by the *nikah* ceremony in the presence of an imam,[7] then the MLSC's jurisdiction would not be easily impugned. The situation might be different if the parties were married under the laws of the United Kingdom. Also, would Muslim communities in the UK in the future continue to turn to their own United Kingdom-based dispute resolution institutions for Sharia-based issues? Could they, for example, resort to Sharia courts in the countries of their origin? Would they be precluded from doing so? If so, on what grounds? These are some of the types of conflict-of-law issues that can arise and on which future research needs to be conducted.

The MLSC is not the only provider of ADR services to Muslims in Hounslow. A number of other alternatives are available and used by the community. The next chapter focuses on these other providers of ADR services.

6

The Many Faces of ADR in Hounslow

People who get caught up in matrimonial and other interpersonal conflicts are often bewildered and do not know which way to turn for help. Just getting someone to listen to their problems often constitutes a major part of the solution, so all the dispute resolution agencies interviewed for this study place a high premium on listening skills. Which forum Hounslow's Muslim residents choose depends mainly on the type of problem they are experiencing. Since there is a propensity not to let anyone outside a very small circle of intimates know what is really going on within a family, family issues are frequently referred to a particular forum through the intervention of a family member, close relative or close friend.

Figure 6.1 summarises the variety of fora that have been used by Muslims in Hounslow to resolve interpersonal disputes. The entities and their positions in the figure do not, in any way, imply a hierarchy or sequence of application. On occasion, disputants may go to more than one forum simultaneously or sequentially, depending on the nature of their needs. Some of the fora interact with each other, either directly or indirectly. Others do not do so for various reasons.

Imams and mosque trustees

The imam is a religious functionary in Sunni Muslim mosques whose main function is to lead the daily prayers. In addition, the

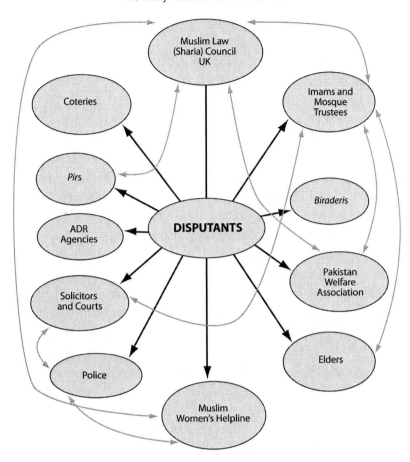

Figure 6.1 Dispute resolution resources used by Muslims in Hounslow.

imam, who is always male, attends to other activities such as rites of passage, funerals and general pastoral care. Three imams of the Hounslow mosque, who had been associated with the mosque for some 25 years, were interviewed for this study.

According to Zaki Badawi, imams came to the United Kingdom from overseas in the 1960s, primarily because the Muslim community urgently needed their services and there was no capability then to train imams locally. The imported imams had a limited remit: to teach Urdu and Arabic to children, acquaint them with the principles of the Qur'an, lead the five daily prayers, attend to different rites of passage and provide the necessary pastoral care. The imams were, by and large, also trained in traditional jurisprudence (*fiqh*) and, while that may not have been part of their initial remit, it has become important in the context of a diasporic community for them to have at least a general knowledge of religious laws and their application in dispute resolution. The imams have played this role in the past and continue to play it even today, but at a primary level.

The imams are often consulted by women wanting to know whether what they have been told by their husbands about their rights during a domestic quarrel really conforms to the principles of Islamic law. By empowering the wife with some knowledge of her basic Islamic rights, an opinion from the imam may serve to disarm an overbearing male. At times, the intervention calls for some sort of mediation. Here, the imam's presence has an authoritative effect. When there is a need for a *fatwa*, the imam issues one, either on the basis of his own relevant knowledge or through referral, often to the MLSC. An imam may also be asked to dissolve a marriage, particularly one that was never registered or recognised under UK law. In effect, the imam is very much a part of the texture of community life, and sometimes even 'unmosqued' Muslims ask him to intervene in disputes.[1]

The imam only intervenes with the consent of both parties to a dispute. He either goes to their home or invites them to the mosque, where the consultation is carried out in privacy and with the guarantee of confidentiality. The imam draws upon his knowledge of the Qur'an and the *sunna* to reach an opinion.[2]

Women interviewed for this study are equally divided over the imams' capability to play an important role in dispute resolution in the community. A negative impression seems to have gained currency for two reasons: first, women have an overall impression that the Sharia is basically patriarchal and that the imam, as a custodian of religious law, is bound to take an approach that is primarily male-biased, and in some cases may have appeared to take such a position; second, women do not attend the mosque for daily prayers, which, *ipso facto*, makes the mosque a bastion of male dominance. I found that, despite this, the imams are consulted on an ongoing basis by women. The imams also participate actively in the resolution of disputes.[3]

Even though not trained in modern mediation techniques, the imams are an important link in the dispute resolution chain.

When necessary, an imam refers an issue to the mosque solicitor for advice on its legal merits under UK law. Complex Sharia issues are referred to the MLSC. If a matter is amenable to resolution without consulting any other institution, the imam resolves it himself. By and large, he allows the disputants to make their own decisions, saying that he only 'facilitates' the process.

Although the imams use traditional methods of dispute resolution, there is much resonance between what they do and what exists in the ADR toolbox. For example, their involvement in dispute resolution may not take the same form as in contemporary mediation practice, but they do so in a manner that is culturally sensitive and appropriate. The imams never see women alone. In the Hounslow Muslim community, they always ensure that a married woman comes to mediation with her husband, brother, father, sister, or other related person. They practise active listening and try to understand the viewpoints of both the disputing parties. They try to keep the disputants calm. They summarise issues and often take a child-focused approach. They do reality-testing, indulge in co-working and use their judgement as to when to close an issue.

In a secular mediation process, all the preceding praxes are often projected in a rights- and responsibilities-based context, while in a faith-based dispute resolution process the Qur'an, the *sunna* of the Prophet and the norms of the community are constantly referred to. The imam takes a strong Sharia approach, but the Sharia rules he enunciates are tempered with justice, fairness and compassion, which are regarded as divine attributes. For example, when one party becomes angry, the imam may cite sayings of the Prophet with regard to controlling the temper, or verses of the Qur'an.

In addition, when advising on Islamic legal rights, he spells out the principles of classical Hanafi law prevalent among the Hounslow Muslims, which he extracts from classical commentaries on the Hanafi law such as the *Hedaya* and the *Fatāwa al-al-imgiriyya*. By virtue of his position in the community, the imam is trusted and held in high esteem. However, even though his words carry weight through moral authority, he has no enforcement capability.

Despite being born and raised overseas, the imams are very receptive to the burgeoning needs of the Hounslow Muslim community as it undergoes multiple transitions. One of the imams interviewed often speaks to his congregation in English as well as Urdu, and in his *khutba*s (sermons) he touches on issues of social significance to the community. For example, on one occasion, after attending a seminar on domestic abuse, he gave a *khutba* on why domestic abuse is not acceptable in Islam – an issue that had never been addressed so openly and emphatically before.

One technique that the imam sometimes uses is the involvement of children in mediation, a practice that is a matter of debate today among ADR practitioners and theorists; and while it has its merits the way he makes use of it could also have some disadvantages. For example, at times, if the children in the dispute resolution process are old enough to understand what is going on in the home, the imam may ask them for their opinions. Since the majority of children generally would want their parents to remain together, the imam tells the parents that, for the children's sake, it would be better for them to compromise and make peace. This technique could cause serious problems if the children are used instrumentally to make one or both of the parents feel culpable or guilty. By asking children to play a judgemental role, even unwittingly, the mediator also risks having the children feel let down when the parents go ahead and divorce anyway, while the parents, for their part, will feel a sense of remorse and opprobrium.

The question of whether and when to include children in mediation has been debated in the UK for over 30 years without any consensus being reached. In the early days of family mediation, a number of authors provided compelling arguments for including children directly in the process (see, for example, Drapkin and Bienenfeld, 1990; Garwood, 1990; Saposnek, 1983, 1991; Wallerstein, 1985). Some research has suggested that their participation carried substantial benefits (Taylor and Adelman, 1986). Despite these early findings, their involvement has been 'patchy' and 'variable' (Walker, 2010). Some court-connected services in England required children over a certain age to attend a conciliation appointment at the court and then left them sitting in a waiting room, to be called in only if negotiations between their parents reached an impasse (Walker et al., 1990). Saposnek (1991) concluded that the decision to include or exclude them appeared to be based not on their needs (or rights) but on arbitrary factors and the discretion of mediators. According to Walker et al. (1990) mediators who were comfortable with, skilled in and adept at, interviewing children were more likely to include them in mediation than were colleagues who were uncomfortable about talking to children.

While most practitioners appreciate the importance of working in the best interests of children and giving them a voice, there are mixed views about when and how to do so. A number of problems are associated with this issue and strategies are still being developed. Some researchers believe that a cultural shift is needed if children's voices are to be routinely heard and their views respected (Smart, 2002). I concur with this view, as in many cultures children are not given much prominence when adult relationships are in dispute and have to be resolved.

Many adults tend to confuse participation with autonomous decision-making and question children's competence to be involved in any family law processes (Murch et al., 1999). However, recent developments in Australia and New Zealand provide an opportunity to revisit the issue. Cashmore and Parkinson's 2008 study with two groups of children found that 91 per cent of the children wanted to be involved. Children in the contested matters group were particularly vociferous on the issue because they wanted acknowledgement that they were part of the family and therefore an interested party; they believed that their participation would produce better outcomes. Most parents agreed that their children should have a say, but they were more cautious about universal involvement and often concerned about putting too much pressure on children.

Another recent study in Australia (McIntosh et al., 2008), comparing child-focused and child-inclusive divorce mediation, indicated, *inter alia*, that children who were included in the process were more likely later to report improved emotional availability on the part of their fathers and greater feelings of closeness; they and their mothers showed preservation of, or improvement in, the mother-child contact arrangements and less inclination to want to change them; and there was greater stability in care and contact patterns in their families. They also showed lower anxiety, fewer fears and fewer depressive symptoms. Therefore, McIntosh et al. see considerable value in parents enabling the mediator to see the children alone at the earliest stage in the mediation process. According to them, that helps parents to focus on the needs of the children rather than on their own interpersonal arguments; the children, for their part, are relieved to have someone from outside the dispute hear them out so that they can offload their problems.

The United Kingdom College of Family Mediators Code of Practice (Welfare of Children) outlines a set of rules on child involvement in family mediation.[4] They include special concern for the welfare of all children in the family, in addition to focusing upon the participants' own needs, and exploring the situation from the child's point of view. They also highlight that mediators should encourage the participants to consider their children's wishes and feelings. Where appropriate, they may discuss with the participants whether, and to what extent, it is proper to involve the children in the mediation process in order to elicit their views about their hopes and aspirations.

When the imams of Hounslow are consulted on family disputes, they are sensitive to context. Realising that women tend to be reticent about domestic abuse because of the notion of shame and family honour prevalent among people from the South Asian subcontinent, they try to probe further to ascertain whether a woman has suffered violence. If she has been abused, they tell her that protecting herself and her children in such a situation is in accordance with the principles of Islam and encourage her to report the matter to the police. In some cases they refer the matter to the mosque committee's solicitor, who takes the necessary steps to ensure legal protection. The lack of understanding of their rights among many women in the Hounslow area can be attributed to their low level of education or lack of a central facility in the mosque where such information could be imparted. The imams are also open to the concept of legal pluralism (*takhayur*) and refer disputants to different Sharia viewpoints by informing them of the Fatwa Committee that sits at the Regent's Park Mosque as well as the *fatwa*s that are available online.

The imams' general understanding of social issues is reflected in the changing nature of their *khutba*s (sermons), which touch on hitherto taboo subjects such as domestic abuse. My research corroborates Zaman's (2002) finding that the *ulama* have a far more flexible understanding of the world and of Islam than is often acknowledged, not just by observers or critics of the *ulama*, but also by the *ulama* themselves. According to Zaman, this flexibility means that, far from having been marginalised in the face of challenges to their authority – emanating for instance from the modern nation-state or from Islamist activists and the new religious intellectuals – the *ulama* have often continued to be, or have become, active and important players in many contemporary Muslim societies.

However, he observes, and I concur, that the type of sweeping changes some *ulama* are calling for today, backed by Muslim modernists like Mohamed Arkoun or Muhammad Shahrur and Fazlur Rahman, are of a very different order than what most *ulama* have been willing to accept. This change is premised on the recognition that the fundamental texts must be interpreted afresh, the religious tradition re-evaluated, critiqued and radically rethought, and only *then* parts of it appropriated for their present 'usefulness'. Zaman maintains that the '*ulama* remain unrelenting' on the privileged status of the classical texts, since it is the central basis of their claim to religious authority and of their identity as *ulama*.

The imams nonetheless enjoy the trust of the congregation and maintain a very high degree of confidentiality. In some cases, they ask the trustees of the mosque to accompany them to meet disputants. The cumulative moral weight of this has great effect. The involvement of the trustees in the process fits in with Lederach's concept of 'conscientisation – awareness of self in context' – that is, people are knowledgeable about, capable of naming, interacting with, and responding to their own realities in dynamic ways (Lederach, 1995).

This study found considerable potential for strengthening the indigenous conflict-resolution resources of the community, such as imams. The community has its own narratives and its own dispute resolvers who have acquired experience and credibility over a period of time. These dispute resolvers have also shown a willingness to embrace new ways of doing things. Empowering them with new skills would yield multiple benefits for the community. The capacity to respond in new ways is extant, and through adequate refurbishment the system could become more responsive to the changing needs of the community.

The question remains: What is the nature of the imams' intervention and where does it fit into the ADR landscape? They are not mediators as such, as they do not really *manage* the process. They enunciate the religious law and see their position largely as 'facilitators' who call attention to the relevant principles of the Sharia. Though they are passive interveners, their position is very influential because they are custodians of the religious law, which generally has a strong hold on the disputants. On one level, their role is facilitative and minimalist, and on another level it is influential and morally directive even though they are clearly seen as impartial and neutral. According to Roberts and Palmer (2005) mediation may range from a minimal intervention that aspires to do no more than set in place or improve the quality of communication between the parties – passing messages between the parties, facilitating information exchange – to an active, direct intervention encompassing the provision of specialist evaluation and advice.

What degree of control do imams have over the outcome? This study found that while imams do not *control* the outcome, they do play a strong directive role, even though it is only by virtue of their very presence. Their role is within the range outlined by Gulliver (1979), moving from virtual passivity to chairman, to enunciator, to promoter, to leader and to arbitrator. Gulliver states that, 'by his very presence, a quite passive mediator can encourage more positive communication and interaction between the parties, stimulating the continuation or the renewal of the exchange of information.'

The next question that arises is: How does an imam do this and at what stages? As enunciator of rules and norms relevant to the issues in negotiation, the imam reminds 'the parties of what they have temporarily forgotten or neglected, which might provide a basis from which to move toward agreement'. He 'reminds the parties, too, of the moral community to which both belong' and 'articulates what may have been left unclear and obstructive between the parties' (Gulliver, 1979). One can ask quite legitimately whether this might not lead to some form of manipulation and abuse. The imam may continue to be impartial, as he always tries to be, but there is opportunity to influence the direction of negotiations and to favour one party or to push towards the quickest outcome available, without giving full consideration to the merits of the case. I have not investigated this issue in any depth but recognise that there are distinct possibilities for such manipulation to take place, particularly in light of the relationship of trust that exists between the imam and the disputants, who, in most cases, are his congregants.

As we have seen, the process used by the imam is neither mediation nor arbitration. He *facilitates* the process of dispute resolution and articulates the religious law and the norms of the community, leaving the decision to the conscience of the disputants, who are generally disposed to submit to legal precepts which, because of their religious source, are deemed to be normative and beyond dispute. On the basis of this, the disputants decide how they want to resolve the dispute. Normally, disputants in societies that are relational, such as that of the Hounslow Muslims, expect an authoritative third party to decide the dispute for them. Contemporary mediation posits that it is the parties *themselves* who make the decision, though in reality that may not always be the case. After the imams enunciate the religious law, they tend to take a more laid-back position. If the matter involves complex Sharia issues, they refer it to the MLSC.

The imam's capacity to resolve disputes has to be evaluated realistically in light of what he does, what he is mandated to do and the authority he wields to achieve results. First, by virtue of their training and the position they hold as custodians of the religious law, imams are not supposed to change the religious law. By and large, they are *muqallid* – people supposed to follow precedents and not indulge in new interpretation of the Sharia (Zaman, 2002). Notwithstanding this limitation, in Hounslow they are open to meting out justice according to the needs of time and place. Second, the imams are employees of the mosque trustees, who, to a large extent, depend on the regular congregants for donations and help to manage the affairs of the community. Thus, the imams have to maintain a very fine balance and ensure that they are always seen to be impartial and neutral. Perhaps unwittingly, by not taking sides the imams are acting in the best tradition of mediation. Third, the imams are constrained by their lack of training in contemporary techniques of dispute resolution. All three imams interviewed expressed a wish to learn mediation skills. Fourth, imams have to lead prayers several times a day, conduct rites of passage, provide pastoral care and oversee the general administration of the mosque; that leaves them very little time to attend to dispute resolution. Last, because mediation is a voluntary process, the imams cannot compel anyone to submit to the process, force anyone to agree to something or enforce any agreement reached. To this extent, their role reflects that of any other mediator.

The imams also play an important role after a dispute has been resolved: that of healing the wounds. Post-dispute rehabilitation cannot only be in a material forum; spiritual healing and prayer play an important role in the whole healing process, particularly when a disputant has to confront important existential questions in life. For many disputants, conflict is a precursor to transformation; after the conflict has been resolved, those involved need emotional and spiritual support to cope with changes in their lives, and a community, with its religious functionaries and support systems , often constitutes the most important environment for facilitating that process.

*Biraderi*s

The great majority of South Asian Muslim households in Britain comprise nuclear families, but most also have close relatives living nearby. Those may include as many as ten or more households. An extended kinship network of this kind is termed a *biraderi*. According to Alavi (1972), the *biraderi* is best understood as a context-dependent idea rather than a rigid and concrete entity.

Thus, besides its local manifestation as a network of co-resident kin, it may also include relatives elsewhere in Britain, and in its widest extent, may span several countries. Particularly when only a few members live locally, a family may well consider this transnational network of relatives as constituting its *biraderi*.

The *biraderis'* approach to disputes would be broadly patriarchal, their effectiveness depending on their influence, with pre-immigration cultural norms and values as the main guiding principles. Given the general reluctance on the part of disputants to speak about family disputes outside the close-knit clan, very few people in the general community – often not even the imam of the mosque – would get to know about a conflict when a *biraderi* is involved. By and large, in the interest of clan harmony and group cohesiveness, disputants are encouraged to settle their disputes amicably within the principles of customary practice; where they help, general Islamic principles are also cited to the parties to effect reconciliation. I was not able to access the *biraderis* because of the very personal nature of conflict within the clans and their reluctance to speak to outsiders about it.[5] The resolution of conflicts through the *biraderi* system is said to be particularly prevalent among the Mirpuris.[6]

Pakistan Welfare Association

The Pakistan Welfare Association (PWA) is a registered charity established in Hounslow in 1966 in order 'to relieve the inhabitants of the London Borough of Hounslow and its adjacent towns, particularly those of Pakistani origin or descent who are in condition of need, hardship or distress'. The Association provides advice and counselling and represents some 6.5 per cent of the population of the borough. The PWA predates the MLSC and ranks as one of the older institutions dealing with dispute resolution in the area.

When it was established, the PWA's main remit was to help newly arrived immigrants from Pakistan to settle in the area. It provided a host of services, ranging from identifying suitable places for worship and negotiating for Muslim burial facilities, to imparting education in Urdu and Arabic to children and helping people find jobs and housing. It also helped people fill out forms concerning their housing needs, and with Department of Social Security matters, general immigration needs and matters associated with the Pakistan High Commission. Dispute resolution was generally ancillary to the main objective of helping with settlement. As the population increased, many of the original activities were transferred to specific committees. Some of the community elders who have helped with dispute resolution over the past 30 years have been affiliated in one way or another to the PWA.

The Association now deals with people's interpersonal problems and has a part-time Community Development Officer. A social worker who trained with the Federation of Independent Advice Centres, she normally handles issues of domestic violence. People without a previous link with the organisation approach it either through referral or after reading about its services in the Muslim Directory. According to the Community Development Officer, 'This is the first stop for them.' People approach the PWA rather than other organisations for various reasons. First, there is already a connection in the case of those whom it has helped to settle in a new, and often alien, environment. Second, some may have known the office-bearers for a long time, since they are prominent in the community and the PWA was the first community agency to be established. Third, the linguistic and cultural affinities are a comfort factor. Finally, the PWA is a gateway to appropriate agencies that can help them.

What the Association provides is clearly more akin to counselling than mediation in the sense that the term is used in contemporary ADR. The Community Development Officer appeared not to know the difference between the two processes. Only one party is usually present, and yet a so-called, neutral third party makes a decision that has an important bearing on a family relationship. The PWA takes depositions from the parties and refers people to the appropriate social services. At best, whatever process is used, it constitutes a good example of how community members derive a sense of comfort from speaking with someone from a similar or the same background in a community organisation. However, it should be noted that people are generally reluctant to discuss their interpersonal problems at the PWA; a staff member said that they merely provide enough information to elicit sympathy so that they can be helped to access the relevant governmental social services.

People ask for advice largely on housing matters and financial issues. The domestic abuse cases are usually linked to a request for alternative housing by a woman. According to the Community Development Officer, women feel more comfortable bringing their issues to the PWA because such facilities are not readily available to them in mosques. She finds that listening to them is the first step in engendering trust, 'where they can disclose to you all the things which they feel they cannot talk to other people about'.

A male co-worker highlighted some of the important social issues the Pakistani community faces today. As with the Somali immigrants, a very important problem is the changed role of families and clans in resolving disputes. During the 1960s, the joint and extended family helped to resolve issues internally, but this is no longer a widespread practice. Nonetheless, while some people do approach the PWA, it has not become a substitute for the family in this regard because people feel that bringing their problems to it would be akin to washing their dirty linen in public. According to the male co-worker, the PWA is regarded as an 'internal' institution, and for broader professional services people often prefer to go directly to the courts or to the MLSC. A second social problem is the plight of estranged male immigrant spouses in a matrimonial dispute. Such a spouse, often the victim of his wife's overbearing extended family who sponsored his immigration into the United Kingdom, is caught in a disproportionate power imbalance and mediation is not able to help him.

While it is not normal for male spouses to be viewed as victims of domestic violence in the context of mediation, it is increasingly acknowledged that males are not always the perpetrators of spousal violence. Some researchers also stress the need to discriminate between families that feature occasional outbursts of (non-gendered) violence by a husband, a wife or sometimes a same-sex partner ('couple violence') and those that are characterised by systematic intimidation and abuse.

Nazroo (1995) emphasises that the methodology of assessing domestic abuse is often flawed, because it only focuses on the incidence of physical attack and does not take into account the context and psychological elements involved. For example, in a domestic incident, after a woman attacks a man and gains the basic advantage of hitting him, she normally stops; but when a man gains the basic advantage, he often continues to hit and inflict injury. Nazroo found that women hit their partners more often than men, but, when viewed in terms of context and meaning, male violence is more likely than female violence to be threatening and dangerous. It is more likely to lead to serious injury and greatly increase the risk of anxiety in the female partner. Female-perpetrated violence seldom has these consequences for male partners. Of the couples studied by Nazroo, 55 per cent of the women and 38 per cent of the men had been violent in their relationship. However, 17 per cent of the women and 79 per cent of the men were violent in ways such that their partners could not defend themselves; and 6 per cent of the women and 20 per cent of the men used violence that could be defined as 'dangerous'. With regard to the level of injury sustained, the study showed that 25 per cent of the women experienced severe injury while only 2 per cent of the men sustained injury of similar magnitude; 30 per cent of the women sustained moderate injury, compared with 15 per cent of the men; and none of the women sustained mild injury, compared with 8 per cent of the men.

The PWA normally refers Sharia issues to the elders of the Association, who, in turn, refer them to the imam or the MLSC, depending on the complexity of the issue. When the research for this study was being carried out, a senior office bearer of the PWA was personally involved in dispute resolution and had handled some cases of forced marriage and intergenerational issues. Some of the elders associated with the PWA are still called upon occasionally to help resolve interpersonal problems.

Elders

Although they do not exist as a formal group, elders undertake some dispute resolution individually and at times are called upon to intervene. Five elders who had acquired a reputation as *adula* (trusted elders) by virtue of their work in the nascent community were interviewed for this study; two of them are (non-practising) lawyers, one a teacher, one a chartered accountant and one a medical practitioner. All of them have been affiliated to the PWA at one time or another. They are noted for their sense of dedication, both in the PWA in the late 1960s and early 1970s as well as in the mosque project, in which most of them were personally involved in one way or another.

By and large, the community's early interpersonal problems were basic and revolved mainly around marital disputes, which the elders were able to resolve within the context of a close-knit, nascent, immigrant community, often utilising approaches that worked in their countries of origin. They usually impressed upon disputing couples the value of compromise by reminding them of the psychological damage that divorce would inflict on their children. At times they would apply gentle pressure on the woman to overlook problems and to try and make the family relationship work.

The elders had no special knowledge of the Sharia as such, except for a general understanding of the ethics contained in its teachings, which emphasise the benefits of 'surrender to the Will of God and of living a virtuous and righteous life leading to felicity and salvation in the Hereafter' (Nasr, 2004: 156). They embodied 'lived wisdom' and their approach was largely traditional. The elders realised that their advice carried no legal weight and that anything agreed upon by the parties could not be legally enforced.

Over time, some of the elders entered public life. For example, one became a town councillor, in which capacity he was able to help people through referrals to the appropriate social security departments. He also became a trustee of the Hounslow mosque. Another elder became a member of the mosque's funeral committee. Another, Bhabi Khatija, a doctor and the only woman elder, who is the widow of a former president of the Pakistan Welfare Association, continues to do social work.

The processual tools they utilised were neither mediatory nor arbitrational. They were a kind of amalgam of techniques that combined counselling, advice, exhortation and cajolery – all closer to the directive end of mediation rather than the facilitative end. Whenever a Sharia-specific issue arose in the early days they would refer it to the mosque, and later, through the mosque, to the MLSC once that institution had been established. In keeping with the general Islamic injunction, they emphasised reconciliation as a virtue and very closely followed the *hadith* of the Prophet that labels divorce the most abhorrent of acts. Hence, their major focus, like that of other Muslim dispute resolvers, has always been on reconciling the disputing parties.[7] Unfortunately, contemporary ADR literature does not seem to have much on this concept, and whatever limited literature exists does not seem to address this specific faith-based dimension.

All the elders interviewed reiterated the desperate need for culturally sensitive counselling services. The influence of the elders has generally declined with the acculturation of the community. In the early days, when social cohesiveness was important to the community, its members were amenable to accepting the elders' advice. However, in later years, when it had reached a certain equilibrium, individual rights became more valued and there was a shift in mentality from one of submission to one of assertion. The initial intervention was more akin to what Doo (1973) describes, in the context of Chinese-American communities, as 'didactic mediation – predominantly authoritarian and characterised by a background of coercion while being persuasive, educational and instructive as to what is required of disputants [...] Enforcement was by ostracism, economic boycott, or the weightiness of imposed moral righteousness. These forms of enforcement, to be effective, require wholehearted community support which exists only in a society where mutual dependence is strong'.

Whether the elders would continue to be heeded by most people today is a moot point. Also, given the complex nature of the interface between the Sharia, custom and the laws of the United Kingdom, it is unlikely that the advice of the elders, which generally does not take this complex relationship into account, would really be that relevant to peoples' daily interpersonal problems. The elders often view this complexity (mistakenly) as one of the negative effects of Westernisation – undiscriminating acceptance of the essentially secular values of the host culture and abandonment of what they perceive as Islamic values. As dispute resolvers, the elders are a fast-disappearing group and the work they did in the early days of settlement is now being undertaken by individuals or institutions with specialised professional skills such as the MLSC.

Doo found that as discrimination against the Chinese community decreased, their method of dispute settlement changed. As court remedies became feasible and opportunities in employment, residence and assimilation increased, voluntary mediation gradually displaced didactic mediation. It is likely that, as the Muslim community begins to feel more integrated into the British way of life, adjudication will tend to be increasingly preferred; mediation will then, for most people, become 'only a favoured custom', to quote a member of the MLSC panel. Rights generally erode or replace the obligations of custom.

Thus, two important phenomena that have had an impact on conflict patterns in the community and its ability to deal with interpersonal disputes have been taking place simultaneously. The first is the positive aspects of acculturation, which have made individuals in the community more aware of their legal rights and provided the opportunity to assert them through appropriate governmental services. This has particularly had an important bearing on how women in the community view their rights, both under the Sharia as well as under the laws of the United Kingdom. Second, and more importantly, a significant number of the second generation, born in the United Kingdom, have tended to become more 'Islamic' in their daily lifestyle and appearance by adopting the *hejab* and, more recently, the *niqab* in the case of women and a beard in the case of men. This phenomenon seems to be a temporary response to the rising tide of Islamophobia observable in Britain and the Western world generally today, and it is likely to subside as and when demonisation of Muslims diminishes in the global media. However, for the present, tensions are running high and they are unlikely to abate in the near future.

Muslim Women's Helpline

The Muslim Women's Helpline (MWH) is a national telephone-based support service established in 1989 by a small group of Muslim women volunteers. The organisation does not practise mediation and reconciliation directly, but provides support and referrals to organisations that can provide such services. As it is self-funding and operates on a very small budget, it experiences constant funding problems.

According to one of the founding members of the organisation, many of the conflicts that are brought to the MWH would be amenable to arbitration and mediation, but Muslim women often do not want external intervention in their problems as they feel that would jeopardise their situation and exacerbate their problems. They fear reprisals because talking to an outsider may be perceived as violation of family honour. The MWH originally operated as a small, stand-alone institution but is now part of a telephone helpline network. It receives technical help from other telephone helpline services and has engaged a trainer who organises in-house training. Though not the only one operating currently, it was the first Muslim telephone-based emotional support service for Muslim women in the United Kingdom. The MWH receives between 1800 and 2000 calls per year. It shies away from immigration and financial problems as it does not have sufficient resources to deal with follow-ups. Matrimonial matters top the list of issues that it normally handles. People who approach it often want to know where they can get help and the MWH refers them to specific statutory agencies or the MLSC. It also refers them to other Islamic helplines and various *mufti*s. According to one of the office bearers of the MWH, some of the *mufti*s take into consideration the local context in which Muslims find themselves today and issue quite enlightened *fatwa*s.

One of the MWH staff members has a background in mediation, but at the time of my research she had only carried out one neighbourhood mediation thus far. An MWH office bearer observed that Muslims in Britain come from communities where they have never had to mediate in a structured manner, and problems in the past were normally resolved by the head of the family or an elder. When mediation is suggested to women with matrimonial problems, many of them respond that their husbands would never agree to it.

Another issue that the MWH often encounters is the need for a refuge where Muslim women can feel comfortable culturally. The women who go to the MWH are often desperate to get out of a deteriorating matrimonial situation and initially they are prepared to go to any women's centre where they can be helped. However, when they reach such a refuge and see the other women smoking and drinking, they begin to have second thoughts. As a result, in some cases. they prefer to remain in their conflictive matrimonial situation rather than live in a refuge where they would encounter practices that they find repugnant and which would be considered a deliberate insult if carried out in their social circle. According to another office bearer of the MWH, there is a Muslim safe-house, but it is located outside London.

Police

The imams have no enforcement powers, but many issues associated with a dispute, such as emergency help in the case of domestic violence, require urgent attention. It is then that the police play an important role. Although they do not 'mediate' in the true sense of the word, their intervention is very much mediatory and critical. Their understanding of cultural issues and religious sensibilities can help, and in the past has helped, to resolve many problems in the earlier stages of a dispute. Many disputants often resort directly to the Hounslow police for help with their interpersonal problems.

One police officer interviewed for this study has spent 15 years of his 35-year tenure with the Metropolitan Police Force in the Hounslow area. Having been a Community Officer for nine of the 15 years, he found himself in the midst of all the problems that arose as a result of the construction of the mosque. He noticed the racism the community was facing and became a member of the committee involved in the mosque development in order to gain 'hands-on' understanding of the issues. Through that involvement, he got to know many of the children who were then growing up in the area and developed a strong trust relationship with them. He saw the community undergoing acculturation and trained other members of the force to understand different cultural mores.

Realising the need to help without causing destabilisation in the community, he developed the concept of 'third-party reporting' of domestic violence, making Hounslow the first borough in London to introduce a system whereby a woman could go to a mosque or a *gurudwara* (Sikh temple) and report a crime, after which a third party could then go to the police station and report the crime on her behalf. Over time the police became socialised to the cultural specificities of the Muslim community in the area. According to the officer, the police force also became sensitive to extended family networks and the continuing need to provide support to women who were victims of domestic violence, which helped them to gain deeper insight into how to manage domestic abuse in the Asian community at large. This developed trust between the police and the Muslim community over three decades, which made the police force an even more important agency for disputants to resort to in interpersonal disputes.

Solicitors

A small number of Muslim lawyers practise in Hounslow, but the mosque mainly seems to have a very close rapport with one of them, Soli Osman, who was brought up in the area and renders voluntary service to the trustees and many of the congregants. Generally, the imam of the mosque refers matters to him that have an immigration dimension or a public law element, or where a matter is one of custody and abduction. Disputants resort to him not only when there is an impasse on an issue, but also in the normal course of a dispute that has a strictly legal dimension; for example, when seeking a divorce through the courts. In such cases, he helps by referring them to other solicitors who deal with divorce matters. As a Muslim solicitor, he tries to help effect reconciliation whenever possible. Whenever parties can be encouraged to reach a negotiated settlement (*sulh*) he promotes the process. Asked how the submission of a matter to a solicitor affects the dispute, he said the couching of the dispute in proper legal terms gives it a juridical complexion so that it can be adjudicated upon in a court of law when reconciliation or a negotiated settlement are not possible.

Lawyers generally present disputes as discrete, bounded and pathological episodes, generated by rule-breach-'messes' which need to be 'cleared up'. From a lawyer's perspective, they are most appropriately cleared up through litigation (Palmer and Roberts, 1998). According to Felstiner, Abel and Sarat (1981) disputes are affairs of 'naming, blaming and claiming', with an individual perceiving himself as suffering some injurious experience, identifying that as originating in a legal wrong, blaming someone for it and instituting a claim against him or her, setting in train a process that will put the matter to rights. Lawyers representing the parties then reshape the dispute into a form suitable for processing in the legal system, typically transforming it while doing so (Palmer and Roberts, 1998).

In most cases, disputants do not really have a choice about whether or not to go to a solicitor. Even if they were on a purely mediatory track, at some point the mediator would be obliged to ask them to consult their legal adviser. This is consistent with good mediation practice. However, my research shows that in a faith-based context, the solicitor is often more than just an independent provider of partisan legal advice. A Muslim solicitor should also be able to advise on the interface between the Sharia, customary practices and the public laws of the United Kingdom. The role of such solicitors, therefore, cannot be viewed from a purely binary perspective any more than law and ADR can be viewed that way.

*Pir*s and coteries

Two other groups that play a role in dispute resolution in the area warrant some mention, even though this book does not focus on their work. They are the *pir*s and professional coteries.

*Pir*s are individuals who head spiritual orders (*tariqah*s) and are influential among a section of Sunni Muslims strongly inclined towards Sufi teachings and traditions. Among South Asian Muslims, *pir*s exist mainly in the Barelwi tradition, which favours an intercessionary concept, as opposed to the Deobandis, who follow a more 'orthodox' interpretation of the faith. When two members from the same *tariqah* have a dispute, the *pir*, as spiritual head, is called upon to help resolve the dispute.

*Pir*s are viewed as people of great spiritual achievement and are therefore regarded as authoritative and neutral persons. They offer moral advice and guidance to their followers whenever it is required and they particularly play an important role in resolving family disputes. The *pir* fits in with Gulliver's concept of the individual with acknowledged prestige and ability, who is not directly concerned with the issues and the potential outcome but whom disputants would be willing to accept as a person of recognised sagacity (Gulliver, 1979).

Coteries are small groups of people belonging to a common profession, such as doctors, dentists, businessmen and so on who support each other; in the event of a dispute, they help to settle it out of court. While not formally constituted, Muslim coteries exist all around Britain, reputedly in fairly significant numbers. Their methods are said to be informal and the norms by which they settle disputes are based on their personal understanding of the general ethical precepts of the faith as well as their own knowledge and background. When necessary they consult a lawyer, an imam or an elder. In some cases they might refer to a book for clarification on a religious issue.

This study has not investigated any coterie, but they are flagged here because of their potential for resolving disputes between their members. In some cases, coteries could be important stakeholders with the necessary sanctioning capabilities; for example, they could influence people to respect agreements. Therefore, it would be worth researching them in future studies of ADR in diasporic Muslim settings in the United Kingdom.

Alternative dispute resolution agencies

In addition to the faith- and community-based resources available to Muslims in Hounslow, there are various ADR agencies or institutions that serve the area and are accessible to all communities. Four main ones are outlined here to complete the picture of the services available in Hounslow.

Relate was established in the 1930s and was known as the National Marriage Guidance Council until 1988. The organisation flourished in the years after World War II as marriages and families came under new pressures. Couple counselling has always been a core service for Relate, but it expanded its services to include psychosexual therapy in the 1960s, counselling for young people in the 1990s, and later, family counselling.

Relate serves 150,000 clients each year, including 22,000 children and young people and 9,000 families. Its adult clients include people who are married, in civil partnerships, single, cohabiting, separated, in same-sex relationships and dating. Relate provides face-to-face services in a variety of locations, including GP surgeries, children's centres and schools, as well as in the Relate 'high street' premises. In addition, it provides counselling over the telephone and via email. Its face-to-face services are provided by 2,000 practitioners working in 78 local centres across England and Wales, including the west London boroughs of Hillingdon, Ealing, Brent, Harrow and Uxbridge; each centre is an independent charity in its own right and a member of the Relate Federation.[8]

Relate is the largest couple relationship counselling service in England. It also provides a family mediation service as well as mediation for the homeless, which at times has domestic violence and immigration dimensions to it. The agency has no contact with the Hounslow mosque or the MLSC. One area where it has great resonance with the mosque and the MLSC is in its emphasis on reconciliation where possible. The agency always leaves it to the parties themselves to come to that decision and offers a counselling service to facilitate that process. The agency normally uses mediation as it is understood in contemporary ADR terminology.

Mediation in Divorce (MID), founded in 1984, provides mediation to families and couples who need to make decisions about the future of their children, finances, property and other important matters. In addition to mediation, MID also offers counselling services for children from five years upwards that are affected by their parents' changed relationship, and for adults (either individuals or couples) who need to talk through unresolved issues related to separation, divorce or relationship breakdown.

MID does not give legal advice to clients, but it has a Community Legal Service ('Legal Aid') franchise which entitles qualifying clients to use mediation without any charge. Their children's counselling service is free of charge for all clients. MID also assists young people to find housing when they want to leave the family home as a result of inter-generational tension. The agency tries to help such people and their parents repair and preserve their relationship.

MID is culturally sensitive but has no formal contact with the Muslim community. When providing counselling services, it asks people whether they would like a counsellor from their own community. Some clients do prefer someone from their own background, while others fear that confidentiality will be compromised if the counsellor is from their own community. The agency also provides all-issues mediation.

The **National Children's Home** (NCH), with its head office in Highbury, offers residential accommodation to children with disabilities when there is conflict in the family. It also provides family group conferencing in cases where the family recognises that the child needs to stay within the family. Space is provided for all family members and close friends to come together and work out a plan for the young person. 'Family' includes the extended family as well, that is, grandparents, uncles, aunts, and so on. The approach is that families themselves are experts on what works best for them; therefore the family itself works out the plan and the child has a say in what is decided. The service operates under the Children Act 1989 and the Children Act 2000. The system is voluntary and any party can leave the process at any time. The NCH does not deal with issues affecting children when their parents are contemplating divorce.

Hillingdon Community Mediation, established in April 2000, provides mediation in neighbourhood disputes. Family disputes are seen to be a specialised area related to the courts, so the service generally refers such cases to Relate in Hillingdon or neighbouring boroughs. However, it can provide family dispute mediation for clients who are prepared to pay for it. The agency is not keen to take on matters for which it is not funded, as it already has more neighbourhood dispute cases than it can handle.

Even with all these possibilities of alternative dispute resolution, people sometimes decide that they have no other recourse than to take their case to the courts. The next chapter highlights some important cases that have been adjudicated by courts in the United Kingdom, including one challenging the MLSC's jurisdiction.

The Case for Court-Invoked Adjudication

Sometimes interpersonal disputes among Muslims end up in court even when they involve matters that are within the purview of the Sharia. It is instructive to outline some important cases of this type that are representative of the sort of issues that frequently occur in diasporic Muslim communities, and then investigate their implications for informal dispute resolution in those communities.

Mahr as a contractual matter

All the legal schools of Islam, both Sunni and Shi'i, accept that there can be no marriage in accordance with the Sharia without *mahr* (dower). The Qur'an (4:4) commands, 'Give women their dower' (Alami and Hinchliffe, 1998: 19). The leading case on this issue in the United Kingdom is *Shahnaz* v. *Rizwan*.[1]

The parties had married in India in accordance with Muslim law. Later, following a divorce, the wife claimed her deferred dower. Islamic law allows polygamy (with certain provisos) but the marriage was not actually polygamous. The husband contended that since the marriage was polygamous or potentially polygamous, English courts had no jurisdiction; or alternatively, the court should not extend jurisdiction to the wife's claim, by reason of the fact that the *mahr* provision in the marriage contract was in consideration of a polygamous or potentially polygamous marriage. In the second alternative, the husband contended that if the court held in the wife's favour, he, the husband, would contend that the judgment was unenforceable because such a contract of (potentially polygamous) marriage and the *mahr* provision were contrary to the distinctive policy and good morals of the law of the country.

The court resolved the jurisdictional problem by treating the wife's claim as a contractual rather than matrimonial matter. Justice Winn held that the right to dower is a 'right *ex contractu* which, while it can, in the nature of things, only arise in connection with a marriage by Muhammadan law (which is *ex hypothesi* polygamous) is not a matrimonial right. It is not a right from the marriage, but is a right in *personam* enforceable by the wife or widow against the husband or his heirs.'

In his judgment, Justice Winn saw no foundation in the cases referred to him for any judicial ruling that the marriage referred to involved any element offensive to the standards of decency accepted by English law. Commenting on the definition of marriage under English law, he emphasised that the court could not give to a person the rights which are the property of a wife or a husband as such, specifically by force of a marriage which was polygamous. He viewed the right to dower, once accrued, as a right in action, enforceable by a civil action without a wife having to take specifically matrimonial proceedings and regarded by Islamic law as a proprietary right assignable under S3 of the Transfer of Property Act 1882 of the Indian Code. Justice Winn held that it was a right for the support or protection of which, should the wife or widow gain physical possession or control of any property of her spouse, she was entitled to assert a lien. 'This right is far more closely to be compared with a right of property than a matrimonial right or obligation.' he said.

With regard to the contention that the court should not extend its jurisdiction to entertain a claim of that nature, Justice Winn's words are far-reaching. He said, 'As a matter of policy, I incline to the view that, there being now so many Mohammedans resident in this country, it is better that the court should recognise, in favour of women who have come here as a result of a Mohammedan marriage, the right to obtain from their husbands what was promised to them and should enforce the contract and payment of what was so promised, than that those women should be bereft of their rights and receive no assistance from the English courts.'

In the absence of many subsequent reported judgments, the presumption must be that the courts continue to follow the decision in *Shahnaz* v. *Rizwan*, that the wife's right to dower is based on a contractual obligation arising from the contract entered into or in contemplation of, or by reason of, a Muslim marriage.[2] According to Doreen Hinchcliff, a barrister and academic who is a specialist on *mahr*, 'as the courts appear to regard dower as a contractual matter we can assume that in the case of a marriage concluded between two Muslims in which no dower is stipulated, the English courts will not seek to impose payment of the proper dower which Islamic law would deem due'.

Another case regarding dower, *Ali* v. *Ali*, came before the English courts in 1999. The parties in the case were Bangladeshis living in England. At the time of the marriage, following considerable discussion between the two families, the dower was fixed at £30,001 – this odd amount being consistent with Bangladeshi customary practice. Following dissolution of the marriage, the wife claimed the stipulated dower of £30,001 but the judge awarded her £30,000. It is assumed that the court was emphasising that the right to make financial provisions following the dissolution of a marriage is, under English law, the right of the court alone; and that while, in making a decision the court would take into account the sum agreed upon as dower by the parties themselves, it did not feel bound by it absolutely. An academic specialist on Muslim family laws in Britain raised another possibility, that the court might have felt that by awarding such an odd amount (that is, £30,001), it would be recognising not a contractual agreement but an incident of a Muslim marriage. Alternatively, it could be argued that the court just rounded off the sum as a matter of convenience.

Forced and arranged marriages

Forced and arranged marriages are a major cause of intergenerational discord among Muslims and other faith groups in the

United Kingdom. Although the two are not synonymous, and neither is sanctioned by Islamic law, the line between them is sometimes thin. Arranged marriages are a cultural custom and have been practised within many communities and countries successfully. However, they can become coercive and intimidatory, especially in a diasporic context. Forced marriages, on the other hand, are often likely to involve a series of crimes, including abduction, kidnap, assault and domestic violence. It is estimated that about 500 forced marriages have taken place in the United Kingdom between 2003 and 2005 (Gibb, 2005).

In the 2000s, the police were reviewing 109 murders committed since 1995 to see whether any could be linked to honour killings. Such murders, which are on the increase and are committed by the victims' families, are linked with forced marriages of women who reject chosen partners or have relationships outside their close-knit, mostly Asian and Arab, communities. The suicide rate among Asian females aged 16 to 24 is nearly three times the national average. Not all victims of forced marriages are women, however; young men accounted for 14 per cent of the 1,682 such cases referred to the Forced Marriage Unit of the Home Office in 2009.[3] According to the Unit, many male victims were forced into marriage because their families knew or suspected that they were gay.

While cases of forced and arranged marriages arguably can be amenable to ADR, attitudes often become so hardened that no real breakthrough is possible except through the official law with its mandatory rules and consequent sanctions. Law-enforcing agencies step in when there is a breach of the criminal law or the immediate apprehension of it, but they do not attempt any kind of mediation, since that might make a woman more vulnerable and place her in greater jeopardy.

In the UK, Scotland has taken the lead in enacting legislation to combat forced marriage. In 2011, the Scottish parliament passed the Forced Marriage (Protection and Jurisdiction, Scotland) Act, which strengthens the power of courts to protect people who face being married forcibly and to annul such marriages. The Act makes breaching of a protection order a criminal offence punishable by a fine, a two-year prison sentence or both.

Thus it goes beyond legislation in England, Wales and Northern Ireland, where breaching a protection order is not a criminal offence. Courts there can only rule such a breach to be contempt of court and then punish the offender with a jail sentence.

Smina Akhtar, director of Amina, the Muslim Women's Resource Centre in Glasgow, lauded the new Scottish law for having 'given a voice to a silent minority and a lifeline to many young people who until now have had nowhere to turn for help and support'. The Law Society of Scotland also welcomed the legislation and noted the additional crucial need to educate 'potential perpetrators, potential victims and also those who may be in a position to spot the danger signs on behalf of that victim' about the issue.[4]

With regard to arranged marriages, the case of *Sohrab* v. *Khan* in the Scottish Court of Session in April 2002 is elucidative.[5] The marriage was arranged by the parties' parents and the parties had met each other on only one occasion prior to the ceremony. They took part in a Muslim wedding ceremony on 13 December 1998. The wife later sought annulment of the marriage on the grounds that her consent to it had been vitiated by duress. She had been aged 16 at the time of the ceremony and her parents had only told her of the marriage one week before the ceremony. Her mother had threatened to commit suicide if she refused to marry the man chosen to be her husband. Her parents had told her that she would be a disgrace to the family, and that she would be sent to Pakistan to be married. There had been two short periods of cohabitation following the marriage, in February and April 1999.

The wife also sought annulment on the grounds that there had been no marriage schedule relative to the ceremony that took place, and no proper registration (as required under the law). The notices of intention to marry had been signed on 14 December 1998, specifying 30 December 1998 as the date of the proposed marriage. The marriage schedule also gave the date of the marriage as 30 December 1998, but the marriage took place at an earlier date. The husband argued that the wife had been willing and happy to go through with the ceremony, but had become unhappy for other reasons.

Section 13 (1) (a) of the Marriage (Scotland) Act 1977 provides that a marriage shall not be solemnised by an approved celebrant unless the parties produce to him, before the marriage ceremony, a marriage schedule in respect of the marriage issued in accordance with the Act.[6]

The Court held, first, that the wife had not given any genuine consent to the marriage, but had been put under such duress by her parents that whatever semblance of consent was exchanged at the ceremony was vitiated; and second, that the need to have a marriage schedule at the solemnisation following upon a notice of intention to marry is not a requirement which can be dispensed with even where registration follows. Therefore, the decree of annulment was granted.

The Lord Ordinary (Lord McEwan) pinpointed the predicament that young Muslims in the United Kingdom are facing today with regard to arranged marriages. He said, 'I am heartily sorry for both the pursuer [the wife] and defender [the husband]. At the time of these events they were both very young, especially the pursuer. I am certain, beyond a peradventure, that each was wholly dominated by his or her respective parents, especially the mothers. These mothers were of a different generation and were both themselves in arranged marriages. No doubt, they thought they were doing the best for their children. However, what they both did, put an intolerable pressure on both of these young people at an age when neither was able to take an informed decision about their future or to act in any way independently. Neither was in a position to resist the will of their parents. It may be that in the multi-cultural society in which we now live, such situations will continue to arise where ancient Eastern-established cultural and religious ethics clash with the spirit of twenty-first century children of a new generation and Western ideas, language and what these days passes for culture. There is inevitable tension, and clashes will happen'.

In an earlier, unreported, case in Scotland in 1999, Nasreen Akmal, an Asian Muslim woman, made legal history when she became the first woman in Scotland to have her arranged marriage annulled by the Scottish courts.[7] Akmal was forced to marry her first cousin in Pakistan, where her parents took her 'on holiday' when she was 14. She was not allowed to return to Glasgow until she provided the family with a grandchild. Soon after the marriage, her husband began to beat her, and when the violence escalated, she was forced to flee back to Scotland. She engaged a lawyer and began proceedings to have her marriage annulled on the ground that, under Scottish law, a bride must be aged 16 or over. As a result, Akmal suffered severe ostracism and threats of physical intimidation. Despite that, she does not regret having had the marriage annulled. In an interview published by *The Scotsman* newspaper on 23 June 1999, she said, 'Over 100 women and men have had forced marriages annulled because of what I did. It has also prevented parents from abducting their children and forcing them into marriages in Pakistan.'

Forced marriages: an extra-judicial approach

Akmal appealed to the courts for annulment once she was back in the UK. However, it is not easy for a woman who is being kept abroad against her will to get away from her husband and his family. Recognising that the women need to be rescued in such cases, the British High Commission in Islamabad has established a special unit to help victims of forced marriages. The team rescued 108 victims in 2005, according to Helen Feather, head of the Consular Section (Walsh, 2006). Most of the victims were between the ages of 18 and 24, and the youngest was 14. Often, women turn up at the High Commission but are torn between leaving their families and thus risking ostracism, and remaining in the family home and continuing to suffer beatings for not being compliant. The programme is sensitive and discreet. Conservative Pakistanis have accused the team of meddling in local affairs, but Feather is adamant that 'this is a human rights abuse and these are British nationals in distress.'

Official support is vital for such programmes, and the High Commission sought permission from the Pakistani government before starting its activities in Pakistan. The then President of Pakistan, Pervez Musharraf, spoke out publicly against forced marriages, but the attitude of the local police continued to vary from sympathy to reluctance to get involved in a 'family matter'.

Hence, the High Commission team, comprising four people, had to become personally involved in the actual rescue operations.

Rescues often follow a pattern. A worried relative or boyfriend in the United Kingdom makes initial contact with the Foreign Office. Sometimes a victim herself sends an SOS to the Foreign Office. The High Commission team then establishes contact through hushed, late-night conversations and secretive text messages, and a time and date are agreed after days or weeks of careful preparation. The element of surprise is crucial. Local police are informed hours beforehand to provide back-up. The head of the High Commission team Jon Turner knocks on the front door and tries to extract the young woman through patient negotiation. Flustered relatives plead with the girl to stay, often resorting to emotional blackmail. They say to her, 'Your father will have a heart attack', or 'Your mother will commit suicide', or 'You will bring dishonour on your family'.

The young woman is taken to Islamabad and lodged in a refuge run by Struggle for Change (SACH), a Pakistani organisation that supports victims of forced marriage and domestic violence. The address of the refuge is kept secret in case relatives try and snatch the woman back. The High Commission issues an emergency passport and, if necessary, provides plane fare to the UK. Within days, the rescued woman travels to the airport. In high-risk cases, she may be hidden under a shawl, flown from a regional airport or escorted onto the plane. Most rescues are resolved peacefully, stresses Turner, but the dangers are real in a country with frequent so-called 'honour killings', in which reluctant family members, usually young women, are murdered in the name of 'family honour'.

SACH has tried hard to spark debate on forced marriage through the media and visits by Muslim scholars who debunk myths about women's role in Islam. 'Forced marriage is part of our customs. It has nothing to do with the law and religion. In fact, it is the very opposite,' says Dr Noreen Khalid, who counsels the runaway brides. British citizens also become trapped in forced marriages in other countries, and British diplomats have carried out rescues in India, Bangladesh and countries in Africa and the Middle East; but no other country comes close in scale to Pakistan, which has an estimated 80,000 dual nationals and accounts for nearly 60 per cent of all cases handled by the Foreign Office's Forced Marriage Unit.

What we see here is a novel approach based on rescuing national hostages. The implications are far-reaching, both legally and socially. From a legal point of view, the young woman would still require a divorce or an annulment in the United Kingdom with all the legal procedures associated with the process. From a social point of view, where does such a woman reside once she is back in the United Kingdom? Who would support her? What about her relationship with her family and her community? What about any possibility of remarriage within her own community? Would she be hounded by the extended family for having brought dishonour on them? What protection would she receive against that happening? These are some of the serious questions that need to be considered following the rescue operation. Whether such situations would be amenable to legal measures or ADR treatment is a moot point.

Children of estranged parents

The issue of custody and contact orders relating to a Muslim child is a vexed one for a number of reasons. First, the majority of Muslim countries are not party to the Hague Convention on the Civil Aspects of International Child Abduction 1980. Second, and most importantly, in the realm of family law most Muslim countries still follow the Sharia, where the minimum age at which a female child can marry varies from country to country. This often causes anxiety to one of the spouses, usually a non-Muslim wife, who fears that the other spouse – a Muslim husband who has contact with the child – will arrange for a female child to be married off under the Sharia laws obtaining in a particular Muslim country. The case outlined below, though not based directly on these concerns, nevertheless highlights an important issue concerning a child of estranged parents, only one of whom is a Muslim.

The case of *Re J*[8] involved a Muslim father seeking two specific orders in relation to his five-year-old son, one requiring the non-Muslim mother to raise the child as a Muslim and the other requiring her to have the boy circumcised. The father acknowledged that he was not a devout Muslim, rarely attending the mosque and ignoring many of the tenets of his faith, but gave evidence that he was very anxious for the son, who was a Muslim under Islamic law, to follow certain basic practices including circumcision. The mother opposed both applications, as did the Official Solicitor acting as guardian *ad litem*.

Rejecting both the applications and prohibiting the father from arranging or permitting the child's circumcision in any jurisdiction, the court held that only in unusual circumstances would the court require that a child be brought up in a religion which was not that of the parent with whom the child was residing. In a case like the one before the court, where the child was unlikely to have much contact with the Muslim world even when staying with his father, it would not be appropriate to require the mother to follow Muslim practices.

The court also held that, while it was lawful for two parents jointly exercising parental responsibility for a male child to arrange for the child to be ritually circumcised in accordance with their religious beliefs, where parents or other persons having parental responsibility for the child, including a local authority, were in dispute over whether or not to circumcise a child, that dispute should be referred to the court for urgent resolution if necessary. The court would then decide the question of applying S1 of the Children Act 1989 to the facts of the case. In this particular case, circumcision was not in the child's interest, as, although it would firmly identify the child with his father and confirm him as a Muslim in the eyes of Islam, it was a painful operation, which was opposed by his mother, and which would make him an exception among his non-Muslim peers.

The case gives rise to a number of interesting issues with regard to Islamic law and what constitutes a Muslim. First, to what extent can a United Kingdom court decide who is a Muslim in contradistinction to the principles of Islamic law? In this particular case, the learned judge made the correct decision, that the child was a Muslim, but on an erroneous understanding of the expert evidence presented in the case. The judge accepted the opinion of one Dr Suhaib Hasan of the 'Islamic Sharia Council' in London, that 'in Islam, children of parents either of whom is Muslim, are considered Muslim; J has a Muslim father, therefore he is a Muslim in the eyes of Islam.' In reality, this is not true under the Sharia. For a child to be Muslim, the *father* has to be Muslim. Immediately thereafter, the judge stated that that opinion was supported by Dr Doreen Hinchcliffe, who reported as follows: 'A Muslim woman may never validly marry a non-Muslim man. The law, however, allows a Muslim male to contract a marriage with a non-Muslim woman, provided she belongs to one of the revealed religions, that is, Judaism or Christianity. Any child of such marriage is a Muslim. It is a principle of Islamic law that the child of a Muslim father is always considered to be a Muslim.' It was submitted that what Professor Hinchcliffe stated as an expert witness was the true position, but her statement did not tally with Dr Hasan's. Yet the judge appeared to say that it did.

Second, according to the judge, orthopraxy seemed to be the defining factor as to who is a Muslim, whereas, under Islamic law, it is the affirmation of the fundamental testimony of faith, the *Shahada, 'La Ilaha Ilalah Muhammadur Rasulilah'* (there is no God but Allah and Muhammad is His Prophet) which is the defining factor. The judge stated, 'In English law, therefore, J would seem to be being brought up as a "non-practising Christian" in accordance with the convictions of his mother with whom he lives and as a "non-practising Muslim" when he stays with his father. He therefore has a mixed heritage and an essentially secular lifestyle. He does not have a settled religious faith.' The judge thus deduced that the child had no 'settled faith'.

Third, the judge rejected a basic cultural ritual, which is incumbent on *all* Muslims, on the assumption that the child, although born a Muslim, was going to have an essentially secular upbringing in England. The question arises: To what extent is a ritual obligation such as circumcision of a male Muslim child dependent on whether such a child will grow up to lead a secular or religious life?

This case also gives rise to a number of other questions, such as: What if the mother insisted on feeding pork to the child, or if he imbibed alcohol during certain rituals? Would these basic

Islamic prohibitions be subject to whether the child was going to lead a secular or religious life in the future?

Inheritance: appeal against Sharia Council ruling

Inheritance issues are normally fairly straightforward and involve basically the filing of a few affidavits and filling in of forms. According to Doreen Hinchcliff, who is a specialist on Islamic inheritance issues, if a Muslim testator wishes his estate to devolve according to the principles of the Sharia, he is at absolute liberty to make a will indicating such a wish. In the absence of a will, the general English laws of intestacy apply.

Al Midani and another v. *Al Midani and others* was a case involving an arbitration agreement entered into by the heirs of an estate where the dispute had been referred to the 'Islamic Sharia Council' in London.[9] The plaintiffs challenged the Sharia Council's jurisdiction and the court had to decide whether the judgement constituted an 'arbitration award', and if not, whether it should be set aside.

The facts were as follows. Sheikh Mouaffak bin Jamil Al Midani, a citizen of Saudi Arabia, died in Los Angeles on 23 September 1991, leaving a substantial fortune. He had made two wills five days earlier, in the presence of his four children. One will dealt with property for which he made Dr Alawi Kayal and Mrs. Kayal the legal testamentary guardians for distribution as follows: one-third to charities in Saudi Arabia and the remaining two-thirds to his four children 'according to the *Shari'te* distribution of inheritance'. The second will dealt with property both within and outside Saudi Arabia. In it, he nominated a 'Trusteeship Council' under the presidency of Dr Kayal, the other members being his son Imad (the first defendant), Sheikh Mohamed Badinjki (the fourth defendant) and Mr. Joseph Dabbous. Subject to certain specific bequests to each of his four children, the estate was to be divided as follows: one-third to charity and two-thirds between his children equally. The Sheikh also gifted US $150 million to Dr Kayal by means of an IOU.

Disputes began to emerge between the first and second plaintiffs, Myrna and Omar, children of the Sheikh's second wife on the one hand; and the first and second defendants, Imad and Amer, children of his first wife, and the Trusteeship Council, on the other. To resolve these disputes, the heirs (Myrna and Omar and Imad and Amer) entered into an arbitration agreement dated 8 September 1993, which provided *inter alia*: first, under clause 1, 'to execute what was mentioned in the "will" of our father, late Sheikh Mouaffak bin Jamil Al Midani. We voluntarily and willingly accept the arbitration of Dr Kayal for all the succession affairs related to our father's estate (the "Estate") whether financial, administrative, legal or successional, to put all these matters under his direct supervision, and to consider his word as "concluding word" and "final decision". So we are legally not allowed, we the four heirs, collectively and individually, to dissent from the judgements and decisions he takes or to contest them or to contravene them or to prevent their execution. That is because of our full confidence in Dr Kayal's sound decision, fair judgement and objectivity in seeking the right and looking for justice.'

Second, under clause 7 of the agreement, 'We, the four heirs undertake, jointly and separately, that in the event of any dispute regarding the implementation of this agreement or the decisions emanating therefore, there would be no way for its resolution and settlement except by having recourse to an "Islamic Judicial Body" appointed by the Trusteeship Council without the participation of any of the heirs in this appointment or the participation of any of their representatives, whether jointly or separately.' Unfortunately, these agreements did not resolve the heirs' disputes and the matter was referred to the 'Islamic Sharia Council' in London by the Trusteeship Council.

The plaintiffs protested the Sharia Council's jurisdiction over the matter of their late father's estate. The Sharia Council issued its judgement, dated 15 January 1997, making various dispositions. On 28 February 1997, the plaintiffs issued a notice of originating motion against the five defendants, claiming a declaration to the effect that the Sharia Council's judgement was not a binding arbitration award and in the alternative claimed to set aside the Sharia Council's judgement under S23 (2) of the Arbitration Act 1950 or for leave to appeal pursuant to S1 (2) of the Arbitration Act 1979. On 24 June 1997, the plaintiffs issued a separate originating summons against the five defendants, in which they claimed a declaration that a Sharia Council's judgement was not an arbitration award and did not contain or give rise to any decision, order, obligation or liability binding on, or enforceable by, or in that court against the plaintiffs or either of them.

It was held by the Queen's Bench Commercial Court per Justice Rix that first, the arbitration agreement did not expressly provide for a proper law; however, it was an agreement made between the heirs to the Sheikh's Islamic wills, was written in Arabic and provided for the appointment of Dr Kayal, a citizen of Saudi Arabia, as arbitrator; its article 8 provided expressly that its text was drafted in Arabic and that in the event of any dispute, only the Arabic text should be adopted to clarify it; the Sheikh's main will described him as a citizen of Saudi Arabia and provided that one-third was to go to projects in the Arab and Islamic world and the remaining two-thirds was to be divided among his children, 'according to the *Shari'te* distribution'. In these circumstances, it was likely that the proper law of the agreement was either Sharia law or such law as modified by the law of Saudi Arabia; and Islamic or Sharia law would be regarded as a branch of foreign law.

Second, the Sharia Council was neither a national court nor an arbitration tribunal; it did not derive its authority from any statute, nor from any consensus between the parties before the court; The Sharia Council described its bench in terms of being a 'quasi-Islamic Court' and its bench's decisions as 'extra-judicial,' so that even in its own opinion, it did not seem to be a judicial body; if it was nevertheless an Islamic Court, it was not one set up under the auspices of any state and did not appear to come within the definition of article 7's 'Islamic Judicial Body' as that phrase would be interpreted in Sharia law.

Third, article 7 could not be regarded as an arbitration clause or as providing for a second-tier arbitration; and the plaintiffs could not be bound by the Sharia Council's judgement on the basis that it was an arbitration award. Fourth, even if article 7 was an arbitration clause and even if the Sharia Council was within the definition of an 'Islamic Judicial Body,' it nevertheless had no jurisdiction over the plaintiffs; article 7 was to be construed as permitting only the parties of the arbitration agreement, namely the heirs and not non-parties to it, to refer a dispute to an 'Islamic Judicial Body'. The fourth defendant, Sheikh Badinjki, had no right to involve the jurisdiction of such a tribunal, either on his own authority or as a representative of the Trusteeship Council; all that the Trusteeship Council had power to do, was to nominate the 'Judicial Islamic Body'. Last, the plaintiffs were entitled to the declarations sought; the judgement of the Sharia Council was not an arbitration award and did not give rise to any decision, order, obligation or liability binding on, or enforceable by, or in that Court, against the plaintiffs.

This case shows that, when they are contested, inheritance provisions can be a complicated issue. The case has important conflict-of-laws dimensions. It has a proper law dimension and, most importantly, it raises the question: what is a proper arbitration agreement? It raises an important issue with regard to the interface between the laws of the land (in this case, the laws of the United Kingdom), the Sharia and the principles of arbitration, which though an ADR process, is subject to much greater legal scrutiny than mediation. The case also shows the importance of proper educational training of extra-judicial bodies that have to grapple with multiple and complex issues in resolving disputes.

Discussion of the cases

The above court cases lead to the following questions: to what extent is ADR, and more particularly mediation, depriving Muslims in a diasporic context of a more definitive understanding of their personal laws and their interface with the laws of the country in which they are living? If these cases had not been taken to the courts, how would the disputants ever have got to know what their rights are and how justiciable they would be?

According to Fiss (1984: 1085–6), courts are reactive institutions which wait for others to bring matters to their attention, relying on them, for the most part, to investigate and present the law and facts. 'A settlement will thereby deprive a court of the occasion, and perhaps even the ability, to render an interpretation.' Fiss' central objection to out-of-court settlement lies in the assertion that a move away from the courts would compromise key legal and political values. He presents the role of judges in resolving disputes as secondary to their function of restating important public values and presents judgments as the means through which the core repertoire of norms in society is publicised and refurbished. Thus, out-of-court settlement divests the courts of the opportunity to articulate central values, and as these values fall from public attention the stability of society is compromised.

In the context of court-invoked adjudication, one can legitimately ask: How valid is Fiss' objection to settlement in the eyes of the disputants? Would Muslim disputants view some of these court decisions positively? Would they be gratified by them? If some of these cases had not gone to the courts for legal determination, would they now feel a sense of deprivation over not having obtained definitive legal decisions?

It is arguable that Muslims in Britain would have never had known how a United Kingdom court would view a *mahr* claim had the *Shanaz* v. *Rizwan* issue not gone for adjudication. Since then, not many *mahr* cases have been reported from the United Kingdom courts. The reasons for this are not clear, but there are several possibilities. First, not many cases regarding *mahr* are taken to the courts. Often, the *mahr* is a token sum and either the husband pays it or the wife forfeits it. It sometimes become an issue at the MLSC, but then it is generally sorted out as part of the negotiated agreement. Whatever cases do come up in courts these days involve much larger sums. According to an academic specialist in the field, such cases can sometimes involve up to a million pounds. Another academic specialist on Muslim family law in Britain says that a fair number of cases involving Sharia issues do not get reported in the law reports at the present time. Furthermore, it is not clear how many people in the Hounslow Muslim community are aware of the way the United Kingdom courts would view a claim for *mahr*.

Nonetheless, Fiss' theory does seem to be valid in the case of *mahr*. If the case had not gone to court, Muslims in Britain would have never had known how such a claim would be adjudicated. According to the academic specialist on *mahr*, by not taking matters involving *mahr* into the adversarial arena for determination today, Muslims in Britain are not necessarily being deprived of clarification of a societal norm, because its judicial treatment *has* already been determined under the United Kingdom laws. It is legally clear that *mahr* will only be treated as a matter of contract and not as an aspect of Islamic law. Unlike in a Muslim country's court, where, if *mahr* is not stipulated, it will be judicially implied in a contract, in a United Kingdom court it is more than likely that no such implication will be made because the laws of the United Kingdom do not recognise *mahr* as an aspect of Islamic law.

However, Fiss' contention is further reinforced by cases of arranged marriage, where the definition of what constitutes arranged marriage and what constitutes forced marriage is so blurred that often arranged marriages can be construed as forced marriages with a heightened level of coercion. In the case of *Sohrab* v. *Khan* it can be argued that if the young woman, born and brought up in the United Kingdom, had not taken her case to court, she would never have learnt what her actual legal rights are and the fact that her Pakistan-celebrated marriage under the Sharia could be annulled under Scottish law. Such cases establish a precedent for a court of law to take due cognisance of the age of the woman or the circumstances under which her apparent consent for marriage was obtained.

The case of *Re J* could cause disquiet to many Muslims in the United Kingdom. The nature of the issues was such that Muslims could legitimately feel that a United Kingdom court is not able to understand their cultural mores fully. Furthermore, rather than feeling a necessity to obtain legal definition of an issue, they could develop a reluctance to take their matters to court, fearing premature judicial determination of the issue without full cultural competence on the part of the court to do so. In fact, the case did have a strong deterrent effect in another, similar, case. A Moroccan national married to a British woman wanted to frame his contact application in predominantly cultural terms, requesting the court for a specific order for the circumcision of his male son. On becoming cognisant of the judgment in *Re J*, the man, on the advice of his family and the imam in Morocco, withdrew the application and instead sought the court's assistance for pure visitation rights. Those were granted to him on his swearing an oath on the Qur'an that he would not unilaterally have the child circumcised without his estranged wife's permission. Arguably, in such cases members of the Muslim community would in future want to ensure that their cultural rights were not in any way eroded; therefore, they might feel that ADR would provide a better alternative.

The inheritance case of Al Midani is yet another one that supports Fiss' assertion. The legal status of the Sharia Council has never really been tested as such. Generally, until now the rulings of the MLSC have been tacitly accepted by Muslim disputants in the United Kingdom and in Muslim countries and the courts of the United Kingdom have not viewed its deliberations in a conflictual way. The MLSC usually enters into a divorce matter after the United Kingdom courts have rendered a decision. However, in the Al Midani case, the court specifically had to decide whether the Sharia Council was an 'Islamic Judicial Body' within the terms of article 7 of the arbitration agreement entered into by the heirs of the late Sheikh Al Midani. It can be argued that, had the matter not gone to the Queen's Bench Division (Commercial Court), the status of the Sharia Council on this point would not have been clarified and defined.

Fiss' contention that settlement deprives society of definitive judicial rulings on important societal issues should be juxtaposed with putative Muslim feelings that premature recourse to a court of law leads to judicial decisions on the Sharia by a foreign court, which sometimes may not have the necessary competence to decide on Sharia issues. Muslims, generally, would have a predilection not to resort to a court of law if they did not have to. Fiss' theory could be better viewed in the context of the formal-informal discourse that Comaroff and Roberts (1981) discuss in their seminal work. According to them, the informal discourse in dispute resolution does not normally undermine the formal code among the Tswana, a tribe in South Africa. However, the Tswana have only two linguistic codes in operation, while discourse among the

Muslims of Hounslow is often at two or more levels. First, at the community level, where certain fora such as the *biraderi*s operate, they would usually use the informal evaluative code. Then at the MLSC level, the formal code, based on classical Islamic jurisprudence, would most certainly be used. Here, while the two codes would generally reverberate, the potential still exists for the informal code to undermine the classical Sharia. This could happen by way of *urf* (customary law) trumping the Sharia.

A case in point would be forced marriages, a practice which classical Islamic law neither recognises nor condones, yet custom seems to accept it. In such a case, the classical Sharia would be seen to be in closer harmony with the law of the land, which in turn would constitute yet another formal code. It is likely that a United Kingdom court would be viewed by some Muslims as a foreign 'anthropologist' imposing a decision on them and freezing out what they perceive to be 'the Sharia' – something that might not find easy resonance with many in the community. According to a lawyer on the MLSC panel, Raficq Abdulla, this perception is difficult to change as long as an individual or a group of people are obsessed with orthopraxy and metonymic details of outward behaviour at the expense of the inner spiritual life and the ethical engagement that the Islamic faith enjoins.

This whole subject can be viewed as part of the larger debate on the relationship between religion and the state, which has engaged the courts in the United States for centuries (Miller and Flowers, 1977). At heart, the issue is: should there be a strict separation between religion and the state or should the state take the position of benevolent neutrality? Ericsson (2007) emphasises that the issue cannot be seen in simplistic, binary terms such as Church versus State. The family also has an important role to play in the equation and the issue in a federal country such as the United States implicates 15 different entities (see Figure 7.1).

With regard to striking the correct balance in the Church-State-Family arena, Ericsson observes that there is always an ongoing tension between the three and the relationship is dynamic. The courts in the United States have developed a

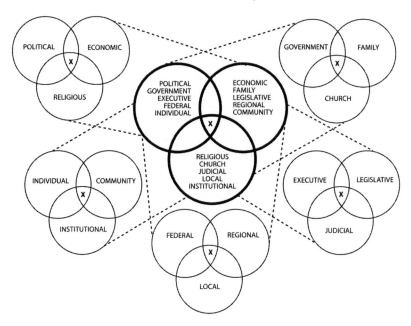

Figure 7.1 Striking a balance among competing interests.
Source: Ericsson (2007).

set of principles, but issues are generally decided on a case-by-case basis.

All religions want freedom and equality, as do individuals and families. It is law that defines the proper role of the State as it relates to the Church and Family institutions. There are large areas of independence for all three institutions. There are also the inevitable areas of overlap where the institutions must interact with one another. In the centre, we find the issues that cause the most tension because all three institutions have a legitimate interest in the core issues of society, such as morals, values, human rights, civil rights and education. The tension is often based on the human drive for power, which makes the struggle for a just balance among competing social interests a never-ending battle.

It is worth noting that, this battle is even more difficult in many developing countries because they have to bring their legal (and other) systems into line with internationally accepted standards quickly. Therefore, they must work on all fronts simultaneously.

In contrast, Western nations have had centuries to adjust their legal systems while trying to strike a balance among competing spheres (Ericsson, 2007).

The case of *Reynolds* v. *United States* is informative on the question of where the state would draw the line between strict separation and benevolent neutrality. The case involved polygamy practised by Mormons in the territory of Utah before it became a state, when it was under federal jurisdiction. The Supreme Court struck down the Mormon practice of polygamy by drawing a distinction between the freedom of belief, which is absolute, and freedom of conduct, which cannot be, stating:

> Laws are made for the government of actions, and while they cannot interfere with mere religious belief and opinions, they may with practices. Suppose one believed that human sacrifices were a necessary part of religious worship, would it be seriously contended that civil government under which he lived could not interfere to prevent a sacrifice? Or if a wife religiously believed it was her duty to burn herself upon the funeral pier of her dead husband, would it be beyond the power of civil government to prevent her carrying out her belief into practice?
>
> So here, as the law of the organization of society under exclusive dominion of the United States, it is provided that plural marriages shall not be allowed, can a man excuse his practices to the contrary because of his religious belief? To permit this would be to make the professed doctrines of religious belief superior to the law of the land and in effect to permit every citizen to become a law unto himself. Government could exist only in name under such circumstances.[10]

Reviewing the cases mentioned in this chapter, it can be argued that British Muslims would not view court-invoked adjudication as being absolutely negative. With regard to *mahr* and arranged marriages, it seems that the United Kingdom courts have bent over backwards to ensure that the true social purpose of the Sharia is asserted. In the case of visitation rights, the court's decision may not be viewed in the same light, because of the influence of socio-cultural rights as well as human rights. In the case of inheritance, the decision was a clarification of the Sharia Council's status within the context of a very specific arbitration agreement and not a generic declaration binding on the entire world.

Ericsson (2007) sees the key to greater religious freedom as lying in the nurturing of legal pluralism through education and law. Pluralism among the various spheres, as well as within each sphere, is the most effective counter to the concentration of power within any dominant political, religious or ethnic group. Legal pluralism, as an integral part of civil society, holds an important potential for balancing societal interests. In a multicultural context it constitutes the best guarantee for a balanced society.[11] However, traditional systems can only contribute meaningfully if they are adequately refurbished with state-of-the-art skills combined with traditional wisdom.

Legal pluralism

Legal pluralism is best understood when we recognise the limitations of the traditional definition of law. John Austin argued in the nineteenth century that laws are only valid when they are issued by a sovereign entity (which could be a person such as a king or a body such as a government); however, we know that laws, such as religious laws or transnational laws, extend beyond the state (Yilmaz, 2005: 9).

A quick survey of the legal literature suggests that 'there are, generally speaking, basically two approaches to conceptualising law, focusing either on justice and morality, or on rules and regulations' (Menski, 2000: 55). Law is not limited to acts, rules, administrative orders, courts, decisions, and so on. It must be understood as cognitive and normative orders generated and maintained in a social field such as a village, an ethnic or religious or cultural community, an association, a state or a transnational community. The term 'law' could refer to any set of observed social norms.

According to Menski (2000), a globally focused understanding of law shows us that, first, law is a universal phenomenon which manifests itself in many different ways. Second, it not only takes different forms but also has different sources. Third, these sources are, in essence, the state, society and religion, which compete and interact in various ways, so any given body of rules may contain components of these three elements. This is endorsed by Yilmaz (2005: 10): 'Legal pluralism must be envisaged as a factual description of the operation of several legal regulations that attempt to achieve justice by responding to cultural and legal diversity in society […] especially when it comes to Muslim law […] legal pluralism is an undeniable factual situation whether the law of the state is secular, laicist or Islamic.' Yilmaz goes on to argue that the paradigm of legal modernity has to be reviewed in order to understand legal pluralism. In his view, legal modernity covers legal positivism and legal centralism, where the former is about the rules that generate law as law and the latter is about the institutions that make those rules work. However, such an understanding of law may be a hindrance to an accurate appreciation of legal modernity. To quote Griffiths (1986: 4), it has 'made it all too easy to fall into the prevalent assumption that legal reality, at least in "modern" legal systems, more or less approximates to the claim made on behalf of the state'.

Galanter (1966) lists 11 characteristics of legal modernity. First, uniformity of rules and their application. Second, transactional basis for rights – people's obligations to each other come from agreements freely negotiated between them, not from unchanging obligations based on personal or group identity. Third, universalism – legal decisions, once made, are kept uniform rather than altered from case to case; the application of law is reproducible and predictable. Fourth, authority is distributed downward from higher officials to lower ones in a hierarchical administrative system. Fifth, the system implies impersonal procedures and the use of written rules and records. Sixth, understandable rules are designed to achieve clearly-stated goals, using demonstrably effective methods. Seventh, the system is run by full-time staff with formal qualifications. Eighth, the system includes specially-trained persons who act as mediators between the specialists of the system and laypersons who must deal with the system. Ninth, the rules and procedures can be modified for the purposes of achieving stated goals. Tenth, modern law exists to serve the purposes of the state, with the state enjoying a monopoly over disputes. Last, the system is independent and separate from other governmental institutions and functions. The judiciary is differentiated in the personnel and technique. That legislative, judicial and executive powers are separate and distinct, is a sacrosanct condition of democratic societies.

According to Galanter (1966) secular motives and techniques have superseded religious sanctions and inspiration. Law-making and its application are now the responsibility of certain professions and operate in the name of central national power. This central national power does not tolerate rivals and the sovereignty and uniformity of the law is seen, in Griffiths' words, as a 'condition of progress toward modern nationhood' (Griffiths, 1986: 8).

Yilmaz (2005: 12) considers the ideological role of law to be of central importance in legal modernity. Law can be used as an instrument of social control and as a mode of organising beliefs and values. Law is viewed in legal modernity in utilitarian terms as a tool, 'an amoral and infinitely plastic device of government' (Coterell, 1989: 124).

Legal instrumentalism has been criticised by a number of scholars. Some scholars (for example, Allott, 1980) emphasise the limits to the capacity of law to transform social life. Moore's (1973) semi-autonomous model explains this phenomenon more succinctly. For her, the social space between legislator and subject is not a normative vacuum. Although the state has the power to use physical force, it does not mean that there are no other agencies and modes of inducing compliance. In other words, even though the formal legal institutions enjoy a kind of monopoly in terms of the legitimate use of power, there are some other forms of effective coercion or effective inducement. Various social fields are interposed between the individual and the political body to which the individual belongs. These social fields have their own rules and means of coercing or inducing compliance.

The state-centric and basically nationalist vision of law has developed over a long period of time and has been described by some comparative legal scholars and theorists as being a 'myth' (Griffiths 1986: 4) or a 'political claim' (Santos; 2002: 89–90).

Regardless of recent public pronouncements on the issue of multiculturalism and its cornerstone of 'Britishness' and what constitutes the elements of this concept in legal terms (for example, Blair, 2006; Cameron, 2005; Phillips, 2005) legal pluralism among British Muslims is very much a fact.

Muslim legal pluralism in Britain

Ballard (1994a: 31) observes that Muslims, as 'skilled cultural navigators', have reconstructed in Britain a home away from home, with the older generation and their British-born offspring continuing to find substantial inspiration in the resources of their own cultural, religious and linguistic inheritance, which they have actively and creatively reinterpreted in order to rebuild their lives on their own terms.

According to Yilmaz (2005: 59), Muslims did not come to England expecting to 'do as the Romans do'. Most of them have desired to maintain their own distinct culture and traditions, including their laws. This desire has been coupled with ignorance of many requirements of English law. From the beginning, Muslims were confronted with a number of problems and tried to find solutions to their problems by themselves in the absence of official response and recognition.

I concur with Yilmaz, with the qualifier that the desire may have been implicit. The research for this study unearthed no evidence that there had been a particular drive among the Hounslow Muslims to maintain 'their laws'. Basically, the rank and file of Muslims in Hounslow were trying to reconstruct their identity in a new environment, and that focused initially on securing a place of worship, being able to obtain *halal* food and finding suitably segregated schools for their female offspring. The Sharia, therefore, was a second thought and resorted to only when specific problems arose that required formal solutions.

Yilmaz (2005) posits four main possible results from the continuing existence of unofficial Muslim laws in the United Kingdom: first, incorporation of the unofficial law into the official English law; second, a recognition of the lack of sensitivity on the part of the legal system and thus the use of informal methods of conciliation; third, continuation of the search for official recognition and formal methods of conciliation compatible with Islamic law; and fourth, development of a hybrid rule system to satisfy the requirements of both official English law and unofficial Islamic law.

Poulter (1990) suggests that Muslims will not only wish to be regulated by the principles of Islamic law when living in a non-Muslim state, they will also seek to formalise such an arrangement within the state's own legal system. During colonial periods, Western powers left Muslim family law untouched, and thus it is 'natural that Muslims expect the application of Muslim family law, even from a non-Muslim government' (Jansen, 1994: 2). This, to Poulter (1990) is something they expect as part of reciprocity for their concession to Jewish and Christian minorities in Muslim lands. However, these attempts have been unsuccessful.

Muslims are trying to obtain acceptance of the use of principles of Islamic law for resolving their family issues in a context where many of them do not consider a Western secular court to be capable of ruling on such issues. For them, 'the secular authority of Western law may lack legitimacy and moral standing to deal with any intricate matter of obligations that may arise in the context of a personal law system' (Menski, 1993a: 255). This, coupled with the issue of *izzat* (honour) explains the preference for informal methods of conciliation. A further reason may also be the lack of response and recognition from the legal system, which has led to the development of an avoidance mechanism that, in the view of Pearl (1986: 32) has led to Muslims withdrawing from state institutions and developing 'their own methods of dispute resolution which operate both on an official and unofficial level'.

There is increasing evidence of the consolidation of such methods. Sharia councils are examples of such concerted efforts to respond to the challenges of the official legal system. These councils are designed to resolve difficult social and legal problems that arise as a result of the application of English law to British Muslims while Muslim law remains in the unofficial sphere.

The Churches' Committee on Migrant Workers in Europe organised a seminar of Christians and Muslims in 1985, at which both sides reached a compromise between two extremes: separate Muslim personal law and the current purportedly uniform legal system of England. David Pearl (1987) suggests the possibility of an informal family court system – a body modelled on the Jewish Beth Din, which in some cases enjoys a quasi-official status in that the state recognises it as being the representative and regulatory body of most Jews in Britain. Sharia councils, it can be argued, fall within this category (Badawi, 1995: 73–80). However, keeping such bodies on an unofficial level has provided an important autonomy to Muslims that would have been lost if the control were given to the state (Yilmaz, 2005). The Hounslow research confirms that this has been the case. Zaki Badawi specifically told me that he always wanted to ensure that the MLSC remained an independent body free of interference from any source.

With regard to the hybrid system of Muslims satisfying the requirements of English law while maintaining their own legal and cultural tradition, Menski (1987) has shown that there is an active interaction between official English law and unofficial South Asian laws, including Islamic law. Rapid urbanisation and modernisation have affected the lives and identities of British Muslims. According to Ansari (2002), British Muslims have sought to adjust to, and accommodate, existing institutions and practices, experimenting and negotiating between the factual and perceived demands and values of British society and their needs, beliefs, and practices as Muslims. While the widely expected assimilation of English cultural patterns has not occurred, their laws and customs have undergone change and modernisation. Yilmaz (2005) observes that, in England, as in other modern countries, the state's legal decisions and positions oblige Muslims to adjust their lifestyles, which also include their laws and customs, in accordance with the state and its norms system.

My research for the thesis on which this book is based shows that, in the case of Muslims in Hounslow, there has been gradual integration but not assimilation. Menski (1988: 65) posits that the assumed assimilation of Muslim ethnic minorities could occur in three stages. First, the initial stage, where they might be ignorant of particular legal requirements; in such situations, customary practices would continue. My research demonstrates this to have been the case. The second stage is when they learn to follow certain rules and requirements of the country where they are residing. My research confirms this. However, Menski's third stage, that Muslims might completely abandon their Muslim law and use only English law, is not borne out by my research. In fact, the research shows that even some of the second-generation and third-generation Muslims prefer to live within the ethical parameters and values of their faith, albeit in a modified form, which are applied to their interpersonal disputes. The older generation of Muslims and their British-born offspring are continuing to find substantial inspiration in the resources of their own cultural, religious and linguistic inheritance, which they have actively and creatively reinterpreted in order to rebuild their lives on their own terms (Ballard, 1994a).

Yilmaz's (2005) contention that this reality confirms his theoretical discussion of Muslim law being placed higher than state law and that Muslims view and treat perceived Muslim norms as crucially binding, is also not borne out by my research. The respondents do not in all cases perceive the 'universal' rules of Muslim law to be superior to the local *lex loci*. Basically, disputants have sought solutions to their problems and have approached their issues in a partial and piecemeal manner. As long as the solutions proffered have not violated basic Islamic ethical values, there has been no self-conscious decision on their part to seek an 'Islamic' solution to their problems.

Also, and most importantly, the research shows that Muslim communities in Britain, contrary to Yilmaz's assertions, have not set up 'an internal regulatory framework to settle disputes' (Yilmaz, 2005: 66). The MLSC concept emerged quite fortuitously, through sheer necessity, and the Council developed a set of basic procedural rules for day-to-day operations; however, a structured and systematic internal regulatory framework applicable to all Muslims does not exist. It will be a welcome innovation and my research shows how receptive the community would be to such a development. I concur with Yilmaz that the assimilation thesis is no longer valid in the contemporary world, that the 'immigrants' are not lost between two cultures, and that the construction of hybrid rule systems has allowed many Muslims to feel at ease.

Some pertinent questions arise that require further research in the future. If legal pluralism is desirable and a new hybrid form of Sharia is in the making, what actual form is it likely to take? For example, does this new hybrid form follow the principles of *takhayur*, that is, drawing from the various schools of Islamic jurisprudence? If so, how are the Shia schools of jurisprudence to be accommodated? Is this process largely driven by the precepts of Sunni Hanafi law, given the demographic preponderance in the UK of Muslims from the South Asian subcontinent, or will it represent the full spectrum of Muslim jurisprudential interpretations in the United Kingdom? In those cases of Muslim family law that end up in a court of law for adjudication, what will be the nature of decision-making and how will the decisions arrived at by an English secular court relate to the principles of classical Islamic law, which themselves have variants depending on the different schools of law, and even within a particular school itself? If the development of an 'angrezi shariat' is very much in the realm of unofficial law,[12] how will developments in this law be recognised by society at large, given the fact that decisions or agreements in the unofficial legal sector are not recorded or reported? How can Muslims in Britain ensure that their cases are adequately reported when they end up in the courts in the United Kingdom? That is, how do they address the issue of the politics of legal reporting of Muslim issues? Finally, how do Muslims ensure that the approaches they follow in ADR practice conform to the original purposes of the Sharia or what is referred to in classical Islamic jurisprudence as the *maqasid-al-sharia*, that is, the protection of religion (*din*), person (*nafs*), offspring (*nasl*), property (*mal*) and reason (*aql*)?

As this book has shown, some Muslims are already exploring questions like these and are suggesting that the *maqasid al-sharia* (the essential higher purpose of the Sharia) be reinstated wherever Islamic law has become egregiously legalistic. Obviously, in resolving their personal disputes, Muslims need to follow a model of ADR that reflects the spirit and ethical values of Muslims today. The next chapter expounds on what the elements of such a culturally appropriate model of ADR could be, with a specific focus on diasporic Muslim communities in the West.

Towards an Islamic Model of ADR

From the preceding chapters, it is clear that appropriate and ongoing training in ADR is critical to strengthening informal dispute resolution processes among the Muslim communities in the United Kingdom. Proper training of dispute resolvers in the mediation techniques of power balancing, domestic abuse screening, normalising, mutualising, positive reframing and 'knowledge for information' on Sharia-specific issues would help obviate the necessity of cases ending up in secular courts for adjudication, and hence premature legal definition of such issues. Proper training would help instil the necessary confidence not only among beneficiaries of the services, but also among personnel providing such services.

In addition, the trustees of various mosques, the imams operating within them, the Sharia councils and the Muslim lawyers advising various congregations need to work together to create a credible, robust and well-resourced ADR system, embedded in the ethical and cultural values of the community. Inevitably, such a system would be viewed against the background of how family mediation is conducted currently in Britain; therefore, before discussing the shape that Islamic ADR could take, it is important to outline the way family mediation has developed over time in the United Kingdom and some of the correspondences with the situation among Muslims in Britain today.

Evolution of family mediation in the UK

Many of the research findings on family mediation in the UK over the past 30 years are relevant to issues that have emerged in this study. For example, while discussing why the rate of divorce has increased so significantly since the 1960s, Walker et al. (1990: 7) remark that 'Experts are in general agreement, however, that explanations for the continued increase in divorce are to be found in broader social, structural and cultural changes which include the greater participation of women in the labour market, smaller family size (largely as a result of widely accessible birth control), economic growth and prosperity, growing secularisation and a greater tolerance of a variety of family forms and living arrangements'. Many of these factors are now found among diasporic Muslim communities in the UK.

Walker (2001) outlines the evolution of divorce reform in England from the nineteenth century, culminating in the Family Law Act 1996. She emphasises that, historically, there has been a reluctance to change the laws of marriage and divorce, often driven by the fear that change might result in unwanted social and political side-effects. She points out that divorce in the UK was a hard-fought-for right for women and that the 1995 Family Law Bill was the first government-led initiative in divorce reform in England since 1857.

In theory, divorce is not such an issue for Muslims because, in accordance with the Sharia, a marriage is a contractual relationship which can be terminated. However, in practice, because of the cultural accretions of relationships, women have always found it difficult to obtain a divorce. Even though there are mechanisms through which the Sharia allows them to get a divorce in a non-contentious way as long as there is no conflict with the religious and ethical principles of the faith with regard to relationships, they often have to go to Sharia councils or courts to dissolve their marriages. This is because their mentors at times fail to have the proper clauses inserted in the marriage contract to enable them to obtain a divorce.

Walker also makes the point that no-fault divorces took some time to be accepted in the UK, citing a 1937 argument 'that to allow divorce by consent would destroy the institution of marriage and undermine the sanctity of marriage and family life: arguments which were used again during the passage of the Family Law Bill, nearly sixty years later' (2001: 19). Once again, in theory, such 'no-fault' divorce is available under the Sharia in the form of a *khula* divorce, which is available largely on the basis that the wife relinquishes her *mahr* (dower right); however, in practice, it is not easy and a woman has to go to a Sharia court or a Sharia council to obtain such a divorce.

In the run-up to the Family Law Bill of 1995, the Law Commission addressed the issue of divorce reform and considered a number of options, rejecting a return to a system based wholly on matrimonial offence. The preferred model for reform was one in which divorce was viewed 'as a process over time' and which granted a decree of divorce only after a period of consideration and reflection. The minimum overall period proposed for consideration and reflection was one year. 'The Law Commission went further to suggest that counselling, conciliation and mediation services would be important elements in developing a new and more constructive approach to the problems of marital breakdown and divorce' (Walker, 2001: 21). However, the divorce reform process outlined in the Family Law Act of 1996 has never been implemented.

Walker observes that mediation as it is practised in England and Wales is future-focused. It has not embraced attempts to deal with ending of the marriage, and in this important respect the government of the day was almost certainly over-optimistic about the potential benefits of mediation. As discussions progressed on the Family Law Bill, the focus on saving and supporting marriage remained at the heart of debates on the Bill, with a very high level of consensus that the legislation should convey strong messages about the significance of marriage. In the early stage of debate, anxiety was expressed that there was too little emphasis on reconciliation as an objective, and too much emphasis on mediation. According to Walker (2001: 31), 'to a large extent, the moving of marriage counselling to centre stage reshaped the Bill from one that began by being primarily focused on facilitating conciliatory divorce to one primarily focused on saving marriage, particularly in Part II'.

Furthermore,

> whereas the Law Commission and the Government's Green and White Papers all promoted mediation as central to a reformed process of divorce, members of both Houses were more circumspect about its role. The Government saw mediation as capable of reducing bitterness and tension, improving communication and reducing cost. Yet the Commons debates led the Government to table an amendment that there would be no presumption in favour of either mediation or legal representation, thus ensuring an even-handed approach to dispute resolution processes.

With regard to S29 meetings with mediators – a requirement before a party to a dispute can receive legal aid – which remained in the Bill and which was subsequently enacted, Lord Mackay, the Lord Chancellor said: '[It] will allow parties to make an informed decision on the basis of the facts, and in the process learn of the considerable benefits of mediation for the parties and the children.'[1]

Stark and Birmingham (2001) found that people attending an information meeting under the Family Law Act still wanted to have a solicitor guide them through the divorce process. It seemed that neither the information meeting in its current format nor mediation could take the place of a solicitor. Some attendees were encouraged to seek the advice of a solicitor, whereas others, who had not had their questions answered, saw a solicitor as the next logical step. As we have seen, solicitors also play a role in the Hounslow ADR processes. Research for this study showed, for example, that in addition to providing partisan advice, Muslim solicitors on the MLSC panel have given advice on UK public laws to the imam of the mosque in cases of forced marriage and abduction and to the MLSC regarding the 'Islamising' of a woman's divorce granted by a UK (secular) court. Moreover, the Sharia is implemented by legal scholars. Though not solicitors in the adversarial sense of the word, they *are* legal scholars and are central to the process of applying religious law to a particular issue.

According to Stark (2001: 489), 'mediation is sometimes regarded by people facing divorce as an either-or option, rather than a process which can be used in conjunction with other legal services [...] Promoting the value of mediation in its own right, rather than merely comparing it with solicitors, may enable more people to see its potential benefits'. However, he concedes that the 'decision as to whether or not to use mediation is a complex one, even if the idea is appealing' (2001: 487). He found that women tend to consult solicitors to get assurance that a mediated agreement is fair in legal terms. In a diasporic Muslim community, disputants do not always have an either/or option. As shown by the present study, certain services, such as the 'Islamising' of a secular divorce, can only be provided by a Muslim Sharia council.

Factors determining an Islamic ADR model

Mediation, with its clearly-defined principles of absolute voluntariness, parties' autonomy, lack of coercion, full confidentiality, absolute impartiality, expeditiousness of process, procedural flexibility, total neutrality and so forth, does not exist in its *purest* form in the processes utilised by the various fora to which the disputants in Hounslow resort. However, various aspects of what is generally called ADR are practised by the Muslim community and it is generally warm to the principles of mediation. Interestingly, the Muslim informants in this study perceive commonality between ADR and the Sharia; they view ADR as being closer than the laws of the United Kingdom to the Sharia. On the other hand, the non-Muslim informants view Muslim ADR processes as being closer than the Sharia (as they perceive it) to UK laws. ADR, and more particularly mediation, thus holds the potential of constituting an important bridge that would be acceptable to all, provided it was conducted in a professional manner in conformity with the public laws of the UK.

However, ADR practitioners need to understand and take account of the complexity of issues that diasporic Muslim communities in Britain have faced and are still facing. Mediation, as an ADR process, will not be received well by Muslims unless it is based on a good understanding of this background. Furthermore, as a process, it will not be responsive to the specific, religio-cultural needs of a diasporic Muslim community. This caution is also applicable to ADR practitioners who interface with Muslims in other countries of the Western world. This study has found that it is possible to interpret the principles of the Sharia to find resonance with basic ADR norms and to use them positively to construct the necessary bridge between Islamic religious law and the laws of the Western countries in which Muslims have settled. The MLSC's work in Hounslow is a very good example of what can be achieved without confronting Muslims with a stark choice of either abandoning their religious law or living in conformity with UK laws.

My research shows that preservation of the community's value systems is an important element in the choice of a particular form of ADR to settle issues outside the adversarial arena of the court system by the Muslims in Hounslow. In this connection, Roberts and Palmer (2005) observe that a panoramic view of conflict resolution processes would show something of an episodic alternation between values of 'formalism' and 'informalism'. Auerbach (1983) emphasises that the rejection of legal processes as an appropriate mode of decision-making in the context of disputes is often part of an attempt to develop or retain a sense of community: 'How to resolve conflict, inversely stated, is how (or whether) to preserve community' (1983: 4). While the nature and characteristics of a community evolve with the passage of time and over several generations, members of that community still retain the need to have a sense of belonging. Therefore, a continuous transaction between the community and the processes and values of the majority is enacted by way of adjustments and compromises.

Roberts and Palmer (2005) observe that this tendency may manifest itself in a variety of specific contexts – religious, political, territorial, ethnic and occupational. They highlight a number of core elements constituting a 'model' of informal justice that could be seen as superior to orthodox formal justice. Those core elements include a non-bureaucratic structure, local nature, and accessibility by ordinary people to informal processes that are reliant on lay people as third-party interveners. These processes are outside the immediate scope of official law and are based on substantive and procedural 'rules' that are vague, unwritten, flexible and intent on promoting harmony between the parties and within the context of local communities. For Roberts and Palmer, the history of the search for alternatives should be seen in a broad historical context and should encompass experiences wider than in Northern Europe and North America.

In the Islamic context, reconciliation is central to conflict resolution. This study found ample evidence that it is a crucial factor in ADR and is followed assiduously. Reconciliation is important in *all* Muslim communities and is often seen as a religious obligation. Its inclusion in the dispute resolution trajectory thus becomes important. General mediatory practice in the West today tends to view itself as a binary to the adjudicative process, with the result that, processually, no serious place is assigned to reconciliation in the dispute resolution trajectory. This is an issue for ADR practitioners to reflect upon generally, because it could be the deciding factor in the response of Muslims to mediation as a process.[2] If mediation is projected merely as an alternative to adjudication with no mention of the possibility of reconciliation during the sessions, it will inevitably only take on the coloration of a cheaper form of adjudication; or, worse still, it will not be embraced.

Understanding the role of secular lawyers in a Muslim mediatory context is also very important. Lawyers *do* play an important role in the whole ADR process (Stark and Birmingham, 2001). While in mainstream mediation practice they are called in mainly to advise the parties on their legal rights, in a diasporic, faith-based situation, the need for them is always at an earlier stage. Their purpose is two-fold: first, to advise the parties on their rights, and second, to advise on how the principles of their religious laws interface with the public laws of the United Kingdom. Lawyers are often called upon to give advice on this aspect and that gives rise to various challenges. Therefore, it is important for them to gain some working knowledge of the Sharia and the *fiqh* traditions of different Sunni and Shia schools of jurisprudence.

Of particular significance to the understanding of Muslim diasporic situations is that *urf*, or customary practice, is an important aspect of dispute resolution. Among the issues that ADR practitioners and theorists need to know about when dealing with Muslim communities in the Western world is that there is often a tension between customary practices and the classical Sharia; and the laws of the United Kingdom are invoked to disentangle the Sharia from its cultural overlays. Whereas disputants often tend to conflate customary practices with their religious law, the religious law does not countenance certain customary practices, such as forced marriages. Thus, Muslims in a diasporic setting constantly have to operate within three concentric circles: the norms of their customs, the laws of their faith and the laws of the land. ADR has to cut across all three circles (see Figure 4). Therefore, mediators need to have some familiarity with each of these areas, not as 'knowledge for use', but rather as 'knowledge for information' in order to enrich and facilitate their practice.

The Sharia and understanding of it, both externally and internally, are very important. The average perception externally is that the Sharia permeates every aspect of a Muslim's life, and particularly his or her interpersonal disputes. However, many Muslims interviewed for this study do not have a clear idea of the Sharia. Often, the understanding is based on their memory

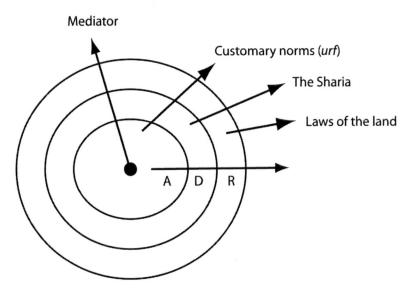

Figure 8.1 ADR in a Muslim diasporic setting.

of what it appeared to be when they left their countries of origin. Where imams of the mosque are concerned, the Sharia is a particular imam's understanding of the classical texts that he refers to by virtue of the particular school of law to which he belongs. At the level of the imams the notion of the Sharia is still very much a positive-law phenomenon of *fiqh* based on various medieval texts. Thus, the imams are not aware of situations that could give rise to conflict of laws. At the level of the MLSC, the *Sharia* assumes a different dimension. It is there that the conflict-of-laws dimensions actually help to give the Sharia today its original purpose, which is to assist the disputing parties to resolve their problems in an equitable and fair manner within the framework of a society's mores and expectations.

Abdalla (2001) sets out several basic factors to take into account when designing an appropriate conflict resolution model in an Islamic context. He refers to the unique position of Islam as a religion and a value system cherished by its followers and emphasises that Islamic sources are rich in conflict intervention principles, values and models that are ripe for exploration and articulation in a language that would adapt them for contemporary practice. Citing the Turkish psychologist Kagitçibasi (1994) he refers to the concept of interdependence and the 'culture of relatedness', which, he says, are characteristics of Islamic communities and could be built upon to improve conflict intervention.

Abdalla sees the involvement of others as a distinct strength in conflict intervention because it would model Islamic norms and principles as described in the Qur'an and the *sunna*. 'A conflict intervener cannot assume that the community is made up of independent autonomous individuals who expect that interpersonal conflict intervention will take place only between primary parties and the intervener. An Islamic setting is likely to engage and involve other entities and parties (for example, extended family members) in any given conflict' (Abdalla, 2001: 176). Additionally, building on the strength of the community and its culture of relatedness would put to useful purposes resources that are otherwise wasted or neglected. Abdalla's views are borne out today in Muslim mediation practice. For example, this 'culture of relatedness' emerges as a strong theme in the mediation training given to the Ismaili Muslim National Conciliation and Arbitration Boards worldwide (Keshavjee and Whatling, 2005).

With regard to the utilisation of Western-developed models, Abdalla observes that many such models stress a strong sense of individual autonomy and have a heavy focus on self-interest. Referring to practices based on the North American model of mediation,[3] he states that 'individualism, individual autonomy, the assignment of more significance to interests rather than to relationship and the "professional" neutrality of third parties are major cultural themes that seem to dominate [that] model'. He calls for serious reconsideration of the model, observing that it would not find resonance in Muslim societies, which are primarily non-individualistic. Discussing the cultural influences affecting various aspects of the North American model, namely conflict definitions, defining issues, third-party neutrality and conflict resolution or management, he emphasises that the Western approach of framing conflict in terms of 'divergent interests' results in the design of techniques that focus only on reconciling the interests between parties. He views such an approach as being 'most suitable to social and cultural norms which profoundly emphasise individuals' autonomy, self-articulated interests and free choices based on individuals' own "standard of fairness"'. In contrast, Islamic settings 'both in theory and culturally, assume a great deal of social interdependence and community involvement even in interpersonal matters, which are more conducive to situational definitions that allow for a deeper and wider analysis of conflict situations' (Abdalla, 2001: 162).

With regard to whether a model or models predicated on the Western assumption can be applied in an Islamic setting, Abdalla observes that, due to increased contact with other societies and cultures, many scholars in the West have now expanded their views of mediation. He concedes that many of the North American concepts have undergone some changes in recent years because of advances in studying communication, relationships, community and the effects of culture and gender differences. These advances have had an impact on mediation theory and practice and have caused many authors to develop models that are less 'individualistic'. Nevertheless, that has not occurred to a degree where the North American model would be suitable for wide implementation in an Islamic setting. While the model might be useful in conflict situations involving relationship issues or value-based issues, it does not provide the tools for addressing conflicts where ethical issues of justice, rights or interpretations of the Qur'an and the *sunna* are prevalent.

Being against indiscriminate acceptance of the underlying assumptions on which most of those models have been predicated and which, until recently, have gone undetected, Abdalla suggests a critical review of the potential principles one can extract from Western conflict resolution models for incorporation in an Islamic context. To develop an appropriate cultural model for Muslim communities, Abdalla uses the distinction between two approaches to cross-cultural analysis presented by Augsburger (1992): the 'emic', which describes a cultural phenomenon in terms of its own units, and the 'etic', which imposes categories that are external to the phenomenon. Abdalla favours the 'emic' approach for its cultural appropriateness, but cautions that due to the 'lack of developed "emic" tools to analyse conflicts in Islamic settings, it seems proper to start the process by using "etic" models, while continuing throughout the research process to refine and enhance the models in order to capture any aspects of conflicts that are not accounted for using an external model' (Abdalla, 2001: 155).

An innovative illustration of Abdalla's proposition is the Ismaili Muslim National Conciliation and Arbitration Board (NCAB) global training programme. The programme, started in 2000 with resources provided by His Highness the Aga Khan, the Imam of the Ismaili Muslims, has been implemented in Africa, Asia ,the Middle East, Western Europe and North America. To date, it has trained over 1,000 mediators, including some non-Ismailis and non-Muslims, in over a dozen countries. It has established its credibility as a culturally sensitive practice and has been used to train family court judges for the Ministry of Justice in Portugal as well as some Sunni Muslim judges in Syria, among other countries. The training programme has been acknowledged in the Middle Temple lectures in the UK and the NCAB processes have been mentioned in the report of the Boyd Commission in Canada as being culturally sound and professionally implemented.[4] The training module for the programme was originally developed in collaboration with the Institute of Ismaili Studies, located in London, and the National Family Mediation and the Centre of Effective Dispute Resolution, both in the United Kingdom. It was subsequently modified through a series of rollouts in different parts of the world to meet the needs of a global Muslim community.

The programme started with 'etic' tools of training, and over a ten-year period, through international experience and interaction with overseas trainers and trainees, added its own 'emic' dimensions to the tool set. The main characteristics of the training module emerged from the challenges posed by the need to balance a programme that sought to bridge the traditional Western individualist approach to mediation with a non-Western communitarian ethic, culture and its subcultures without compromising the irreducible basic principles of mediation. Therefore, the module had to be open to adaptation. Its main characteristics can be described as eclectic, reflective, multicultural and adaptive to the predominant culture and subcultures in any country. Utilising an 'etic', Western approach, it has embraced cultural dimensions of different Muslim countries as well as a diasporic Muslim community. The training module is designed to undergo ongoing modification to suit local conditions as long as such changes do not conflict with the basic principles of the law of those countries, the ethical values of Islam or those of sound mediation practice.

On the basis of my experience with the NCAB training programme since 2000, I concur with Abdalla that it would be worthwhile to start with an 'etic' model first and then, as the rollout takes place and interaction ensues, to modify the training module. The Hounslow Muslim community today has neither a systematic dispute resolution system in place nor a training module. In its case, starting with an 'etic' approach and building systematically on it would be the most sensible and practical way of proceeding, provided that the training given is consistent, qualitative and open to knowledge updating through ongoing refresher programmes.

Abdalla also cautions against indiscriminate absorption of principles from the existing Islamic literature relevant to conflict, which could lead to an 'entrapment in circles of legalistic interpretations developed centuries ago, which lack the spirit of conflict resolution as a movement for social change and an interdisciplinary field of research' (2001: 151). He opines that, due to 'historical misuses, abuses and misinterpretations of Islamic sources', there has been a dilution of the strong emphasis on 'justice, equality and freedom in Islam as a value system'. For him, an Islamic conflict intervention, to be of benefit to Muslim communities and individuals, has to have as its major objective 'to restore to Islam its principles and values of justice, equality and freedom' (2001: 152).

He observes that certain methodological parameters would need to be taken into account while developing models for dispute resolution in an Islamic setting. In any discussion of dispute resolution within an Islamic setting, the focus should be removed from the jurisprudence to interdisciplinary research, from legality to morality, from the letter of the law to its spirit, and from the application of law to the pursuit of justice (2001). The focus of the research, then, would no longer be legal interpretations and precedents which have been laboured over and documented by legal scholars over the centuries and are known in the Islamic heritage as *fiqh*. *Fiqh* becomes only a part of a larger research project, which encompasses culture, history, sociology and psychology. 'Dispute resolution thus attempts to operate within the larger Islamic worldview, not just within its traditional legal system' (2001: 158).

The research for this book confirms this. The MLSC has aspired to carry out dispute resolution innovatively but without in any way undermining the Sharia or causing a disequilibrium in the community; in Zaki Badawi's words, 'without breaking either the Sharia or the law' (Badawi, 1995: 78). That approach has been a good example of 'change within a steady state' (morphogenesis). To succeed, it has to be done in an evolutionary manner and have the full concurrence of the community with the involvement of *all* the stakeholders of the community, including imams of mosques.

Abdalla emphasises the social justice and social change functions of dispute resolution in relation to Islamic principle and cultural traditions, and draws a clear distinction between the two, stressing that mixing of the two has often led to 'depriving

Islam of its egalitarian democratic drive'. He continues, 'abuses of power by Islamic rulers, and abuses against women and minorities, at times, were triggered by inherent tribal and traditional norms, which overshadowed the pure Islamic message or forced extreme interpretations of the sources in order to justify these practices' (Abdalla, 2001: 158). For him, 'if the dispute resolution as a social movement is considered to be an agent of change, it will be the responsibility of Islamic dispute resolution professionals to restore the Islamic principles of equality, justice and freedom through their practice' (2001: 158). Thus, setting an example of dispute resolution research, which is geared towards social justice and change, is the essence of the exercise.

Abdalla cautions that it is neither sufficient nor acceptable to generate dispute resolution models in the Islamic setting that will only maintain the status quo, or to impose Western models without careful review of their advantages and limitations. 'If the challenge for dispute resolution professionals in the west is against persistent racism, discrimination and capitalist injustice, for Muslims the challenge is to restore justice and equality by liberating Islam from the doctrine and cultural elements which subjugated its followers to political and social oppression' (2001: 159). For this, he advocates adhering only to Islamic sources using interpretations that are consistent with the spirit of Islam, citing hadiths related to women which state that it is fundamentally important to recognise the Qur'anic emphasis on the equality of gender in terms of creation, action and accountability (Wadud-Muhsin, 1992).

Abdalla's assertion that an Islamic model needs to reflect Islamic values, goals and processes is a valid one. In addition, he feels that the model must respond to the specific needs and circumstances of Muslim culture. It is in this context that he highlights his three guiding principles: first, restoring to Islam its message of justice, freedom and equality; second, engaging the community in the intervention and resolution processes; and third, adjusting the intervention techniques according to the conflict situation and its stages. These principles need to be examined more closely.

As far as restoring to Islam its message of justice, freedom and equality is concerned, meritorious as the sentiment may be, one needs to ask the fundamental question: how viable and practicable would this be in today's global geopolitical context? The world of Islam, as well as of Muslim societies in the diaspora, are at present undergoing multiple, often painful, processes of transition. There is urgent need for a new epistemology to address the types of issues that the Muslim *umma*, comprising over a billion people and spanning the entire globe, is facing at the present time of heightened conflict and globalisation. Fortunately, a number of modern Muslim thinkers have emerged, ranging from Mohamed Arkoun of Algeria and Abdul Karim Soroush of Iran to Farid Essack of South Africa and Abdulahi an-Naim of Sudan, who are calling for new learning approaches in various disciplines – a new hermeneutics – by which subjects such as Islamic history, philosophy, ethics and law can be reappraised. In brief, what all of them are saying is that there is a desperate need to harness new methods of interpretation to understand modern-day challenges confronting the Muslim world. Muslim societies today need to critique the dominant discourses of the day, including the Western notions of modernity. The imperative is to excavate from the Islamic sources the essential spirit that informed Muslims at the apogee of their civilisations, and to make that spirit speak with a renewed vigour to the issues of the present time. It is crucial for Islamic law itself to be subjected to this process in a systematic and methodically sound manner.

The role of Muslim dispute resolvers, through a culturally sensitive ADR model, could be an important *contributory* factor in this whole process, but it cannot be carried out in isolation from this bigger endeavour that calls on Muslims to adopt a new worldview regarding their history, theology, philosophy and various other facets of the social framework. To expect Muslim dispute resolvers alone to play this role in isolation from a larger enterprise would be expecting too much of a group of people who do not as yet fully comprehend even the basic principles of contemporary mediation practice and how this form of dispute resolution interfaces with the national laws of various countries, let alone the religious law and its application in any particular context. Having said this, it is quite feasible, by the very nature of ADR, for Muslim dispute resolvers to make a sufficient contribution to this change while at the same time adhering to the essential principles of the Sharia without becoming embroiled in its formal rigidity.

According to the Pakistan Muslim thinker, Fazlur Rehman (1985), Muslim law has historically trumped Muslim ethics because, by the time early Muslim thinkers such as Miskawayh (d. 1030), al-Ghazalli (d. 1111) and Nasir al-Din Tusi (d. 1274) had written their opuses on ethics, the four Sunni schools of law had already solidified and produced their legal manuals. That was accompanied by the so-called 'closure of the gates of *ijtihad*'. Hence, the system of law was formalised before ethics were clarified; the Sharia came to place *fiqh* and other expressions of legal normativity above the basic ethical tenets of the faith that underlie it. Such a process was part of the political and religious hegemony that was established in the Muslim world under the rule of the Abbasid dynasty. Thus, the Sharia became institutionalised and wedded to state power.

Rehman calls for a reversal of this process by retrieving the ethical from the legalistic strictures of the Sharia – in essence, a recapturing of the original spirit of the Sharia as a dynamic and evolving compass. This project raises a number of issues, including the question of legitimacy, such as: Who has the authority to engender this reappraisal? Arguably, ADR can help retrieve the more nimble – fairplay – aspects, extricating them from the more rigid, logocentric and formalistic layers that the Sharia has acquired historically (Rehman, 1982). How can such a process be seen as authentic, and hence acceptable to Muslims generally? It is here that the use of Islamic discourse could be critical. For example, the utilisation of *hadith*s showing how the Prophet extolled the virtues of compromise and forgiveness could be an effective way of demonstrating that the principles of ADR are embedded in Muslim praxis.

Since ADR, and more particularly mediation, is conceived to be a modern concept, it is possible that the process might be painted as 'westoxification'. To obviate this, the social philosopher Charles Taylor's (2002) argument of 'multiple modernities' serves us well. In Taylor's pluralist formulation, one may have a discourse that is modern outside a hegemonic Western one; that is, not an alternative to modernity but an *alternative* modernity that is not technocentric, rigidly secular and highly individualistic. That would allow for a Muslim modernity – among other alternative discourses – which commands indigenous legitimacy. If such an approach were taken, ADR would have the serious potential to reintegrate ethics with Muslim law.[5]

With regard to Abdalla's second guiding principle, that is, engagement of the community in the intervention and resolution processes, it should not only be an aspiration, but an imperative. In a community where the 'culture of relatedness' is embedded, the community's involvement becomes a sine qua non. Here, Abdalla's perception of 'Islam, as a religion of modelling' is apposite. He states that 'for the majority of Muslims, passionate sentiment attaches them to their Islamic heritage'. He cites examples from the history of early Islam that are taught to the young at home, in school, at the mosque and in the community, highlighting examples of courage, solidarity, love and compassion, justice and equality. He emphasises that 'this heritage is not subject to the confusing scholarly interpretations, or the abusive institutions that have overshadowed the social and political history of Islam.' For him, this 'represents to Muslims the pure ideals of their religion' (Abdalla, 2001: 167). Abdalla's observation is borne out by my research, which found that both religious functionaries as well as secular individuals often cite examples from Islamic history to inform their thinking on conflict-related issues.

However, Abdalla does see some obstacles inherent in this process. First, there is likely to be scholarly disagreement over the interpretation of several models of behaviour found in the Qur'an and the *sunna*. Second, there would be an intermixture of religious and traditional values, attitudes and behaviours – many of which are 'not only foreign to Islam,' but also contradictory to 'Islamic divine values' (2001: 170). Third, there would be 'selective recall' of certain Qur'anic verses, or Prophetic practices or statements would be taken out of context. This study has shown that while these are real issues that are important and potentially problematic, they are not insurmountable problems. Muslim communities, particularly those in the diaspora, are today beginning to come to grips with many issues involving the Sharia, and the work of the MLSC has shown that, in the hands of a competent, enlightened and non-aligned institution, the Sharia can speak with a renewed voice to the contemporary needs of diasporic Muslim societies.

Abdalla's third principle, which deals with adjusting the intervention techniques according to the conflict situation and its stages, is indisputable. ADR discourses today are sensitive to the need for more culturally sensitive models of mediation, and mediation practice in cross-cultural settings has shown how critical this flexibility to adapt is to the very acceptance of mediation as an ADR tool. In the Ismaili Muslim National Conciliation and Arbitration Board training programmes, not only did the intervention techniques have to be adjusted according to the local context, but greater use of mediatory arbitration – known popularly in the ADR field as Med-Arb – also had to be encouraged, given the nature of the culture of the community concerned and its basic approach to conflict resolution.

This readiness to adjust the intervention techniques according to the conflict situation is very much in keeping with the philosophy of Lederach, (1995: 109–18) who highlights five principles. First, the *in situ* principle, which he describes as seeing something in its original position; that is, looking at conflict resolution modalities in a given setting as *present* and *functioning*. Here, he calls for exploring and identifying people 'who are wet up to their ears standing midstream in the river of conflict from within each cultural group that makes up a multicultural setting'. Second, he refers to *indigenous empowerment*, in which people from that very setting are the key resources for any training. The strategic question here is to identify, validate and empower such persons to create the opportunity for cross-fertilisation and interaction with their counterparts in other communities.

The third principle highlighted by Lederach is *conscientisation*, which he calls 'awareness-of-self-in-context'. It is based on the acceptance that people are knowledgeable about, capable of naming, interacting with, and responding to, their own realities in dynamic ways. Lederach calls for reflection to probe the awareness of conflict and of self in a context that spans the cultural and ethnic groups living within a community. The fourth principle is *recycling*; that is, working with groups that have experienced or are experiencing significant cultural change and transition. Minority immigrant communities in the Western world find themselves in the process of acculturation, where the social resources for handling conflict in their home setting are no longer available in the host context, yet the situation does not adequately deal with those needs.

Finally, Lederach refers to *facilitation*, which suggests that trainers working in multicultural settings should assume a posture of leadership that is closer to that of a facilitator of a group process than that of an expert in a particular model of conflict resolution. The trainer, as facilitator, envisages the overall training group as made up of unique cultural and ethnic groups, 'more like a garden salad than a melting pot'. According to Lederach, 'each has valid and important insights and knowledge about the problem, the possible options, the mechanisms and resources their particular community has or needs, and the viability of proposed solutions.'

Lederach's findings are also corroborated by my research and work experience. There *is* a system of dispute resolution that is extant in the Hounslow community, regardless of how rudimentary it may be. People from that particular setting are best suited to train others. While this is true to a large extent, the Ismaili Muslim National Conciliation and Arbitration Board training programme has shown that a combination of overseas and local trainers works best. Overseas trainers bring to the programme state-of-the-art training which, when combined with the wisdom and experience of local people, yields the best results. People relate to their own issues in dynamic and creative ways, and when given the opportunity, come up with creative and innovative ideas.

The involvement of elders is also something that the present study calls for. Elders have a great deal to offer in any community; they constitute a bridge with the past, and if judiciously brought into play, could facilitate change without causing disequilibrium. The role of the trainer as a facilitator is critical. Even though such societies may be communitarian and espouse a more didactic approach to mediation in practice, with regard to training they seem to appreciate a more facilitative approach provided it is done in an evolutionary and culturally sensitive way. The best learning is experiential, for it enables people to bring important insights to bear on problems they have encountered in the field. This has led to enhancement of the learning process and enrichment of the original teaching module.

My research in the Hounslow Muslim community also shows the importance of using a nuanced approach to the problem of domestic abuse in such a setting. Domestic abuse, which is a very complex phenomenon, is prevalent in the community but is not readily apparent in the conflict-resolution process. The culture is one where women do not readily speak about domestic abuse, since any mention of it is tantamount to besmirching of family honour (*izzat*). Various agencies, including the police, prefer to leave resolution of such conflicts to the parties themselves. For a mediator from either the community or the majority host culture, this poses a serious challenge; how is one to discern whether a party has been a victim of domestic abuse in a culture where, often, people who have been physically beaten do not even admit that has happened?

Greater cultural understanding here would imply a more sensitive reading of the situation than a mere perfunctory session with the disputants as present ADR practice seems to suggest. Since prima facie evidence of domestic abuse precludes mediatory intervention, a proper reading of domestic abuse is critical. ADR agencies, without being fully aware that domestic abuse is being perpetrated, sometimes continue with mediation, to the jeopardy of a spouse. This study found that in a diasporic situation, a more nuanced approach is necessary and a simple cursory session may not reveal sufficient insights into whether or not domestic abuse is taking place.

Counselling remains an urgent need in the Hounslow Muslim community. Quantitative analysis on the basis of a survey has not been carried out, but most of the data in the study attest to the fact that people desperately need to be listened to. Listening constitutes part of the curative process. It has a therapeutic effect. Also, many disputants suffer from depression as a result of conflict. The community could gain immensely from good counselling services that are culturally sensitive.

Education about the value of counselling is also needed. This is significant if mediation, as a process, is going to be viewed as a holistic exercise. The Muslims in Hounslow, for the most part, seem to have come to Britain with certain preconceptions and an aversion to speaking to others about their own personal issues. Such communal reticence is intertwined with cultural taboos and is also found in other diasporic Muslim communities as well as other Asian communities. However, this attitude is slowly changing because of transformations in the socio-cultural milieu and weakening or breaking down of traditional support systems. Greater educational efforts need to be made to socialise people to the need for culturally sensitive counselling services. Adequate counselling services at an early stage of grievance can prevent a disagreement from becoming a dispute.

Adequate support mechanisms are equally crucial. Mediation is not simply an intervention, it is a process. All the fora canvassed showed concern over the lack of support mechanisms for those involved in conflict, both in the social services as well as within the community itself. That often frustrates the ability of the various organisations to deal effectively with domestic abuse. Agencies tend to shy away from handling this issue for fear of leaving the victim in a more vulnerable position vis-à-vis his/her family and society. If ADR is to work effectively, genuinely supportive mechanisms need to be put in place; in the absence of such mechanisms, victims, mainly women, are likely to continue to suffer in silence and mediation may work only to their detriment.

This study has shown that men, too, are victims of domestic abuse, and that in a cross-cultural diasporic setting negotiation takes place in the shadow of different laws. Immigration law is an important determinant, where one spouse, often an overseas male sponsored by the wife's family, is a disputant. Thus, support mechanisms could include community-sponsored legal services, immigration advice bureaus, community-sponsored social welfare committees, welfare boards and community-run women's refuges. Additionally, the community could help divorced women to acquire new skills through training, so that they are able to support themselves. Post-conflict rehabilitation may require psychological, material and spiritual support. Volunteer doctors and support workers from within the Muslim community could be mobilised to provide such support through the mosque and the institutions of the community.

Diasporic Muslim communities today have a unique opportunity to do something creative that would be difficult to do in a Muslim country, and that is to improvise and think innovatively about their personal laws vis-à-vis the law of the land, provided they are prepared to organise themselves in a manner that respects the public laws of the countries in which they live. ADR provides them this opportunity. Through ADR they will be able to extract the essential ethical principles of the Sharia and apply them to interpersonal disputes. Simultaneously, they will also be able to draw from the equitable principles underlying the laws of the UK. In this way, they will infringe neither the Sharia nor the law of the land, and draw on the essential ethical principles of both.

If competently handled, the principles of classical Sharia can be invoked to promote legal pluralism both within Islam and in secular contexts. The MLSC utilises the principles of both Shi'i and Sunni schools of law to deal with issues brought before it. Were it operating in Muslim countries, their national constitutions might not allow such a practice. In a diasporic Western setting, however, the MLSC has been successful in disentangling the Sharia from the *fiqh* – the jurisprudence derived from the Sharia – a task that is critical to Muslim legal modernity. This study shows that reinterpretation of the religious law (through *Ijtihad*) is not only possible, but also necessary if Muslim communities want to live in congruity with the demands of the contemporary world without sacrificing the essential ethical values of their faith.

9

Policy Considerations

It can be argued that this book has come at an opportune time. There is a significant Muslim presence in the Western world today, and as a minority, Muslims are constantly grappling with the issue of finding a balance between adhering to the principles of their faith, and living in the Western world and respecting the public laws of the countries of their adoption. This is happening when the world of Islam and the Western world are entangled in an ongoing confrontation where the Sharia often gets implicated but very little thought is given to the Sharia's essential purpose and how ADR can help restore its original spirit.

For Muslim countries that may now have to move towards institutionalising mediation, a study of this nature provides much-needed insights as to what will work and what may not work. For diasporic Muslim communities, the study provides insights into how they could arrange their legal orderings in a manner that is true to their traditions, while at the same time respecting the public laws of the countries in which they have chosen to settle. For ADR practitioners, the study shows the complex nature of issues they need to be cognisant of in order to make diasporic Muslims more family-mediation friendly. A familiarity with one of the world's major faith-cultures, with a population of some 1.6 billion people in some 57 countries, is important in order for ADR as a whole to evolve further.

Overall implications

The implications of my research have a primary bearing on the diasporic Muslim communities in the United Kingdom, where there are some 3 million Muslims today. The lessons learnt about the various fora to which diasporic Muslims resort in order to resolve their interpersonal disputes, and how they interrelate with each other, and how the Sharia is inferred, could have an important impact in other countries with substantial Muslim minority populations. However, we should not forget that the Muslim communities in Britain today have different interpretations of the faith within the context of Islam's fundamental unity, which raises the question of whether one model would be suitable for *all* Muslim communities in the Western world. This question can also be raised with regard to other faith communities.

Over the past few decades, mediation has been increasingly used as an alternative process for resolving disputes. As mediation has evolved and become more institutionalised, mediators have come under increasing pressure to take a more directive approach to practice in order to generate agreements more rapidly and to solve problems. As Bush and Folger (1994) and Le Baron and Pillay (2006) observe, the result is that the transformative potential of mediation has thus not been fully realised. Greater involvement of different societal institutions could help towards the realisation of this potential. In this context, the findings of my research call for a serious rethink of the original purpose of mediation and whether the models that are presently being used worldwide are really capable of addressing the complex and polyvalent needs of different communities in transition in a world that is undergoing rapid globalisation.

Implications for ADR

Although human societies have been practising informal dispute resolution from time immemorial, ADR in its contemporary form, with discrete processes, terminology and techniques, is relatively new.[1] The models being used for mediation today are highly individualistic, problem-solving ones, largely conceived and developed in the Western world. As this study has found, such models may not fully resonate with the polyvalent needs of many non-Western societies. Experience has shown that, in order to be acceptable and applicable, the models have to be adapted to different needs.

Much work has been done in the field of family mediation in the United Kingdom since the mid 1970s. Work has also been done on cross-cultural mediation since the promulgation of the Family Law Act in 1996, and the difficulties experienced in that endeavour provide useful lessons for the strengthening of ADR in diasporic communities today. To gain better insight into this issue, we need briefly to review the evolution of family mediation in the UK, building on the information provided in the previous chapter.

Walker highlights this evolution by emphasising that the Family Law Act was a watershed in the development of family mediation in England and Wales; it not only envisaged a central role for mediation in the resolution of matrimonial disputes, but also provided a statutory basis for public funding of family mediation. Yet, though enshrined statutorily, 'Family mediation continues to struggle for universal acceptance and professional respect' (Walker, 2001: 401). Walker feels that family mediation has been seen 'to hold the key to reducing conflict and promoting civilised divorce,' but has failed to receive funding. With successive governments failing to act on the recommendations of the Finer Committee's *Report on One Parent Families*, it was left to a small group of divorce-associated professionals to spearhead the development of mediation in the voluntary sector and through the family court welfare arm of the probation service.

The paucity of mainstream central government funding, or the lack of any coherent national strategy, led to the development of family mediation in 'a piecemeal and fragmented fashion'. A host of different organisations undertook mediation and 'as a consequence of this ad hoc development across a wide variety of previously existing agencies, family mediation has pursued a somewhat hazardous course with ambiguous and confused terminology, at least in the early years, differing ideologies, a multiplicity of practices and a distinct tension between legal principles and the theoretical perspectives of social welfare' (Walker, 2010). It was only in the early 1990s that some of the groups involved in mediation came together to promote greater consistency in policy and practice, but tensions have remained between them.

Walker traces the parliamentary discussions that preceded enactment of the Family Law Act, observing that 'the primary focus was not on dispute resolution as such, but on the role of mediation in helping parties to communicate better, to reduce conflict between themselves and to make arrangements for the future' (2001: 405).

Referring to the low take-up of mediation following the pilot information meetings prescribed under the Family Law Act, she suggests that a change in strategy might help. 'Governmental concerns [over the low take-up] require consideration of whether information meetings or information provision in some other form could and should be attempting to divert people along certain pathways, or whether, as in the pilots, it is more appropriate and acceptable to provide objective information which equips people to make better informed choices' (2000: 412). 'If a diversionary approach is favoured, this would shift the provision of information away from being presented in the form of a "technical guide", as in the pilots, towards it being presented as an unashamedly persuasive "consumer manual" which attempts to "sell" mediation as the preferred route through the divorce process.' Nonetheless, 'even if these shifts were made, there would still need to be a greater sense of realism about just how many couples could and would use mediation effectively' (2000: 412).

Rosenberg (1992), influenced by studies demonstrating that the take-up of mediation was low, hypothesises that the people who chose mediation were likely to be those willing to try something new and who had a college education and a relatively high income and status, indicating the relevance of socio-economic factors. He argues in favour of a mandatory process (Kressel and Pruitt, 1989).

As general family mediation developed, certain members of National Family Mediation (NFM) felt there was a need for more 'culturally sensitive mediation', and a task force made up of a few trainers associated with NFM was set up.[2] According to Tony Whatling, an NFM trainer, the task force produced a two-day training module, which initially taught about different faiths on the basis of assumptions about what it *meant* to be somebody (for example, 'what it means to be a Muslim,' or 'what it means to be a Hindu'). That in itself left the module open to serious challenge. Also, once the training module was being used, other problems began to emerge. It was found that the module was too heavily focused on race and ethnicity. The other major flaw was the assumption that if someone learnt something about Islam, then he or she would know how to act towards somebody in an 'Islamic' manner. Whatling observed, that this did not work, as 'there are 20, 30, 40 different subcultural groups: maybe 20 to 25 different languages [alone] within the Indian culture'. Whatling did not mention the complexities created by the diverse countries and continents from which Muslims come, nor the significant differences between Sunni and Shia Muslims, and further subdivisions within those communities of Islam.

Even in an area like Hounslow, where the majority of the Muslims are from the Sunni branch of Islam, there are a number of significant differences within the branch: Hanafi versus Shafi; Deobandi versus Barelwi; Mirpuri versus Kashmiri; early immigrants versus indigenous, locally born Muslims. There are also differences between Sunni and Shia; and further, within the Shia branch, itself, there are Ismailis, Ithna Asharis, Zaidis and Bohras. Spanning both the branches of Islam, there are also Sufis – those who follow an esoteric path emphasising the spirit rather than the letter of the scriptural text.

The trainers began to question the very content of the course, with its major focus on race and ethnicity, and came to realise that what was needed was understanding of diversity and difference, which could be within the same racial group as much as across racial and ethnic divides. Therefore, according to Whatling, mediators should be just as concerned and just as challenging of themselves about gender differences *within* the same ethnic group as they are about inter-ethnic differences. The trainers then decided to introduce into their core training programme elements of mediating diversity, that is, differences relating to class and culture and what it means to be from, say, Northern Ireland as compared with coming from Somerset. According to Whatling, the NFM instilled a sensibility in mediators 'to find out from them [the disputants] what it is in their culture that is going to have an impact on their ability to separate as a couple in legal terms [as well as in] social and religious terms.'

The NFM soon realised that cultural assumptions did not hold water and that mediators needed to have an understanding of the generational level of the person to whom they were talking. As one Muslim female mediator from the Midlands explained, within 'the course of a single day, I needed to change my whole world-view, depending on whether I was talking to my grandparents, my parents or my siblings'. Muslims, generally, would expect another Muslim to know instinctively how to interact with different generations and they would be more forgiving of a European mediator who did not know the nuances. To quote Whatling, 'As long as they [non-Muslims] were respectful and as long as they would ask the appropriate questions about culture, about, if necessary, the religious divorce compared with the legal divorce, then the Muslims would be happy to "teach" an outsider what he or she needed to know, in order to help them.' Whatling constantly emphasises that 'one has to be sensitive, to be respectfully enquiring, to be constantly learning, to be asking our clients to teach us what it is *we* need to know [from them] in order to help them. By and large, they will respect you for that.' In a sense, mediation is an in-depth conversation between all the parties, which implies a level of trust.

As a consequence of the work of a cross-cultural mediation task force set up by the NFM, the UK College of Family Mediators (now the UK College of Mediators) adopted a set of principles and practice rules, which include issues such as gaining insights into attitudes to conflict, marriage, divorce, child upbringing, property, finance, family structure, role of family members and expectations. The list also includes issues such as community values, legal issues, immigration and its impact, religious values and structures of religious communities – the role of teachings, elders and religious leaders. Whatling's experience in the Peterborough area of England was that Muslims 'were not at all sure that they would be understood if they went to a predominantly white mediation service or counsellor or any other number of help advisors. They were not sure that they would be understood in terms of cultural differences. They were not sure that they would be seen sympathetically.'

The initial endeavour to provide mediators with deeper cross-cultural insight was frustrated by various factors, such as inappropriate course content, apathy and lack of adequate resources. According to Whatling, not many people these days can afford to give the amount of time required for this type of specialisation. Nor can many people spare the time required for training and upgrading. In addition, trainees themselves have to pay the costs of a supervisor to help them gain accreditation with the UK College of Mediators. Many mediators do only one session per week or per fortnight, so the financial burden is very high.

On the Muslim side, the take-up of family mediation is low, probably due to factors such as insufficient familiarity with mediation, lack of trust in outside mediators, and passivity coupled with cultural inhibitions. The Sisyphean task of making Muslims more family-mediation friendly could legitimately be seen to be deeply discouraging. However, it is a task that needs to be carried out if we are to make mediation more acceptable in the Muslim community. Such an endeavour could be initiated by respected elders of the community, such as, for example, mosque trustees. This is very much an educational issue – how to get those leaders to go and see how ADR actually works so that they can familiarise themselves with its processes, and to discuss with them the pros and cons of their respective communities in order to convince them that ADR is useful to them.

This book has identified the different dimensions of interpersonal disputes among diasporic Muslims with which ADR practitioners need to be familiar to increase their effectiveness in such a setting. If national non-Muslim mediators are unfamiliar with some of these aspects, they will be inhibited from extending their mediatory services to British Muslims; on the Muslim side, it will result in lack of confidence in, and therefore reluctance to go to, non-Muslim mediatory services. Worse still, it may make mediation appear to be a foreign intervention, one not worth embracing.

Implications for Muslims in Britain

British Muslims, like all other diasporic Muslims, are undergoing multiple transitions through the process of rapid acculturation. In such a situation, there is an understandable tendency to hold on to traditions in the face of relentless globalisation. Although this tendency may have been a bulwark in the past, it can become a source of conflict in the future. British Muslims need to develop their own structures to deal with interpersonal disputes. As a starting point, the communities' own traditional systems can be refurbished to make them more responsive to conflict at a more basic level.

This study found that the community in Hounslow has specific needs. By extrapolation, these can be extended to other areas of Britain. For example, there is a dire need for culturally sensitive counselling services. Though the study did not conduct a quantitative assessment of the depression caused by conflict, it is apparent that many people, particularly women, desperately need counselling help. This is also true with regard to intergenerational problems. Because of the culture of reluctance to air problems, the community needs to be socialised to resort to counselling services. That could be done in a three-step process: first, the community could be socialised to the value of counselling; then it could be encouraged to avail itself of the services offered by government agencies; finally, promising young men and women from within the community could be encouraged to become counsellors. Thus, the community would gradually develop a cadre of counsellors proficient in community languages and sensitive to its cultural mores.

The community could help to strengthen existing institutions that play a referral role. For example, the Muslim Women's Helpline (MWH) has gained extensive experience in telephone counselling and seems to have been effective in helping women in distress. The community could help the MWH with resources and develop meaningful links with it, without compromising the helpline's basic integrity with regard to confidentiality and so forth. The community could encourage a small group of promising counsellors to work with it on an internship basis each year. That would reinforce the MWH as well as help the interns to gain experience in the field while at the same time working in the community, and to apply their learning to the community, thus bridging counselling theory and practice.

A major resource that the community can avail itself of is the imams, who are in touch with the congregants on a daily basis. As this book has shown, the imams are the custodians of tradition and are trusted individuals. Moreover, counselling is a skill that would naturally appeal to them. Sending them for short university courses on counselling, which would enable them to combine their experience in the community with a new skill, could be of immense value to the Hounslow Muslims. The imams have expressed a wish for this type of training. For it to become possible, the mosque trustees would have to help finance the training and give the imams the necessary time off to pursue their studies. The benefits to the community would far outweigh the training costs. Bursaries could be given for specific studies at institutions such as Thames Valley University and Brunel University. The study also found that the imams in the Hounslow community, as elsewhere in the UK, are open to new learning influences and do reach out to the young. This is one area where the education of the imams is of vital importance to the health of the Muslim communities.

Training in mediation techniques would provide diasporic Muslims with a new language for communication with the younger generation. The community could also gain considerably from its young men and women being instructed in contemporary mediation techniques. Special training programmes could be set up through British training institutions. The Ismaili Muslim National Conciliation and Arbitration Boards' programme could be a good example for emulation, with suitable adaptation. The training programme could also utilise older community members as well as past and present mosque trustees who could share their experiences with younger potential dispute resolvers. In Hounslow, experienced police officers could be invited to share their experiences with potential young dispute resolvers. In addition, Muslim secular lawyers and some of the new, young, female Muslim solicitors in the area could teach aspiring mediators where and how ADR and the official laws of the United Kingdom intersect. MLSC personnel could share their experiences of the last 25 years and provide some insights into conflict prevention. Refresher programmes could be held once every two years to ensure that the dispute resolvers keep up to date with new ADR techniques and new knowledge in the field.

The trustees of the mosque could consider providing appropriate physical facilities to both men and women so that the mosque can play a more pivotal role in dispute resolution. These could include an office within the precincts of the mosque that affords adequate confidentiality and privacy. Additionally, a small committee could be set up to help disputants by referring them to appropriate fora. Consideration could also be given to the establishment of a Muslim refuge for battered women. Such a refuge could be run with the help of volunteers from within the community.

The Muslim community in Hounslow could help the MLSC in ways that would also benefit itself. The MLSC is overworked and under-resourced and a fair amount of its work at the primary level could be done at the community level. For example, counselling could be carried out at the community level provided there are suitably trained counsellors. In many cases, mediation could also be done within the community if the imams and some trustees were trained in it. In addition, and most importantly, the community could help the MLSC with resources so that it does not have to struggle constantly for adequate funding. This help should be given without compromising the MLSC's integrity as an independent institution that is able to dispense justice within the principles of the Sharia without becoming mired in any sectarianism or particular interpretations of the religious law on an exclusivist basis.

The MLSC itself needs to step back and take serious stock of its work over the past 25 years. Its processes need to be reviewed and upgraded through proper training and affiliation to regulatory bodies. For one, it needs to utilise the tools in the ADR toolbox more judiciously with a better sense of discernment, so that while it has the liberty to use whatever processual tool it feels is best able to deal with an issue, it does so consciously. The MLSC needs to be fully aware of the role its dispute resolvers are playing at any particular time. With proper training programmes, the UK College of Mediators would probably grant the MLSC the necessary accreditation as a single-faith ADR service.

Implications for government agencies
and policy-makers

There is a tendency today on the part of organisations dealing with law or alternative forms of dispute resolution to overlook field realities. A very public example of this occurred after the then Archbishop of Canterbury, Dr Rowan Williams, gave a speech in London on 7 February 2008, entitled 'Civil and Religious Law in England: a Religious Perspective'.[3] The Archbishop appeared to suggest that the introduction in Britain of some aspects of Islamic law was unavoidable. That particular section of his speech was given extensive and sensational media coverage, leading to a major controversy in Britain over the issue. The Archbishop faced a torrent of criticism, with some newspapers even calling for his resignation. His comments were condemned by Downing Street, the Conservatives and the Chairman of the government's Equalities and Human Rights Commission, among others. In an interview with the BBC on the same day as his speech, Dr Williams noted that some provisions of the Sharia were already recognised under British law and that Orthodox Jews were allowed to use their own courts to settle some issues on the basis of religious law.

Hounslow is not the only area in Britain where Sharia law is applied among Muslims in some situations today. On 10 February 2008, the Dubai newspaper *Gulf News* reported that the Islamic Council in Leyton had handled over 7000 divorce cases. Other councils in areas with high Muslim populations, including Dewsbury in West Yorkshire, Birmingham, and Rotherham in South Yorkshire, also apply Sharia law in family disputes though it is not recognised under the laws of the United Kingdom.

The *Khaleej Times*, another leading Dubai newspaper, reported on 10 February 2008 that at least 10 Islamic courts, dealing mainly with divorce or financial disputes, operate in Britain. An editorial in the *Gulf News* of 10 February 2008 entitled 'Ignorance of the Law Is No Defence' commented that the furore surrounding the Archbishop's comments 'demonstrates more than anything else that either people did not hear the broadcast, have not read a transcript of the interview, do not understand Sharia law or are unaware of the present situation in British religious society'.

The newspaper noted that Dr Williams had not called for the introduction of Sharia law into England's civil or criminal law. What he had actually said was: 'as a matter of fact, certain provisions of Sharia are already recognised in our society and under our law'. When asked if 'the application of Sharia in certain circumstances – if we want to achieve this cohesion and take seriously peoples' religion – seems unavoidable,' he had agreed.

The *Gulf News* observed that 'What Dr Williams is calling for is not English civil and criminal law becoming Sharia law, but the acceptance of certain Sharia practices being acknowledged and accepted by the English and Welsh and Scottish Courts of law, as already exists with Jewish communities, which have long-established religious community courts.' This study concurs with Dr Williams' viewpoint, with the caveat that the acceptance of some Sharia principles should be subject to the public laws of such jurisdictions and subject also to a proper regulatory framework being put in place. However, it is not clear why the Archbishop chose to make an issue of principle out of the pragmatic evolutionary approach adopted by English courts. It is doubtful whether the majority of the Muslim population in the UK were in favour of the position taken by the Archbishop, and it can be argued that it has done some harm to the status of Muslims in the UK who already suffer from an endemic form of Islamophobia that is kept alive by media reports and bias.

In July 2008, the Lord Chief Justice, Lord Philipps of Worth Matravers, backed the Archbishop's suggestion, saying: 'It is possible in this country for those who are entering into a contractual agreement to agree that the agreement shall be governed by law other than English law'. He said he could see no reason why the Sharia should not be used to settle disputes in the UK. 'There is no reason why principles of Sharia, or any other religious code, should not be the basis for mediation or other forms of alternative dispute resolution'.[4] Politicians responded by expressing fear that at a time of heightened tensions, encouraging Muslims to live by their own distinct rules could make it harder for different communities to integrate.[5]

Regardless of the debate, it seems that ADR is here to stay. If it is going to be a wave of the future and an integral part of civil society, greater resources need to be allocated to the training of mediators, both nationally as well as within various communities. Government policy could be geared towards ensuring greater training opportunities for all mediators, with faith communities being asked to make a financial contribution to their own training programmes. The Hounslow Muslim community would most likely be receptive to such an idea. The mosque trustees, the imams, the consulting solicitor and some other members of the community have shown a willingness to set up a community mediation training programme. Cross-cultural training could also be made available to the police to increase their awareness of the needs of the different diasporic communities with whom they are working.

Most importantly, the Government needs to consider the possibility of appropriate regulatory frameworks for Muslim mediation in order to ensure that informal justice in their dispute resolution fora does not unwittingly degenerate into inferior justice. This is also salient in the case of other faith-based arbitration systems where religious laws are applied and where there are often concerns about potential human rights violations. The training and upgrading of mediators should be given the same importance as in other service professions in the United Kingdom. Community mediators could be given 'single-faith' accreditation by the UK College of Mediators, which would formally entitle them to provide services exclusively within their own communities as volunteers. Those who want to make a full-time career in mediation could also develop further skills and serve the wider public.

Implications for law schools and universities

Law schools in the United Kingdom would benefit considerably by providing teaching programmes on both law and ADR that encompass more cross-cultural dimensions. British and overseas law students could be required to do ADR at the LLB level as a compulsory subject, which would temper the overall culture of over-reliance on the adversarial approach that permeates modern legal educational thinking.

Law students could be encouraged to take courses on religious laws, such as Islamic law and Jewish law, and to try to understand their rich diversity of interpretations and the various cultural mores that impact on dispute resolution, including the role of forgiveness and the power of apology in different cultures. These subjects should be taught in a *creative* way, not as monumental relics to be reified but as living organisms interfacing on a daily basis with different branches of national laws such as family law, contract law, conflict of laws and comparative law. Appropriate modules on ADR and Islam could draw on the rich experience of various Muslim communities across Britain, highlighting the Qur'anic inspiration with regard to negotiated settlement and how principles embedded in Muslim juridical thought are actually played out in the ADR processes in various communities in a diasporic setting.

Universities could also conduct more purposive research on Muslims and ADR in the United Kingdom and make scholarships available to students to do field research among various Muslim communities. Such research could draw upon the experiences of indigenous Muslim institutions such as the United Kingdom Sharia councils, helplines and others in order to gain insight into what is happening in Muslim institutions that are involved in dispute resolution.[6] Very little is known about, or has been written on, issues such as *mahr*, child abduction in Muslim communities, and generally about the Sharia, in a language that is comprehensible to the average dispute resolver. Universities in cities with large Muslim populations, such as London, Bradford and Leicester, could develop meaningful linkages with Muslim communities in their vicinity and gain practical insights into their dispute resolution practices, learn from their experiences and help them devise appropriate training programmes.[7]

Implications for the legal profession and ADR practitioners and theorists

Finally, this study has important implications for legal practitioners, ADR agencies and the judiciary. Muslim diasporic interpersonal issues are complex and intertwined with the official law of the land, the Sharia and customary practices. In mediation, lawyers are called into the process at various stages to advise the parties on whether what they are negotiating is consonant with their overall rights and obligations. In some cases, lawyers practising within the United Kingdom legal system also have to advise on Sharia issues.

It would be valuable if lawyers were generally familiar with some of the issues that Muslims in diasporic settings confront when they have an interpersonal dispute. For example, not many lawyers are familiar with the concept of *mahr*, or know how child custody orders granted in the United Kingdom would be viewed in a Muslim country. The latter would be of importance because child abduction occurs occasionally, regardless of who has the *de facto* or *de jure* custody of the child. Familiarity with such issues could also increase the chances of settling such cases out of court. A short training course or module could be taught on some of these issues. Members of the judiciary, too, would benefit immensely from such a programme as they often have to rely on expert witnesses in such cases.

The ADR agencies, too, need to be more aware of Muslim laws, customs and practices. This study found minimal or no contact between them and the Hounslow mosque or the MLSC. In many aspects of mediation, the support of, for example, community elders could be elicited and issues such as *mahr* be allocated for determination to the MLSC; where reconciliation is still possible, the imam could be called upon to help. All these institutions could work in a synergistic manner without in any way undermining their own basic mandates or the mandates of those they are working with.

There are many advantages to providing ADR services for diasporic Muslim communities, but ADR can only work if there is a sustained effort among all the stakeholders to provide such services at the level of proficiency required to meet today's fast-evolving needs. ADR services for diasporic Muslims, who are by and large organised around their mosques, can be reinforced through some practical steps. ADR agencies need to make these communities more aware of the value of their services, to reduce resistance arising from misconceptions. For optimum effectiveness, this can be done jointly with the mosque imams, community elders and trustees. Community human resources have to be nurtured in a number of disciplines, such as law, sociology, counselling and mentoring, family therapy and communications.

ADR agencies need to investigate the possibilities of enabling their personnel to obtain further training, for example through courses offered at good universities in their vicinity. Community workers who enjoy the trust of members in the community as counsellors and mediators also need to be given formal training. Furthermore, mosque imams should be socialised to the value of mediated settlements so that they, in turn, can advise their congregations on the advantages of mediation vis-à-vis litigation.

The way forward

As a dispute resolving mechanism, mediation has enormous potential and the time to harness its full scope may now have arrived. As this book has shown, diasporic Muslims, because of the interface of their interpersonal issues with the laws and structures of Western society, may be better placed to bring about the necessary and appropriate synthesis between their religious heritage and their contemporary needs in a manner that is true to the ethics of their faith while at the same time in accordance with the principles of public law in the countries where they have settled. This synthesis would be of value to Muslim communities everywhere. In a knowledge society, and given the expectations of the youth in the Muslim world today, who are clamouring for a more effective civil society contributing to greater social justice, this seems to be a major way forward. The knowledge on which this synthesis is based has to be underpinned by a commitment to the ethical values that the faith enjoins, and which transcend both time and space, drawing inter alia on the wise words of Caliph-Imam Ali' when he says, 'No belief is like modesty and patience, no attainment is like humility, no honour is like knowledge, no power is like forbearance, and no support is more reliable than consultation'. Only a non-adversarial process like ADR with 'limitless remedial imagination' can engender such values and help disputants experience the transformative potential that conflict, which is an inevitable part of human life, often gives rise to.

Appendix

Some Perspectives on ADR

The contemporary discourse on ADR, and more particularly mediation, focuses heavily on the works of Western writers and not much is known of Muslim thinkers in the field. As this book shows, some important research by Western scholars touches on issues that are pertinent to Muslim ADR principles and practices, and some Muslim scholars have drawn from Western writers. The book draws from the work of both groups of writers. This Appendix provides more information on their contributions to the literature on ADR.

Views of Muslim writers on ADR

Some interesting and useful research has been done by a few Muslim writers in the Occident over the past decade.[1] The themes that emerge from these studies are that there is a need for a more indigenous model of dispute resolution for Muslim communities and that ADR practice should be founded on the essential higher values of the Sharia, that is, its message of justice, freedom and equality, through engagement of the community in the intervention and resolution processes. All the writers concerned also see value in integrating the scholarship that has been developed in Western countries with what is learnt in Muslim contexts, but not indiscriminately.

Abu-Nimer (1996) urges scholars and practitioners of ADR to be aware of procedures of conflict resolution already being applied in local communities. Such awareness would herald 'the acceptance and recognition of the proposition that Islam and Islamic societies contain beliefs, customs, attitudes and a history which can serve as rich bases for identifying constructive conflict resolution frameworks and processes'. He proposes integrating existing religious and social patterns with the appropriate concepts and experiences that can be derived from Western experience. Abu-Nimer sees a pressing need to examine the principles and procedures that exist within Islamic society – a process which he feels is still in its initial phase – and poses some important questions for exploration, such as: how does the Qur'an relate to the causes and types of conflicts, and what principles of conflict resolution are reflected in the Qur'an?

Abdalla (2001) highlights the relational dimension of conflict resolution within Muslim communities, compared with the highly individualistic, problem-solving, Western approach. While calling for judicious appropriation and adaptation of the Western models of dispute resolution, he exhorts Muslims to build upon the concepts of interdependence and their 'culture of relatedness', which are characteristic of their communities. He feels this should be done, to develop their own model with a view to restoring to Islam its message of justice, freedom and equality through engagement of the community in the intervention and resolution processes. Abdalla calls for exploration of Islamic sources, which, he says, are not limited to jurisprudence – *fiqh* – but attempt to operate within the larger Islamic worldview. For him, the challenge for Muslims 'is to restore to Islam justice and equality by liberating Islam from the doctrine and cultural elements which subjugated its followers to political and social oppression'.

Pakistani scholar M.A. Chaudhary shows how power dynamics are always at play in informal justice and that mediation has to always ensure that there is a level playing field. Analysing the resolution of disputes in a village in Punjab province, Pakistan, Chaudhary (1999) finds that, despite the existence of state laws, the villagers predominantly continue to utilise their own customary processes. While the state legal forums are expensive and slow and sometimes corrupt, in theory they follow the principle of 'the same law for all'. The traditional system, in contrast, is fast and cheap, but justice is provided according to the social status and position of the disputants. As the villagers put it, 'The one who owns the stick owns the buffalo', that is, might is right. The resolution of conflicts in the village is closely linked to the nature and type of conflicts.

Views of Muslim writers on Qur'anic interpretation

Over the last 25 years, some Muslim women scholars have questioned the correctness of interpretations of the Qur'an and the *sunna* (conduct of the Prophet) that are often used to justify cultural relegation of women.[2] Such liberal Islamic rethinking on the rights of women addresses, among other things, verses in the Qur'an that discuss male polygamy, men's unilateral rights to divorce, men's greater inheritance rights and the greater weight of male legal testimony, as well as parts of the *sunna* that discuss veiling, gender segregation and women's unsuitability for leadership of a Muslim community.

Kurzman observes that liberal Islamic scholars challenge these interpretations in three main ways. First, they re-examine the sources on which they are based, finding them less hostile to women's rights than previously supposed (Kurzman, 1998). They attribute women's position in early Islam to the persistence of pre-Islamic social customs in Arabia. For instance, Wadud Muhsin (1992) adopts this approach in extensive discussions of Qur'anic verses that are often interpreted to justify male domination over women. A similar argument has also been put forward by some male scholars, most famously Hasan Turabi, whose widely read 1973 pamphlet on women and Islam states that the seclusion of women and restriction of their rights is a result of customary misreadings of the Sharia.

In addition, some women scholars argue that the apparently limited rights given to women, while perhaps applicable to the conditions of seventh-century Arabia, are not suitable for other times and places. The controversial verses are then weighed against more liberal parts of the Sharia. For example, Zein-ed-Din (1998) suggests that God's Revelation permitted the continuation of pre-Islamic Arab customs such as polygamy and slavery only in order to ease the Arabs' transition to Islam, and that the Prophet intended to eradicate those customs but died before he could do so. Some women who use this logic accept the existence of seemingly misogynistic statements but contend that they do not prohibit women from organising to protect their rights. Thus, feminists in Iran have campaigned for and succeeded in having legislation passed requiring couples to sign a prenuptial agreement granting women divorce rights equal to men.

Some liberal scholars on women in Islam point to possible multiple interpretations of statements that seem to place women in an inferior social position. Instead of replacing an incorrect interpretation with a more faithful one, this approach contends that all interpretation is human and fallible. For example, Sharour (1998: 139-42) argues that 'jurisprudential ruling bears the historical stamp of the era in which it was created and the society in which it was shaped'. Writing in the same vein, Mernissi (1998) posits that following the Prophet's death, his companions, who are revered in Islamic scholarship as the source of testimony about the *sunna* of the Prophet, disagreed about certain religious injunctions concerning women. She cites the example of one Companion being hesitant to provide testimony for fear that his memory might be incorrect. Ruthven (1997: 113) regards this 'indigenous feminist' approach as a strategy to defuse the accusation that the Muslim feminist critique of Islamic attitudes is simply a 'Western-inspired' commentary.

All the above authors see a basic contradiction between the ethical principles of Islam, with its commitment to social justice regardless of gender, and the restrictions to which Muslim women became increasingly subjugated over time. Ahmed notes that, 'among the remarkable features of the Qur'an, particularly in comparison with the scriptural texts of other monotheistic traditions, is that women are explicitly addressed (1992: 64). One passage (30:35) 'declares by the very structure of the utterance, as well as in overt statement, the absolute moral and spiritual equality of men and women'. She also points to other Qur'anic verses, such as one declaring the identicalness of men and women and indicating the equal worth of their labour,[3] as being similar in their emphasis and thrust. There are 'two distinct voices within Islam, and two competing understandings of gender, one expressed in the pragmatic regulations for society [...] the other in the articulation of an ethical vision [...] the unmistakable presence of the ethical egalitarianism explains why Muslim women frequently insist, often inexplicably to non-Muslims, that Islam is not sexist. They hear and read in its sacred text, justly and legitimately, a different message from that heard by the makers and enforcers of orthodox, androcentric Islam' (Ahmed, 1992: 65-6).

Not all Muslim women scholars fit neatly into the above framework. A notable exception is Shah-Kazemi (2000), whose focus is on the cultural dimension of mediation in family disputes. She notes that the question of how individuals view disputes and their resolution through the prism of their cultural identity is often neglected by mediators from outside the community to which the disputants belong. For her, it is often precisely within the parameters of a marital relationship that individuals are motivated to practise their normative ethics.

Other perspectives on ADR

Many issues in this book cross the cultural divide, and the work of Western authors has proved useful as a prism through which to see the empirical data more clearly. Several trends are noteworthy in their work. First, they recognise that the field of ADR is richer for its multiple insights and sensitivity to the interactive effects of law and legal institutions with other social institutions. 'We will not be cabined to teaching from law and legal theory alone' (Menkel-Meadow, 2003: 3). Second, they consider the social and cultural contexts to be important (Abel, 1973; Avruch, 1998; Nader and Todd, 1978). Third, they call for solutions beyond choosing between two obvious alternatives: 'We hurt ourselves whenever we see ourselves imprisoned' in an 'either-or-situation' (Graham, 1993). As Follett (1996) puts it, 'integrative' solutions require innovation and imagination, requiring dynamic, participative and creative problem-solving'. The fourth trend is exemplified by Fuller (1971), who postulates that the conciliatory process, which does not require a decision based on state-made law, would help reorient disputing parties to each other and bring about a harmonious relationship between them. Last, adjudication is unsuitable in situations where a 'decision on one legal issue might unravel other interrelated issues or relationships' (Fuller, 1971: 326).

The concept of trust is critical to this present study. In this connection, Gadlin and Davis (1998), Govier (1998) and Le Baron (2002), though not directly related to ADR in Muslim societies, are highly pertinent for Muslims because they touch on issues that are also relevant to them as a result of what is said about such concepts in the Qur'an.

Gulliver (1979) provides an excellent review of the multi-disciplinary literature on negotiations, distilling the findings of empirical studies drawn from various cross-cultural studies and labour negotiations to develop a general theory of negotiation processes. He essentially tries to specify the structure of processes that occur in all negotiations, regardless of subject matter or culture. However, his discounting of cultural influences has attracted criticism from Shah-Kazemi (2000), whose views on the importance of cultural factors in ADR are mentioned in the Appendix.

A number of authors see dangers in informal provision of justice on an extensive scale. For example, Fiss (1984) suggests that if too many cases are diverted from the courtroom into settlement, appellate judges will have an insufficient number and quality of cases on the basis of which to make law. If true, argues Menkel-Meadow (2003: 198) that 'could have grave implications for the legitimacy of the entire legal system'. A critical question posed by her is whether new forms of dispute resolution will transform the courts, or whether, in a more likely scenario, the power of our adversarial system will co-opt and transform the innovations designed to redress problems in the justice system.

Partly because of the institutionalisation of ADR, some of its earliest proponents, including anthropologist Laura Nader, now oppose it because it does not foster communitarian and self-determination goals. Instead, it is used to restrict access to the courts for some groups, just at a time when these less-powerful groups have achieved some legal rights (Menkel-Meadow, 2003). Some critics have argued that ADR actually hurts those who are less powerful in society, for example, women (Delgado et al., 1985; Grillo, 1991) or racial or ethnic minorities.

However, many have argued against such criticisms, particularly Kelly and Gigy (1988, 1989) who found that some 75 per cent of men and women in their sample agreed that mediators are skilful, show concern for disputants' feelings, provide sufficient information, help identify important issues and remain impartial. Furthermore, in another sample, 82 per cent of women and 71 per cent of men felt that the mediator helped them protect their individual rights. Indeed, women were significantly more likely than men to say that mediation gave them an opportunity to express their point of view and helped them put aside their anger and focus on their children's needs (Kelly and Duryee, 1992). No evidence exists that women as a group tend to fare worse in negotiations as a result of their greater interest in cooperation and maintaining good relationships (Rosenberg, 1992). Nor are women more likely than men to drop out of mediation. A survey by Kressel and Pruitt (1989) found that when parents were required to accept mediation (even when they would have preferred not to) between 75 and 85 per cent were satisfied with the process and glad that they had been ordered to participate.

Menkel-Meadow (2003) takes a number of major precepts from the intellectual founders that have greatly informed the field of dispute resolution, some of which are given here. She views conflict as good and a potential source of creativity, which, if handled appropriately, can put the parties in a better position than they were before the conflict arose. Good resolution of conflicts and problems in the law occurs when people realise that valuing different things differently is good; that money need not be a proxy for everything. She notes that different dispute-resolution processes require different approaches; for example, in disputes that involve several interrelated issues, mediation or negotiated consensus may be better than a single-issue, externally imposed decision. Competitive behaviour and outcomes are more probable when single issues are at stake; and integrative or problem-solving processes and outcomes are more likely when multiple issues are at stake or when parties can exploit differential value structures or needs. Thus, creative solutions and integrative outcomes may be achieved by exploring different values and underlying interests. Menkel-Meadow observes that there are no universal processes that will always be better, fairer or more efficient than others.

Both Menkel-Meadow (2003) and Fisher et al. (1991) consider the communal context important. Menkel-Meadow regards dispute processes as part of the larger culture in which they are embedded and as contributing to the creation of a community's sense of self. Fisher et al. describe 'a wise agreement [...] as one which meets the legitimate interests of each side to the extent possible, resolves conflicting interests fairly, is durable, and takes community interests into account'.

Asking whether mediation is intended to do anything more than help facilitate solutions to disputes or problems, Menkel-Meadow cautions that mediators need to be realistic. For her, 'the grandiose claims made on behalf of mediation have had to be more modestly stated as the analyses and evaluations of our work have demonstrated that parties do not always share the transformative visions of the mediators – they just want their problems solved' (Menkel-Meadow, 2003: 190).

She deprecates the 'limited remedial imagination of courts' and posits a problem-solving model, asking negotiators 'to think of categories of human needs – legal, economic, social, psychological, religious, moral and political – to be considered in each case to maximise the number of interests that might be pursued and thus to avoid, as much as possible, having to divide single conflicting demands' (Menkel-Meadow, 2003: 277).

She believes that the current theoretical and practical technology of ADR approaches to legal problems would be better described as 'appropriate' dispute resolution, than 'alternative' dispute resolution. Matching different techniques with different goals can help in assessing what process is most appropriate for accomplishing the outcome that is best suited to the particular kind of problem. Finally, she says that if ADR practitioners take multiculturalism seriously, both domestically and internationally, they must avoid legal ethnocentrism that is already threatening some international ADR processes as well as public interest work in other nations.

With regard to the qualities required of a mediator, while American legal culture seems to prefer a 'neutral' who is supposedly impartial, non-partisan, and objective with respect to the parties and the dispute itself, some historical forms of ADR prefer engaged, enmeshed and totally involved third parties to act as arbitrators or mediators. These third parties serve as 'wise persons' who know the community, the nature of the dispute, the disputants, or all three (Auerbach, 1983; Shapiro, 1981).

Notes

Chapter 1.   Introduction

1. A Muslim woman can, of course, marry a non-Muslim in the United Kingdom without an Islamic divorce. However, such a marriage might not be accepted by some Muslim countries, which could then leave her vulnerable to a charge of adultery were she to go to those countries.

2. There are two major branches in Islam, Shi'i and Sunni. The Shia believe that Ali succeeded the Prophet Muhammad (peace be upon him and his progeny) in order to continue to safeguard and interpret the Divine Revelation as Imam, a role that was to pass on to a designated successor from among his sons and their descendants. The Sunnis, who comprise the majority in Islam, recognise the first four caliphs as legitimate rulers and successors to the Prophet.

3. 'Imamia' here refers to the Shi'i Ithna-Ashari community.

4. Zaki Badawi passed away in January 2006.

5. Tradition or report of a saying or action of the Prophet Muhammad.

6. Singular, *beth din*.

7. This information about the Divorce (Religious Marriages) Act 2002 was kindly provided by Ian Edge, Barrister at Law and Director of the Centre of Islamic and Middle East Law, Law Department, SOAS.

8. As of February 2013, 187 countries have ratified the Convention.

9. According to Rauf (2000: 35) and Coulson (1964: 60) *ijtihad* is often translated as interpretation or interpretive effort. In its broadest sense, it means the use of human reason in elaboration of the law and covers a variety of mental processes, ranging from interpretation of texts to assessment of the authenticity of the Prophetic Traditions.

10. This school emerged in Kufa, Iraq, under the eponym of Abu Hanifa (d. 767) but was developed by his students Abu Yusuf (d. 798) and al-Shaybani (d. 805).

11. Al-Shafi'i (d. 822) was the eponymous founder of this school. He demanded the use of systematic reasoning without arbitrary or personal deduction in formulating the law and thus created a system

that was far more cohesive on a theoretical level than had previously been the case.

12. The Southall Black Sisters was established in 1979 to meet the needs of Asian-Caribbean and African-Caribbean women. It has helped thousands of women facing domestic violence and abuse. In addition to providing welfare services and support, it runs campaigns to highlight and bring about changes in the social, political, economic and cultural conditions of women in need.

13. The in-house scholar of the MLSC spoke personally to some of the disputants on more than one occasion to ascertain whether they would participate, with the guarantee of complete anonymity, but they declined to do so. Many of them said they had moved on in life and did not want to revisit their past since the dispute which made them relevant to this study had not been a pleasant experience.

14. Some of their major findings are summarised in the Appendix, along with a broad outline of ADR as expounded by non-Muslim scholars.

15. Both Jack Straw's and Philip Hollobone's comments are from 'Champion of UK Burka Ban Declares War on Veil-wearing Constituents', *The Independent*, 17 July 2010.

16. The comments are from Wilders' speech during a function organised for him at the House of Lords premises in London on 5 March 2010. <http://www.geertwilders.nl/index.php?option=com_content&task=view&id=1662&Itemid=1>, accessed on 5 October 2010. The coalition government parties in the Netherlands had failed to win a majority in the Lower House of Parliament, so they signed a 'conditional support agreement' with Wilders under which the MPs of Wilders' party, *Partij voor de Vrijheid* (Party for Freedom) would vote with the ruling coalition as long as the government implemented some of the policies favoured by Wilders. Thus, although the government says it disagreed with his stance on Islam, his statements carried more weight than they would otherwise.

Chapter 2. The Muslim Community in Britain

1. Sufis are those who have chosen the path of mystical understanding and devotion to God. Sufism is the spiritual dimension of Islam.

2. For 2011 census see http://www.ir/detail/2012/12/12/277699/Muslim/. Accessed 14 December 2012.

3. *Umma* literally means 'people'. The term occurs many times in the Qur'an to refer to the people of a religious community, such as the '*umma* of Abraham'. The word has now come to represent the concept of the Muslim community as a whole.

4. 'British Muslims Want Islamic Law and Prayers at Work', *The Guardian,* 30 November 2004. <www.Guardian.co.uk/uk_news/ story/0,,1362533,00.html>. Accessed on 20 February 2005.

5. However, it differs from the Christian notion of marriage; Christians view marriage as a sacrament, whereas for Muslims it is a form of contract with obligations attached to it.

6. Divorce obtained by a wife when she gives, or agrees to give, a consideration to the husband for her release and the husband accepts the offer.

7. For the purposes of this research, a mixed marriage is where one party is Muslim and the other non-Muslim.

8. For an elucidation of this, see Keshavjee (2011).

9. http://www.policyresearch.org.uk/publications/policy-focus/214-census-2011-first-releaseof-data. Accessed 15th December 2012.

10. The Muslim Women's Helpline was established in 1989 to help Muslim women who felt that existing services were not meeting their requirements. It is an independent, voluntary organisation which maintains confidentiality. It provides a listening service, an emotional support service, Islamic counselling, referrals to Muslim and other consultants, and practical help.

Chapter 3.   Overview of the Hounslow Muslim Community

1. <http://www.statistics.gov.uk/census2001/profiles/00at.asp>. Accessed on 22 July 2002.

2. 'Forces Used Millions of Champion Plugs', *Middlesex Chronicle,* 6 April 1946.

3. For example, a speech by E.S. Adamson of the Conservative Central Office to Brentford and Chiswick ex-servicemen, reported in the *Brentford and Chiswick Times,* 21 February 1947.

4. People from the Pakistani side of the disputed territory of Kashmir.

5. People from the Mirpur district of Pakistan Punjab, many of whom were displaced when the Mangla Dam was constructed in the 1960s. A large number of those received compensation, which they used to migrate to Britain.

6. During afternoon prayers at the mosque, I found the congregation, which averaged around 60 people, to be largely made up of people of Pakistani origin; in addition, there were some Arabs, Somalis and East Europeans.

7. The *biraderi* is best understood as a context-dependent idea rather than a rigid, well-defined entity. Thus, besides its local manifestation as a network of co-resident kin, it may also include relatives

elsewhere in Britain, and at its widest extent, may span several countries and include members resident in Britain, Pakistan and the
Middle East. When only a few members live locally, a family may
well consider its transnational network of relatives as constituting its
biraderi (Alavi, 1972).

8. The Pakistan Welfare Association was founded in the 1960s. Among
other things, it helped people to file tax returns, find suitable marriage partners and resolve family disputes.

9. According to one elder, in his 36 years of service he has dealt with
hundreds of cases; in about 50 to 60 per cent of them the conflicts
were resolved.

10. Muslim parents' attempts to control their children's marriages continue to be the focus of considerable controversy in Britain because
of the grey area that exists between 'arranged' and 'forced' marriages. See Bradford Congress (1996: 21) and Home Office (2000)
for elaboration on this. The latter report, of the Working Group
on Forced Marriage, recommended that forced marriage be treated
like domestic violence or child abuse. In November 2001, a Home
Office Minister declared that government initiatives in this area
were not a move against Muslim traditions but a human rights issue.

11. 'About Turn in Mosque Plan', *Middlesex Chronicle*, 26 March 1986.

12. When I asked the imam why he had delivered this homily on a
weekday, the imam responded that two people in the congregation
had had a heated altercation in the mosque the previous night. Since
they were both in the mosque that day, he wanted to send a gentle
message to them.

13. They requested anonymity and have been given pseudonyms for this
account.

14. The five obligatory tenets of the faith: belief in one God and
Muhammad as His last and final Messenger; *salat*, or prayer; *sawm*,
or fasting during the month of Ramadan; *zakat*, often translated as
'poor due' or 'charity'; and *hajj*, the pilgrimage to Makkah, to be performed at least once in a lifetime if possible.

15. The Qur'anic term for marriage and the rules governing it.

16. However, they are not typical of all young Muslims, many of whom
have little education.

17. 'Young, Muslim and British', *The Guardian*, 30 November 2004,
pp. 17–20.

18. 'British Muslims Want Islamic Law and Prayers at Work', *The
Guardian*, 30 November 2004, <www.Guardian.co.uk/uk_news/
story/0,,13625533,00.html>. Accessed on 15 January 2005.

19. This has not so much a linear correspondence to their being second-generation British-born Muslims as to the fact that, with the
process of acculturation over four decades, the problems leading to

disputes within, and between, families have changed radically and become much more complex.

Chapter 4.   The Sharia, Religious Law of Muslims

1. The word 'Sharia' is often conflated with 'fiqh' – Islamic jurisprudence. However, there is an important difference between them: while the former is considered divine and immutable, the latter is a man-made construct and subject to change. For further elaboration, see Badawi (1995: 73).
2. *Wakf* is an endowment or trust stipulated for a specific purpose. It represents the manner of institutionalising the philanthropic aspect of Islam, by which a Muslim gives property or wealth to be used in perpetuity for a specified cause, such as a school, mosque, hospital or any other humanitarian purpose.
3. Literally, 'roots of understanding'. The *usul al-fiqh*, comprising the Qur'an, *sunna*, *ijma* and *qiyas* (analogical reasoning), are the main sources of jurisprudence in Sunni Islam.
4. In addition to the main Sunni and Shia schools of law, there is the Ibadi school which is neither Sunni nor Shia and is followed by Ibadi communities who follow their own distinct interpretation of Islam. They are mainly found in Oman, the coastal areas of East Africa, the Mzab Valley of Algeria, the Nafus Mountains of Libya and the island of Jerba in Tunisia.
5. On the history and different communities of the Shia, see Halm (2004).
6. See also message of H. H. the Aga Khan to the International Islamic Conference, Amman, Jordan, 4–6 July 2005. <http://www.iis.ac.uk/view_article.asp?ContentID=105673>. Accessed on 22 November 2005.
7. The Abbasid dynasty of caliphs ruled from 750, through the era of the flowering of Islam, until 1258. They had lost any meaningful power some centuries earlier with the rise of the Buwayhids, a Shi'i Persian military dynasty which took over power in 945 and ruled until its overthrow by the Sunni Seljuq rulers in 1050.
8. A *fatwa* is a formal opinion rendered by a Muslim scholar having appropriate status and training. Such opinions may be sought from scholars who are known as *mufti* in the Sunni tradition and as *mujtahid* among the Shia, but are not necessarily binding. The practice of issuing a *fatwa* has continued in modern times as a mechanism for dealing with personal, social, legal and religious issues.
9. Various *ayat*s in the Qur'an exhort the believer to behold the signs of God and to try to understand them. For example, (2:164) states: 'Behold! In the creation of the heavens and the earth; in the alternation of the night and the day; in the sailing of the ships through the

ocean for the profit of mankind; in the rain which Allah sends down from the skies, and the life which He gives therewith to an earth that is dead; in the beasts of all kinds that He scatters through the earth; in the change of the winds, and the clouds which they trail like their slaves between the sky and the earth; (here) indeed are signs for a people that are wise.' See also 3:108; 3:109; 41:53; 10:5 and 10:6 for similar references.

10. Abdul Wahid Hamid, 'Companions of the Prophet', vol. 1. <http://web. umr-edu/-msaumr/reference/companions/>. Accessed on 15 October 2004.

11. However, there continues to be much controversy about whether 'the closure of the gate of *ijtihad*' actually occurred or whether it is a rationalisation to explain the ossification of law over a period of time. See Hallaq (1984: 3–41).

12. This was the codification of the basic law of obligations (mainly Hanafi) that was undertaken by scholars of the Ottoman Empire in 1876 as part of the Tanzimat reforms.

13. Translated by Hamilton (1979: 343).

14. *The Sunday Times*, 29 October 2006.

15. *Ratio decidendi* is the reasoning on the basis of which a particular decision is made in a case. The case itself thus becomes part of the corpus of case law.

16. For an elaboration on how *fatwa*s are used online, see Bunt (2003) and Eicklemann and Anderson (1999).

17. There are four Hudood ordinances in Pakistan. They were promulgated by the former President Zia-ul Haq in 1979 and discriminate against women; for example, only the evidence of males is acceptable in cases where a woman is accused of a sexual offence.

Chapter 5.   The Muslim Law (Shariah) Council (UK)

1. Unless otherwise specified, all information and quotations from Zaki Badawi are from interviews with him between 2002 and 2005.

2. *The Tablet*, 4 February 2006. In any case, this is a title that he could not have held in a non-Muslim state.

3. In this context, a Pareto-optimal situation is one where it is no longer possible for either party to make gains at the expense of the other party.

4. *Takhayur* is akin to legal pluralism; that is, the process of selecting a course of legal action from the various juristic opinions of the different *madhaib*.

5. In this connection, the United Kingdom-Pakistan Protocol on Child and Family Law, a bilateral agreement dealing with the issue

of transnational child abduction, was signed by senior judges of the two countries in January 2003. Pakistan, like many Islamic countries, is not a party to the Hague Convention on the Civil Aspects of International Child Abduction 1980. See also Keshavjee (2011).

6. *Al Midani and another* v. *Al Midani*, which concerned an inheritance dispute. The case is elaborated in Chapter 7.

7. *Nikah* is an Islamic marriage ceremony largely by way of recital of a marriage contract. It may be, but is not always, preceded or followed by a civil ceremony under the laws of the United Kingdom.

Chapter 6.   The Many Faces of ADR in Hounslow

1. One of the imams refers to the following *hadith* about helping a non-practising Muslim whenever he needs assistance. A man had murdered many people in a city and then had repented and sought forgiveness. However, the people in the city could not forgive him and a pious man suggested that he migrate to another city where his past misdeeds would be forgiven more easily by the residents. Unfortunately, he died before arriving in that other city. The question then arose: could he be forgiven? Opinion was divided on this because he had not yet reached his destination and had only had the *intention* of transforming himself. The matter was referred to the Prophet, who advised that the position of the body should be checked to see if the man had travelled more than halfway to the destination city. When the distance to the body was measured, it was, indeed, found to be beyond the halfway point, indicating that he had been genuine about his repentance, and so the man was forgiven his past misdeeds.

2. During the process of dispute resolution, imams often cite the following Qur'anic *ayats*: 'All those who believe, be conscious of God and fear Allah and always speak the truth and be straightforward'; 'By this, Allah will make *sulh* [negotiated settlement] or reform between you both'; 'And Allah will forgive you, your shortcomings and sinfulness'; 'All those who obey the teachings of Allah, the Qur'an and the *sunna* [the teachings of the Prophet], they will be blessed with success and peace.'

3. I personally witnessed this while studying for my LLM at School of Oriental and African Studies. One of my student colleagues was an imam, then affiliated to the Hounslow mosque, who would frequently receive calls on his mobile phone from Muslim wives in the area asking about their Sharia rights after their husbands wanted them to leave the matrimonial home and the children. Also, when I had just begun the research for this study, while the MLSC *Alim* was

introducing me to the incumbent imam of the Hounslow mosque, an agitated man burst into the office and pleaded with the imam to help him in a matrimonial matter. He said his in-laws had obtained an injunction restraining him from contacting his estranged wife, who was a banker.

4. College of Mediators (2008).

5. Nevertheless, I did glean some information through third parties. For example, one young banker recalled the family's *biraderi* getting involved when his parents experienced marital problems which eventually resulted in divorce. He was too young then to fully understand the role they played, but in retrospect he realises that it was constructive and supportive.

6. One respondent estimated that Mirpuris (people from the Mirpur district of Pakistan Punjab) constitute about 25 to 30 per cent of the population in Hounslow.

7. In the course of conducting mediation training programmes in a number of countries, I have also come across this issue in the Ismaili Muslim National Conciliation and Arbitration Boards. The Board members, as dispute resolvers in a faith-based context, see an important part of their remit as 'reconciling' the parties rather than mediating their divorce. If 'reconciliation' fails, the parties are encouraged to go for either arbitration or mediation. If there is the slightest chance of saving the marriage, the parties are urged to do so.

8. See <http://www.relate.org.uk/Documents/Measuring_Outcomes_2008.pdf>. Accessed on 13 November 2008.

Chapter 7.   The Case for Court-Invoked Adjudication

1. [1965]1 QBD 390.

2. See also *Qureshi v. Qureshi* [1971] 2.W.LR 518, in which the institution of dower was virtually taken as judicially known. According to Pearl and Menski (1998), 'the absence of subsequent case reports may be taken as an indication that Shahnaz v. Rizwan is applied as the law on the subject'.

3. <http://www.bbc.co.uk/news/10469935>. Accessed on 28 November 2011.

4. Both quotations are from <http://www.bbc.co.uk/news/uk-scotland-15909237>. Accessed on 28 November 2011.

5. 2002. S.L.T 1255.

6. Section 23A (1) of the Act provides that subject to sections 1 and 2, and without prejudice to sec. 24 (1) of the Act, where the particulars of any marriage at the ceremony in respect of which both parties were present are entered in a register of marriages by, or at the behest

of, an appropriate registrar, the validity of that marriage shall not be questioned, in any legal proceedings whatsoever, on the ground of failure to comply with a requirement or restriction imposed by, under or by virtue of, the Act. Section 1 prescribes a minimum age for marriage, sec. 2 specifies forbidden degrees of relationship between the parties, and sec. 24 (1) specifies various criminal offences.

7. This case was mentioned in Chapter 1 as one of those referred to the MLSC.
8. 1999 2 FLR at 678.
9. Queen's Bench Division (Commercial Court) [1999] 1 Lloyd's Rep 923. It is not clear from the case report whether the 'Sharia Council' was the MLSC. However, an MLSC official confirmed to me on 20 September 2007 that Zaki Badawi had handled this matter.
10. *Reynolds* v. *United States*, 98 U.S. 145 (1878), pp. 108–9.
11. For a dissenting view, see S. Roberts (1998).
12. As noted earlier, the term 'angrezi shariat' was coined by Pearl and Menski (1998: 74) to describe what they perceive as a new form of Sharia specific to British Muslims, 'which remains officially unrecognised by the state but is now increasingly in evidence as a dominant legal force within the various Muslim communities in Britain'.

Chapter 8. Towards an Islamic Model of ADR

1. The Lord Chancellor, Lord Mackay of Cleshfern, Official Report (H.L.), 27 June 1996 at col. 1104.
2. This became evident in the Ismaili Muslim National Conciliation and Arbitration Boards training programme (which will be described later in this chapter). It was initially over-dependent on a module that focused on a Western satisfaction-seeking, problem-solving, individualistic model where reconciliation did not figure, and that created discomfort among dispute-resolution practitioners from 16 countries. Subsequent programmes incorporated this dimension and the teaching module was suitably modified with each successive rollout that took place. In Ismaili ADR practice, the possibility of reconciliation is explored at various stages in the dispute-resolving trajectory.
3. It must be emphasised that there is no one particular model of mediation as such. There are a number of models and practices based on thinking that has largely emerged in the Occident, and to that extent, most of those models take an individualistic, Western, satisfaction-seeking problem-solving approach.

4. Knowledge and experience gained from these programmes have been fed back into training programmes in the UK. See M. Roberts (2007: 157–8). Roberts taught in the initial NCAB programme in London; her book builds on the experience gained by her colleague Tony Whatling, who was the lead trainer in all the NCAB training rollouts globally.

5. In this connection, see Keshavjee (2010).

Chapter 9.   Policy Considerations

1. A fair number of anthropological studies were conducted in the twentieth century, contributing much to the development of ADR, but the most compelling ADR discourses have occurred only from the 1970s.

2. NFM was established with government funding as an umbrella body to support new family mediation services across the UK. It developed the first-ever national mediation training programme in the UK.

3. See <http://www.archbishopofcanterbury.org/1575>. Accessed on 1 March 2008.

4. <http:www.telegraph.co.uk/news/uknews/224340/Muslims-in-Britain-should-be-able-to-live-judge-html>. Accessed on 21 July 2008.

5. What promises to be an interesting addition to this debate is expected in April 2013, with the publication of *Islam and English Law: Rights, Responsibilities and the Place of Sharia*, a collection of papers edited by Robin Griffith-Jones. The papers, by 20 theologians, lawyers and sociologists, 'explore the evolution of English law, the implications of Islam, sharia and jihad, and the principles of the European Convention on Human Rights, family law and freedom of speech', according to the publisher Cambridge University Press.

6. This book focuses mainly on the work of one Sharia Council, the MLSC, based in London. For information on some of the others, see Samia Bano (2012) *An Exploratory Study of Shariah Councils in England with Respect to Family Law*, <www.reading.ac/nmsruntime/saveasdialog.aspxIID=80963>. See also J.R. Bowen (2011) 'How Could English Courts Recognise the Shariah?', *University of St. Thomas Law Journal* 7(3): 411-35.

7. See Keshavjee (2004).

Appendix.   Some Perspectives on ADR

1. For example, A. Abdalla (2001) 'Principles of Islamic Interpersonal Conflict Intervention: A Search Within Islam and Western Literature', *Journal of Law and Religion* 15 (1 and 2): 151-84; M. Abu-

Nimer (1996) 'Conflict Resolution in an Islamic Context: Some Conceptual Questions,' *Peace and Change* 21 (1): 22-40.

2. For example, F. Mernissi (1987) *The Veil and the Male Elite: A Feminist Interpretation of Women's Rights in Islam*, translated by Mary Jo Lakehead, Addison-Wesley Publishing Company, Reading, MA; A. Wadud Muhsin (1992) *Quran and Women*, Penerbit Pajar Bakti San Bhd., Kuala Lumpur; N. Zein-ed-Din (1998) 'Unveiling the Veil', in C. Kurzman (ed.) *Liberal Islam – A Sourcebook*, Oxford University Press, New York; M. Sharour (1998) 'Islam and the 1995 Beijing World Conference on Women', in C. Kurzman (ed.) *Liberal Islam – A Sourcebook*, Oxford University Press, New York; L. Ahmed (1992) *Women and Gender in Islam: Historical Roots of a Modern Debate*, Yale University Press, New Haven, CT.

3. 'I suffer not the good deeds of any to go waste, man or woman: The one of you is of the other' (3:195).

Glossary of Arabic, Persian and South Asian Terms

adula   Trusted elders from within the community.

ahl al Bayt 'People of the house'; a term referring to the family and descendants of the Prophet.

alim   A religious scholar, a learned man; from the root *ilm* (pl. *ulama*).

aql   Reason; intellect.

arkan   Pillars of the faith; includes *salat, sawm, hajj,* Ramadan, and *zakat* (alms giving).

*ayat*s   Verses of the Qur'an; also means 'signs' in creation that signify God's power and presence.

barakah   Blessings; a term often associated with spiritual Islam.

biraderi   Extended kinship networks.

darar   Harm, damage, prejudice. In the context of divorce, cruelty.

darura   Necessity; principles of law in understanding the Sharia.

din   Religion.

faqih   An expert on Islamic jurisprudence.

fatwa   A religious opinion issued by a *mufti*.

fiqh   Jurisprudence; outcome of legal methodology; positive law.

gharar   Uncertainty, risk, particularly in relation to commercial contracts.

gurudwara   Place of religious gathering for Sikhs.

hadith   'Tradition' or report of a saying or action of the Prophet Muhammad.

hajj   Pilgrimage to Makkah.

halal   Qur'anic term for that which is lawful and permissible for Muslims.

hejab   Veil or headscarf worn by Muslim women.

hisba   In its widest sense, the function of ensuring that the precepts of the Sharia are observed.

ibadat   Acts of worship.

iddat   A period of three menstruation cycles following the dissolution of an Islamic marriage.

ifta	An institution that issues a *fatwa*.
ijma	Consensus of opinion, normally of scholars on a religious or legal issue.
Ijtihad	To exert, to use one's mind in order to make meaning of something; by its very nature, it gives rise to reinterpretation of the law.
ikrah	Duress.
izzat	Honour.
juma	Friday; normally associated with Friday congregational prayers.
khula	A divorce that is available under Islamic law to a Muslim woman.
khutba	A sermon which is usually delivered on a Friday after congregational prayer.
maal	Property.
madhab	School of Islamic law.
madrassa	Institution for learning; school for religious instruction.
mahr	Dower right due to a wife under an Islamic marriage contract.
maqasid	Purpose; the higher value behind something.
maslaha	Public welfare/interest.
mazalim	Lit. 'complaints'. The prerogative jurisdiction exercised by political authorities.
muamalat	The relationship between Muslims, as opposed to *ibadat*, which demonstrates a Muslim's relationship to God.
mufti	Jurisconsult.
muhtasib	An official exercising the function of *hisba*.
mujtahid	Interpreter; one who exercises *ijtihad*.
muqallid	One who strictly follows a particular jurist or school of thought.
muslihun	Conflict resolvers; one who brings about *sulh*, negotiated agreement.
nazar fi'l-mazalim	Investigator of complaints about miscarriage of justice.
nikah	An Islamic marriage ceremony.
niqab	A black face-veil that covers the whole face except for the eyes.
pesh imam	Incumbent imam who leads daily prayers in a mosque.
pir	A spiritual head in a Sufi *tariqah*.
qadi	A judge appointed to implement Muslim law.
qiyas	Reasoning by analogy.
salat	Prayer.

sawm	Fasting during the month of Ramadan.
shahada	Fundamental testimony of truth in Islam: *La Ilaha Ilalah Muhammadur Rasulilah* (which states that there is no God but Allah and that Muhammad is His Messenger).
sharia	Lit. 'the way'; term used for Muslim Law.
sheikh	A community elder, respected wise man.
siyasa	Administrative law dealing with issues of governance and administration of the state.
sulh	Negotiated settlement.
sunna	The conduct of the Prophet.
tahkim	Arbitration.
takhayur	Legal pluralism; the process of selecting a course of legal action based on juristic opinions of different schools of law.
talaq	Divorce by unilateral revocation of marriage by a husband.
tariqah	Way, path, persuasion.
ulama	Body of religious scholars; pl. of *alim*.
umma	Community of believers; the Muslim community as a whole.
urf	Customary practice.
usul al-fiqh	Principles of jurisprudence; legal methodology.
waqf	A charitable endowment.
zakat	Often translated as 'charity' or 'alms giving'.
zina	Offence of illicit sexual relations.

Bibliography

Abdalla, A. (2001). 'Principles of Islamic Interpersonal Conflict Intervention: A Search Within Islam and Western Literature', *Journal of Law and Religion* 15 (1 and 2): pp. 151–84.

Abel, R. (1973). 'A Comparative Theory of Dispute Institutions in Society', *Law and Society Review* 8: pp. 217–347.

El-Ahdab, Abdul Hamid. (1993). *Arbitration Within the Arab Countries*. The Hague: Kluwer Law International.

Ahmad, K. (1974). *Family Life in Islam*. Leicester: The Islamic Foundation.

Ahmed, A. (2002). *Islam Today*. London: I.B.Tauris.

Ahmed, I. (2002). 'Communal Autonomy and the Application of Islamic Law', *Newsletter of the Institute for the Study of Islam in the Modern World* (October): p. 32.

Ahmed, L. (1992). *Women and Gender in Islam: Historical Roots of a Modern Debate*. New Haven: Yale University Press.

Ahsan, M. (1995). 'The Muslim Family in Britain', in Michael King (ed.) *God's Law Versus State Law: The Construction of an Islamic Identity in Western Europe*. London: Grey Seal Books, pp. 21–30.

Alami, D.S. and Hinchcliffe, D. (1998). *Islamic Marriage and Divorce Laws in the Arab World*. London, The Hague and Boston: Cimel and Kluwer Law International.

Alavi, H. (1972), 'Kinship in West Punjabi Villages', *Contributions to Indian Sociology*, New Series 14 (6): pp. 1–27.

Allott, A. (1980). *The Limits of the Law*. London: Butterworths.

Amin, S.H. (1989). *Islamic Law and Its Implications for the Modern World*. Glasgow: Royston.

Ansari, H. (2002). *Muslims in Britain*. London: Minority Rights Group.

Anwar, M. (1979). *The Myth of Return: Pakistanis in Britain*. London: Heinemann.

Anwar, M. (1991). 'Muslims in Britain: Some Recent Developments', *The Islamic Times* (July-September): p. 32.

Auerbach, J.S. (1983). *Justice Without Law*. New York and Oxford: Oxford University Press.

Augsburger, D. (1992). *Conflict Mediation Across Cultures: Pathways and Patterns*. Westminster: John Knox Press.

Avruch, K. (1998). *Culture and Conflict Resolution*. Washington, D.C.: United States Peace Press.

Badawi, Z. (1995). 'Muslim Justice in a Secular State', in Michael King (ed.) *God's Law Versus State Law: The Construction of an Islamic Identity in Western Europe*. London: Grey Seal Books, pp. 73–80.

Ballard, R. (1990). 'Migration and Kinship: The Differential Effects of Marriage Rule on the Processes of Punjabi Migration to Britain', in C. Clarke, C. Peach and S. Vertovec (eds) *South Asians Overseas, Migration and Ethnicity*. Cambridge: Cambridge University Press.

Ballard, R. (1994a). 'Introduction: The Emergence of Desh Pardesh', in R. Ballard (ed.) *Desh Pardesh: The South Asian Experience in Britain*, pp. 1–34, London: Hurst and Co.

Ballard, R. (ed.) (1994b). *Desh Pardesh: The South Asian Presence in Britain*. London: Hurst and Co.

Ballard, R. and Kalra, V.S. (1991). *The Ethnic Dimension of the 1991 Census: A Preliminary Report*. Manchester: Manchester Census Group.

Bhatia, P. (1973). *Indian Ordeal in Africa*. Bombay: Vikas Publishing House.

Blair, T. (2006). 'The Duty to Integrate: Shared British Values', speech given at the Runnymede Trust, 8 December, <http://www.number-10.gov.uk/output/Page10563.asp>, accessed on 2 May 2007.

Boyd, M. (2004). *The Boyd Commission Report 2004. Dispute Resolution in Family Law: Protecting Choice, Promoting Inclusion*. <http://www.attorneygeneral.jus.gov.on.ca/english/about/pubs/boyd>, accessed 5 May 2005.

Bradford Congress. (1996). *The Bradford Commission Report: The Report of an Inquiry into the Wider Implications of Public Disorders in Bradford Which Occurred on 9, 10 and 11 June 1995*. London: Stationery Office Books.

Bridgewood, A. (1986). 'Marriage, Women and Property: Turkish Cypriots in North London', PhD Thesis, University of London.

Bush, R.B. and Folger, J. (1994). *The Promise of Mediation: Responding to Conflict Through Empowerment and Recognition*. San Francisco: Jossey Bass.

Cameron, D. (2005). 'Speech given at Foreign Policy Centre', London, 24 August 2005, <http://fpc.org.uk/fsblob/560.pdf>, accessed on 2 May 2007.

Cashmore, J. and Parkinson, P. (2008). 'Children's and Parents' Perception on Children's Participation in Decision-Making after Parental Separation', *Family Court Review* 46 (1): pp. 91–104.

Chaudary, M.A. (1999). *Justice in Practice: Legal Ethnography of a Pakistani Punjabi Village*. Karachi: Oxford University Press.

Chiba, M. (ed.) (1986). *Asian Indigenous Law in Interaction with Received Law*. London and New York: Kegan Paul International.

Chippendale, N. (ed.) (1993). *Reminiscences from the Asian Community in Hounslow*. London: Heritage Publications Hounslow.

Clarke, C., Peach, C., and Vertovec, S. (eds) (1990). *South Asians Overseas, Migration and Ethnicity*. Cambridge: Cambridge University Press, p. 167.

Coker, N. (2003). 'British Muslims and Health'. Unpublished paper.

College of Mediators. (2008). *UK College of Family Mediators Code of Practice*, <http://www.collegeofmediators.co.uk/index.php?option=com_rokdownloads&view=file&Itemid=18&id=5:code-of-practice>, accessed on 21 April 2011.

Comaroff, J. and Roberts, S. (1981). *Rules and Processes: The Cultural Logic of Dispute in an African Context*. Chicago and London: University of Chicago Press.

Coterell, R. (1989). *The Politics of Jurisprudence*. Austin: Butterworths.

Coulson, N. (1964). *A History of Islamic Law*. Edinburgh: Edinburgh University Press.

Coulson, N. (1969). *Conflicts and Tensions in Islamic Jurisprudence*. Chicago: University of Chicago Press.

Delgado, R., Dunn, C., Brown, P., and Lee, H. (1985). 'Fairness and Formality: Minimizing the Risk of Prejudice in Alternative Dispute Resolution', *Wisconsin Law Review* (1985): pp. 1359–91.

Doi, A.R. (1984). *Sharia: The Islamic Law*. London: Ta-Ha Publishers.

Doo, Leigh-Wai. (1973). 'Dispute Settlement in Chinese-American Communities', *American Journal of Comparative Law* 21 (627): pp. 652–4.

Drapkin, R. and Bienenfeld, F. (1990). 'The Power of Including Children in Custody Mediation', in C.A. Everett (ed.) *Divorce Mediation: Perspectives in the Field*. New York: Haworth.

Ericsson, S. (1994). 'Striking a Balance in Church-State Relations', paper presented at Religious Liberty Commission Consultation, held in Guernsey on 3–6 May 1994. Unpublished.

Ericsson, S. (2007). 'Religious Freedom and the American Experiment: Moving from Establishment and Partiality to Freedom, Equality and Neutrality While Guarding Against Hostility and Sterility', paper presented at the Conference on Religious Freedom sponsored by the Portuguese Ministry of Justice in Lisbon, 16–17 March. Unpublished.

Esposito, J.L. (1980). 'Perspectives on Islamic Law Reform: The Case of Pakistan', *New York University Journal of International Law and Politics* 13 (2): pp. 217–45.

Fadl, K.A.E. (1994). 'Islamic Law and Muslim Minorities: The Juristic Discourse on Muslim Minorities from 2nd/8th Centuries', *Islamic Law and Society* 1 (2): pp. 141–87.

Felstiner, W.L.F., Abel, R., and Sarat, A. (1981). 'The Emergence and Transformation of Disputes: Naming, Blaming, Claiming, etc.', *Law and Society Review* 15: pp. 631–54.

Fisher, R., Ury, W.C., and Patton, B. (1991). *Getting to Yes: Negotiating Agreement Without Giving In.* 2nd ed. New York and London: Penguin Books.

Fiss, O. (1984). 'Against Settlement', *Yale Law Journal* 93: pp. 1073–90.

Folger, J. and Bush, R.A.B. (1994). 'Ideology, Orientations to Conflict, and Mediation Discourse,' in J.P. Folger and T.S. Jones (eds). *New Directions in Mediation: Communication, Research and Perspectives.* Thousand Oaks, CA, London and New Delhi: Sage Publications, pp. 3–25.

Follet, M.P. (1996). 'Constructive Conflict', in Pauline Graham (ed.). *A Celebration of Writings from the 1920s.* Boston: Harvard Business School, p. 81.

Fuller, Lon L. (1971). 'Mediation: Its Forms and Functions', *Southern California Law Review* (1970–71): pp. 305–39.

Gadlin, H. and Davis, A. (1998). 'Mediators Gain Trust the Old-Fashioned Way: We Earn It!', *Negotiation Journal* (January): pp. 55–62.

Galanter, M. (1966). 'The Modernization of Law', in Myron Weiner (ed.). *Modernization*, pp. 153–65. New York: Basic Books.

Garwood, F. (1990). 'Children in Conciliation: The Experience of Involving Children in Conciliation', *Family and Conciliation Courts Review* 28 (1): pp. 43–51.

Gibb, F. (2005). 'Who Forces This Woman To Be Married to This Man?', *The Times*, 24 May.

Govier, T. (1998). *Dilemmas of Trust.* Montreal and Kingston: McGill-Queen's University Press.

Graham, J.L. (1993). 'The Japanese Negotiating Style: Characteristics of a Distinct Approach', *Negotiation Journal* (9): p. 123.

Griffiths, J. (1986). 'What Is Legal Pluralism?', *Journal of Legal Pluralism and Unofficial Law* 24: pp. 1–56.

Grillo, T. (1991). 'The Mediation Alternative: Process Dangers for Women', *Yale Law Journal* 100: pp. 1545–1610.

Gulliver, P.H. (1979). *Disputes and Negotiations: A Cross Cultural Perspective.* New York and London: Academic Press, pp. 200–25.

Haddad, Y. and Lummis, A. (1987). *Islamic Values in the United States.* New York: Oxford University Press.

Hallaq, W. (1984). 'Was the Gate of Ijtihad Closed?', *International Journal of Middle East Studies* 3 (16): pp. 3–41.

Halm, H. (2004). *Shi'ism.* Edinburgh: Edinburgh University Press.

Hamilton, C. (tr.) (1979). *Hedaya al-Mirghinani.* New Delhi: Kitab Bhawan (reprint).

Home Office. (2000). *A Choice by Right. The Report of the Working Group on Forced Marriage.* London: Home Office Communication Directorate.

Hounslow. (1990). 'Hounslow Borough Profile, 1990', document coordinated by the Policy Unit, Chief Executive's Office, Hounslow.

Hussain, E. (2007). *The Islamist.* London: Penguin Books.

Jansen, J.G. (1994). 'Islam and Civil Rights in the Netherlands', in Bernard Lewis and Dominique Schnapper, (eds). *Muslims in Europe.* London and New York: Pinter, pp. 39–53.

Jenkins, R. (1967). *Essays and Speeches.* London: Collins.

Jomier, J. (1989). *How to Understand Islam.* New York: Crossroads Publishing Co.

Jones, R. and W. Gnanpala. (2000) *Ethnic Minorities in English Law.* Stoke on Trent: Trentham Books.

Kagitçibasi, Ç. (1994). 'A Critical Appraisal of Individualism and Collectivism: Toward a New Formulation', in Uichol Kim et al. (eds). *Individualism and Collectivism: Theory, Methods and Application.* Thousand Oaks, CA: Sage Publications.

Kelly, J.B. and Duryee, M.A. (1992). 'Women and Men's Views on Mediation in Voluntary and Mandatory Mediation Settings', *Family and Conciliation Courts Review* 30 (1): pp. 34–49.

Kelly, J.B. and Gigy, L. (1988). 'Client Assessment of Mediation Services (CAMS): A Scale Measuring Client Perceptions and Satisfaction', *Mediation Quarterly* 19: pp. 43–52.

Kelly, J.B. and Gigy, L. (1989). *Divorce Mediation: Characteristics of Clients and Outcomes*, in K. Kressel, D. Pruitt and Associates, (eds). *Mediation Research: The Process Effectiveness of Third-Party Intervention.* San Francisco, CA: Jossey-Bass, pp. 263–83.

Keshavjee, M. (2002). 'Alternative Dispute Resolution: Its Resonance in Muslim Thought and Future Directions', speech delivered at the Ismaili Centre, London, 2 April, <http://www.iis.ac.uk/learning/life_long_learning/alternative_dispute_resolution/alternative_dispute_resolution.htm>, accessed on 15 June 2006.

Keshavjee, M. (2004). 'Multiculturalism and the Challenges It Poses to Legal Education and Alternative Dispute Resolution: The Situation of British Muslims', address to Department of Peace Studies, University of Bradford, United Kingdom, 6 May, <http://

www.iis.ac.uk/ view_article.asp?ContentID=104713>, accessed on 15 June 2006.

Keshavjee, M. (2006). 'The Ismaili Alternative Dispute Resolution Training Programmes and the Potential for New Directions in Mediation', address to members of the Judiciary of British Columbia, Canada, on 2 December, <http://www.iis. ac.uk/view_article.asp?ContentID=108757>, accessed on 31 May 2008.

Keshavjee, M. (2010). 'Dispute Resolution', in Amyn B. Sajoo, (ed.). *A Companion to Muslim Ethics*. London and New York: I.B.Tauris, pp. 151–66.

Keshavjee, M. and Whatling, T. (2005). 'Reflective Learning from the Training Programmes of the Ismaili Muslim Conciliation and Arbitration Boards Globally', paper presented at the 5th International Conference of the World Mediation Forum in Crans-Montana, Switzerland on 8 September. Published in *UK College of Family Mediators Journal* (December): pp. 23–8. Also available at <http://www.iis.ac.uk/view_article.asp?ContentID=106246>, accessed on 15 June 2006.

Keshavjee, M. (2011). 'Cross-Border Child Abduction Mediation in Cases Concerning Non-Hague Countries', in Christoph C. Paul and Sybille Kiesewetter, (eds). *Cross-Border Family Mediation. International Parental Child Abduction, Custody and Access Cases*. Munich: Wolfgang Metzner Verlag, pp. 96–122.

Kieswetter, S. and Paul, C. (eds) (2011). *Cross-Border Family Mediation*. Frankfurt Am Main: Verlag.

Kressel, K., D. Pruit and Associates, (eds) (1989). *Mediation Research: The Process and Effectiveness of Third-Party Intervention Research*. San Francisco, CA: Jossey-Bass.

Kurzman, C. (ed.) (1998). *Liberal Islam: A Sourcebook*. New York: Oxford University Press.

Laue, J. and Cormick, G. (1978). 'The Ethics of Intervention in Community Disputes', in Gordon Bermant et al. (eds). *The Ethics of Social Intervention*. Washington, D.C.: Halsted Press, p. 205.

Le Baron, M. (2002). *Bridging Troubled Waters: Conflict Resolution from the Heart*. San Francisco: Jossey-Bass.

Le Baron, M. and Pillay, V. (2006). *Conflict Across Cultures*. Boston and London: Intercultural Press.

Lederach, J.P. (1995). *Preparing for Peace: Conflict Transformation Across Cultures*. Syracuse, NY: Syracuse University Press.

Lewis, P. (1994). *Islamic Britain: Religion, Politics and Identity Among British Muslims*. London: I.B.Tauris.

Lewis, P. (1997). 'British Muslims and the Search for Religious Guidance', in J. Hinnel and W. Menski (eds). *From Generation to Generation: Religious Reconstruction in the South Asian Diaspora*. London: Kegan Paul.

Lewis, P. (2007). *Young, British and Muslim*. London: Continuum International Publishing Group.

McIntosh, J.E., Wells, Y.D., Smyth, B.M., and Long, C.M. (2008). 'Child-focused and Child-Inclusive Divorce Mediation. Comparative Outcomes from a Prospective Study of Postseparation Adjustment', *Family Court Review* 46 (1): pp. 105–24.

Madelung, W. (1997). *The Succession to Muhammad: A Study of the Early Caliphate*. Cambridge: Cambridge University Press.

Marshall, J. (1995). *The History of the Great West Road: Its Social and Economic Influence in the Surrounding Area*. London: Borough of Hounslow.

Masud, K. (1996). 'Islamic Law', in Azim Nanji (ed.) *The Muslim Almanac*. Detroit: Gale Research, pp. 269–74.

Menkel-Meadow, C. (2003). *Dispute Processing and Conflict Resolution*. Aldershot: Dartmouth Publishing Company, and Burlington, MA: Ashgate Publishing.

Menski, W.F. (1987). 'Legal Pluralism in Hindu marriage', in R. Burhart (ed.). *Hinduism in Great Britain: The Perpetuation of Religion in an Alien Cultural Milieu*. London and New York: Tavistock, pp. 180–200.

Menski, W.F. (1988). 'English Family Law and Ethnic Laws in Britain', *Kerala Law Times* 1: pp. 56–66.

Menski, W.F. (1993a). 'Asians in Britain and the Question of Adaptation to a New Legal Order: Asian Laws in Britain', in Milton Israel and Narendra Wagle (eds). *Ethnicity, Identity, Migration: The South Asian Context*. Toronto: University of Toronto Press, pp. 238–68.

Menski, W.F. (1993b). 'Angrezi Shariat: Plural Arrangements in Family Law by Muslims in Britain', unpublished paper at SOAS.

Menski, W.F. (1996). 'Law, Religion and South Asians', unpublished paper at SOAS.

Menski, W.F. (2000). *Comparative Law in a Global Context: The Legal Systems of Asia and Africa*. London: Platinum.

Mernissi, F. (1987). *The Veil and the Male Elite: A Feminist Interpretation of Women's Rights in Islam*. Translated by Mary Jo Lakehead. Reading, MA: Addison-Wesley Publishing Company.

Mernissi, F. (1998). 'A Feminist Interpretation of Women's Rights in Islam', in C. Kurzman (ed.) *Liberal Islam: A Sourcebook*. New York: Oxford University Press.

Miller, R.T. and Flowers, R.B. (1977). *Toward Benevolent Neutrality: Church, State and the Supreme Court*. Waco, TX: Markham Press Fund.

Mirza, K. (1989). 'The Silent Cry: Second Generation Bradford Muslim Women Speak', *Muslims in Europe* 49. Birmingham: Centre for the Study of Islam and Christian Relations.

Mnookin, R. and Kornhauser, L. (1979). 'Bargaining in the Shadow of the Law: The Case of Divorce', *The Yale Law Journal* 88: pp. 950–97.

Modood, T. and Berthoud, R. (1997). *Ethnic Minorities in Britain: Diversity and Disadvantage*. London: Policy Studies Institute.

Momen, M. (1985). *An Introduction to Shi'i Islam: The History and Doctrines of Twelver Shi'ism*. New Haven: Yale University Press.

Moore, C.W. (1996). *The Mediation Process: A Practical Strategy for Resolving Conflict*. 2nd edition. Hoboken, NJ: Josey-Bass.

Moore, S.F. (1973). 'Law and Social Change: The Semi-autonomous Social Field as an Appropriate Subject to Study', *Law and Society Review* 7 (4): pp. 719–46.

Moore, S.F. (1978). *Law as Process: An Anthropological Approach*. London: Routledge and Kegan Paul.

Muhsin, A.W. (1992). *Quran and Women*. Kuala Lumpur: Penerbit Pajar Bakti San Bhd.

Murch, M., Douglas, G. , Scanlon, L., Perry, A., Lisle, C., and Bader, K. (1999). *Safeguarding Children's Welfare in Uncontentious Divorce: A Study of S41 of the Matrimonial Causes Act 1973*, Research Series 7/99, Lord Chancellor's Department, London.

Nader, L. and Todd, H. (1978) *The Disputing Process: Law in Ten Societies*. New York: Columbia University Press.

An-Naim, A. (1990). *Toward an Islamic Reformation: Civil Liberties, Human Rights and International Law*. Syracuse, NY: Syracuse University Press.

Nasr, S.H. (2001). *Ideals and Realities of Islam*. 4th revised edition. Cambridge: The Islamic Texts Society.

Nasr, S.H. (2004). *The Heart of Islam*. Lahore: Suhail Academy.

Nazroo, J. (1995). 'Uncovering Gender Difference in the Use of Marital Violence: The Effect of Methodology', *Sociology* 29 (3): pp. 475–94.

Nielsen, J. (1991). *Muslims in Western Europe*. Edinburgh: Edinburgh University Press.

Nimer, M., abu (1996). 'Conflict Resolution in an Islamic Context: Some Conceptual Questions', *Peace and Change* 21 (1): pp. 22–40.

ONS. (2004). *2001 Census*. London: Office for National Statistics, <http://www.statistics.gov.uk/census 2001>, accessed on 21 March 2005.

Palmer, M. and S. Roberts. (1998). *Dispute Processes: ADR and the Primary Forms of Decision Making*. London, Edinburgh and Dublin: Butterworths.

Pasha, S.A. (1977). 'Muslim Family Law in Britain', paper presented at a meeting at the House of Commons, London, January 20. Unpublished.

Peach, C. (1990). 'The Muslim Population of Great Britain', *Ethnic and Racial Studies* 13 (3): p. 13.

Pearl, D. (1986). *Family Law and the Immigrant Communities*. Bristol: Jordan and Sons.

Pearl, D. (1987). 'South Asian Immigrant Communities and English Family Law: 1971–1987', *New Community* 14 (1–2): pp. 161–9.

Pearl, D. and Menski, W. (1998). *Muslim Family Law*. London: Sweet and Maxwell Ltd.

Pelikan, J. (1971). *Christian Tradition: A History of the Development of Doctrine: The Emergence of the Catholic Tradition, 100–600 AD*. Vol. 1. Chicago: University of Chicago Press.

Phillips, T. (2005). 'After 7/7: Sleepwalking to Segregation', speech delivered at the Manchester Council for Community Relations, 22 September 2005, <http://www.cre.gov.uk>, accessed on 2 May 2007.

Pospisil, L. (1971). *Anthropology of Law*. New York: Harper and Row.

Poulter, S.M. (1990). 'The Claim to a Separate Islamic System of Personal Law for British Muslims', in Chibli Mallat and Jane Connors (eds) *Islamic Family Law*. London: Graham and Trotman, pp. 147–66.

Poulter, S. (1992). 'The Muslim Community and English Law', *Islam and Christian-Muslim Relations* 3 (2): p. 266.

Poulter, S. (1995). 'Multiculturalism and Human Rights for Muslim Families in English Law', in Michael King (ed.). *God's Law Versus State Law: The Construction of an Islamic Identity in Western Europe*. London: Grey Seal Books, pp. 81–7.

Rashid, K.S. (2004). 'Tahkim or Arbitration in the Sharia', *Newsletter of the Regional Centre for Arbitration, KDN* 1505 PP 6818/6/2004, pp. 24–8. Kuala Lumpur.

Rauf, F.A. (2000). *Islam: A Sacred Law*. New York: Qiblah (Threshold) Books.

Rehman, F. (1982). *Islam and Modernity: Transformation of an Intellectual Tradition*. Chicago: University of Chicago Press.

Rehman, F. (1985). 'Law and Ethics in Islam', in R. Hovannisian (ed.) *Ethics in Islam*, pp. 3–15. Malibu, CA: Undena Publications.

Rippon, A. (1990). *Muslims, Their Religious Beliefs and Practices*. Vol. 1: *The Formative Period*. London: Routledge.

Roberts, M. (2007). *Developing the Craft of Mediation: Reflections on Theory and Practice*. London and Philadelphia: Jessica Kingsley Publishers.

Roberts, S. (1998). 'Against Legal Pluralism: Some Reflections on the Contemporary Enlargement of the Legal Domain', *Journal of Legal Pluralism* (42): pp. 95–106.

Roberts, S. (2001). 'Family Mediation After the Act', *CFLQ*.13(3).

Roberts, S. and Palmer, M. (2005). *Dispute Processes: ADR and the Primary Forms of Decision Making*. Cambridge: Cambridge University Press.

Rosenberg, J.D. (1992). 'In Defense of Mediation', *Family and Conciliation Courts Review*. 30 (4): pp. 422–67.

Rubin, J.Z. and Sander, F.E.A. (1991). 'Culture, Negotiation and the Eye of the Beholder', *Negotiation Journal* (7): p. 249.

Runnymede Trust. (1997). *The Runnymede Commission on British Muslims and Islamophobia*. London.

Sachdeva, S. (1993). *The Primary Purpose Rule of British Immigration Law*. Oakhill: Trentham Books.

Sachedina, A. (1996). 'Law, Society and Governance in Islam', in Azim Nanji (ed.) *The Muslim Almanac*. Detroit: Gale Research, pp. 263–8.

Sacks, J. (1991). *The Persistence of Faith*. London: Weidenfeld and Nicholson.

Santos, Boaventura de Sousa (2002). *Toward a New Legal Common Sense*. London: Butterworths.

Saposnek, D.T. (1983). *Mediation Child Custody Disputes*. San Francisco, CA: Jossey-Bass.

Saposnek, D.T. (1991). 'The Value of Children in Mediation: A Cross-cultural Perspective', *Mediation Quarterly* 8 (4): pp. 325–42.

Sardar, Z. (2005). *Desperately Seeking Paradise*. London: Granta Publications.

Schact, J. (1993). *An Introduction to Islamic Law*. 5th edition. Oxford: Oxford University Press.

Shah-Kazemi, S.N. (2000). 'Cross Cultural Mediation: A Critical View of the Dynamics of Culture in Family Disputes', *International Journal of Law, Policy and Family* (14): pp. 302–25.

Shah-Kazemi, S.N. (2001). *Untying the Knot: Muslim Women, Divorce and the Shariah*. London: Nuffield Foundation.

Shapiro, M. (1981). *Courts: A Comparative and Political Analysis*. Chicago: University of Chicago Press.

Sharour, M. (1998). 'Islam and the 1995 Beijing World Conference on Women', in C. Kurzman (ed.) *Liberal Islam: A Sourcebook*. New York: Oxford University Press, pp. 139–42.

Shaw, A. (1988). *A Pakistani Community in Britain*. Oxford: Oxford University Press.

Smart, C. (2002). 'From Children's Shoes to Children's Voices', *Family Court Review* 46 (3): pp. 307–19.

Stark, C. (2001). 'Choosing a Route Through the Divorce Process', in J. Walker (ed.) *Information Meetings and Associated Provisions with the Family Law Act 1996. Final Evaluation Report*. Vol. 2. London: Lord Chancellor's Department.

Stark, C. and Birmingham, C. (2001). 'The Role of Lawyers in Divorce', in J. Walker (ed.) *Information Meetings and Associated Provisions with the Family Law Act 1996. Final Evaluation Report*. Vol. 2. London: Lord Chancellor's Department.

Swann Report. (1985). *The Report of the Committee of Inquiry into the Education of Children from Ethnic Minority Groups*. London: HMSO.

Taylor, C. (2002). 'Modern Social Imaginaries', *Public Culture* 14 (1): pp. 91–124.

Taylor, L. and Adelman, H. S. (1986). 'Facilitating Children's Participation in Decisions that Affect Them: From Concept to Practice', *Journal of Clinical Child Psychology* 15 (4): pp. 346–51.

Walker, J. (2000) 'Whither the Family Law Act, Part II?', in M. Thorpe and E. Clarke (eds). *No Fault or Flaw: The Future of the Family Law Act 1996*. Bristol: Jordan Publishing.

Walker, J. (ed.) (2001). Divorce Reform and the Family Law Act 1996', in J. Walker (ed.) *Information Meetings and Associated Provisions with the Family Law Act 1996, Final Evaluation Report*. Vol. 1. London: Lord Chancellor's Department. London: Lord Chancellor's Department.

Walker, J. (2009). *Assessment of the Family Mediation Service in Ireland*, International Benchmarking (forthcoming).

Walker, J. (2010). 'Family Mediation: The Rhetoric, the Reality and the Evidence', *Journal of the Norwegian Psychological Association*, 37: pp. 676–87.

Walker, J., McCarthy, P., Simpson, R., and Corlyon, J. (1990). 'Family Conciliation in England and Wales: the Way Forward?', *Family and Conciliation Courts Review* 28 (1): pp. 1–8.

Wallerstein, J.S. (1985). 'The Over-Burdened Child: Some Long-Term Consequences of Divorce', *Social Work* 30: pp. 116–23.

Walsh, D. (2006). 'The Rescuers', *Reader's Digest* UK edition (June): pp. 138–45.

Weiss, B.G. (1998). *The Spirit of Islamic Law*. Athens, GA: University of Georgia Press.

Wolfe, C.L. (2006). 'Faith-Based Arbitration: Friend or Foe? An Evaluation of Religious Arbitration Systems and Their Interaction with Secular Courts', *Fordham Law Review* 75 (1): pp. 427–69.

Wolpert, S. (1984). *Jinnah of Pakistan*. Oxford: Oxford University Press.

Yilmaz, I. (2003). 'Muslim Alternative Dispute Resolution and Neo-Ijtihad in England', *Alternatives: Turkish Journal of International Relations* 2 (1): pp. 117–39, <http://www.alternativesjournal.net/volume2/number1/yilmaz.htm>, accessed on 15 May 2007.

Yilmaz, I. (2005). *Muslim Laws, Politics and Society in Modern Nation States: Dynamic Legal Pluralisms in England, Turkey and Pakistan.* Aldershot: Ashgate Publishing.

Zaman, M.Q. (2002). *The Ulama in Contemporary Islam.* Princeton, NJ: Princeton University Press.

Zein-ed-Din, N. (1998). 'Unveiling the Veil', in C. Kurzman (ed.) *Liberal Islam: A Sourcebook*, pp. 101–6. New York: Oxford University Press.

Zelcer, H. (2007). 'Two Models of Alternative Dispute Resolution', *Hakirah: The Flatbush Journal of Jewish Law and Thought* 4 (Winter): pp. 69–113, <www.Hakirahorg.Hakirahflatbush@msn.com>, accessed on 4 March 2008.

Index

Abbasid dynasty, 64, 101, 175, 210n
Abdulla, Raficq, 13, 82, 148
Abu Bakr, Caliph, 48, 58
ADR similarities between Islam
    and Judaism, 5–6, 69
ADR resources in Hounslow, 13,
    104–29, 148, 163, 164, 196
ADR resources in Hounslow,
    chart, 105
Afghans, 22, 24, 80
Aga Khan, the, 170, 210n
Aga Khan III, 20
Akhtar, Smina, 134
Akmal v. *Akmal*, 4, 135–6
Al-Azhar University, 35, 82
Algeria, 20, 174, 210n
Ali, Abdullah Yusuf, 20
Ali (first Shi'i Imam), 59, 60, 61,
    197, 206n
Ali, Syed Ameer, 20
Ali v. *Ali*, 132
amanat (trust), 57
Amin, Idi, 24
'aql (intellect), 9, 10, 60, 100, 158
Arabs, 21, 22, 38, 57, 63, 68, 93, 133,
    141–3, 200, 208n
arbitration, 4, 5, 6, 9, 64, 67–9,
    85, 87, 97, 122, 141–3, 169, 170,
    177, 178, 190, 194, 213n, 214n
arranged marriage, 26, 32, 132–3,
    134–6, 146, 150
Assam, 19
Azmi, Aisha, 73–4

Bangladesh, 14, 21, 22, 23, 52, 132, 137
Barelwi Muslims, 54, 126, 186

Barkatullah, Mufti Abdul Kadir, 74
Baroda, 21
Bengal, 19, 22
beth din, bathei din, 5, 7
Bhabi Khatija, 45, 119
Bharuch, 21
*biraderi*s, 43, 114–5, 148, 208n, 213n
Blair, Tony, 73
Bosnians, 21, 22, 24

Central Africa, 41
chained spouses, 3
child abduction, 29, 92, 138, 195,
    196, 211n
Children Act 1989, 128, 139
Children Act 2000, 91, 128
children of estranged parents,
    138–41, 147
China, 15, 62
Commonwealth Immigration Act
    1962, 22
conciliation, 4, 9, 67, 87–8, 98,
    108, 155, 162, 169, 170, 177,
    178, 190, 213n, 214n
Convention on the Elimination of
    all Forms of Discrimination
    Against Women, 9, 37
Convention on the Recognition
    and Enforcement of Foreign
    Arbitral Awards 1958, 68
coteries, 126
counselling, 32, 46, 50, 54, 85–9,
    115, 116,120, 127, 128, 162,
    179–80, 189, 190, 191, 196,
    208n
Crescent, The, 19